ALSO BY MICHELE WEINER-DAVIS

In Search of Solutions: A New Direction in Psychotherapy
(with William Hudson O'Hanlon)

Nancy

DIVORCE BUSTING

A Revolutionary and Rapid Program for Staying Together

Michele Weiner-Davis

SUMMIT BOOKS

New York   London   Toronto   Sydney   Tokyo   Singapore

SUMMIT BOOKS
Simon & Schuster Building
Rockefeller Center
1230 Avenue of the Americas
New York, New York 10020

Designed by Carla Weise / Levavi & Levavi
Manufactured in the United States of America

3   5   7   9   10   8   6   4

Library of Congress Cataloging in Publication Data
Weiner-Davis, Michele.
Divorce busting : a revolutionary and rapid program for staying
together / Michele Weiner-Davis.
p.   c.m.
Includes bibliographical references and index.
1. Marriage.   2. Interpersonal relations.   3. Communication in
marriage.   4. Marital psychotherapy.   I. Title.
HQ734.W4373   1992
646.7'8—dc20   91-34520
CIP

ISBN: 0-671-72598-X

To my mother, father, and two brothers.

To my children, Danielle and Zachary, who continually remind me of what's important in life.

Most of all, to my husband, Jim, whose never-ending support, charitable ear, down-to-earth advice, and painstaking editorial suggestions made this book a reality. He selflessly nurtured me during my intense year-long affair with writing and did so without complaining. The gift of his friendship has not gone unnoticed or unappreciated.

Acknowledgments

Although only one name appears on the book's cover, many people have generously contributed their time to making this book a reality. I am fortunate to have colleagues, friends, and family who have provided support and/or insightful feedback on the manuscript, such as George Enns, Eve Lipchik, Tony Heath, Rich Simon, Mike Nichols, Suzanne Barrows, and Diane Woodruff. A special thanks to Mike Nichols for having spread good rumors about my work.

I am also extremely appreciative of my colleagues at the American Association for Marriage and Family Therapy, particularly Diane Sollee and Virginia Rutter, for their support and for providing me with the opportunity to "spread the word."

In addition, there are many colleagues who have greatly influenced my thinking during the years I've been practicing therapy. The staff at the Brief Family Therapy Center has been one such major influence. I especially want to thank Steve de Shazer, who taught me to be "simple-minded." He undoubtedly inspired many ideas presented throughout this book.

In particular, I am grateful to Arnold Woodruff for his intellectual support and friendship, for his never-ending assistance with the manuscript and, most important, for his not allowing me to take myself (or anything else for that matter) too seriously. I am lucky to have numerous family members cheering for me. Standing in front of the cheering crowd are Leah and Bill Davis and Lila Weiner, all of whom I love dearly.

My clients are also owed special gratitude. They have allowed me to become an intimate part of their lives and placed their faith in my ability to help them improve their marriages. By so doing, they have taught me a tremendous amount about helping couples change. For this, I am greatly indebted.

I want to thank Suzanne Gluck, my talented literary agent, for navigating my way through the publishing maze. Finally, special thanks to Laura Yorke, my patient editor, for her enthusiasm about my ideas even before the manuscript was a twinkle in my eyes, for providing insightful editorial comments and, most of all, for tolerating me.

Contents

Introduction:
Love the One You're With

ANN WAS THOROUGHLY CONVINCED THAT HER MARRIAGE OF FIF-
teen years was over. She believed she had tried everything hu-
manly possible to straighten things out between her and Steve.
Nothing ever worked. The more she tried reasoning with him, the
more unreasonable he became. Appealing to his sensitivity only
brought out his insensitivity.

Years ago when their problems began, Ann thought, "This is
just a stage we're going through." But now she knew she was just
fooling herself. She sadly admitted that their marriage had gotten
progressively worse, not better. As she reminisced about the past,
she recalled nostalgically that, despite their difficulties, they occasionally shared good times. Recently, the constant war at home
served as a painful reminder that much of what they had together
appeared to be lost forever. To make matters worse, their battles
had not gone unnoticed by their three children. Bedtime had
become fraught with tears, questions about divorce, unusual
nighttime fears and anger.

Desperate for some answers, Ann reflected on what went
wrong. Though things were never perfect, she thought the birth
of Melissa, their oldest child, marked a turning point in their
marriage. Initially, both Steve and Ann were ecstatic about their

new baby, but their mutual joy was short-lived. Ann became totally immersed in motherhood as Steve spent increasing amounts of time with his buddies participating in whatever sport happened to be in season. At first, Ann frequently expressed her hurt and resentment about his long absences, but since Steve seemed unresponsive, she stopped trying.

Now, five years later, Ann and Steve appear more like roommates: separate bedrooms, few shared activities and, when not fighting, verbal exchanges limited to "Pass the salt." While watching a talk show about women who feel lonely and alienated within their marriages, Ann saw her own marriage as if a reflection in a mirror; it even seemed that the camera crew secretly moved in and candidly filmed the story of their lives. She finally realized that her struggles with Steve had reached life and death proportions. If she stayed unhappily married to Steve, she would die a slow and torturous death; if she divorced, she might live.

Ann's story is all too familiar. During the past ten years that I have worked with couples who have marital problems, I have heard many stories like Ann's. The scenes and the actors change, the specifics vary, but the dynamics are strikingly similar. When problem-solving efforts prove ineffective, divorce seems the only solution.

Early in my career, Ann's pessimism would have convinced me that her marriage was irreparable and that it was time for her to take care of her needs. "The handwriting is on the wall," I would have said. "You certainly have tried everything." I would have furnished her with further evidence that, regardless of what she might do, Steve was unlikely to change. "Let go of the past and look toward a brighter future without the arguments and tensions of life with Steve" would have been my next recommendation. We would have rehearsed how she might break the news to her children. After she wiped her tears, I might have suggested, "Perhaps you should join a support group for divorced and separated people to help you through the transition." And as she left my office I would have handed her a long reading list to guide her through the process.

DIVORCE IS NOT THE ANSWER

But those days are gone. Now I do whatever I can to help people find solutions to their marital problems so that they can stay together. I do not get sidetracked by pessimism and hopelessness as I did in days past. Now I know that hopelessness is a reasonable response to an unreasonable situation. Nothing more, nothing less. It is natural for people to feel pessimistic when, day after day, month after month, nothing improves, problems never get resolved. Feelings of pain and rejection are always present. But now I am convinced that pessimism and hopelessness are feelings based on past performances; feelings that are changeable, feelings worth changing. People can and should stay together and work out their differences.

Why the switch? There are many reasons. Over the past several years I have witnessed the suffering and disillusionment that are the predictable by-products of divorce. I have seen people who have been divorced for five years or longer with wounds that won't heal. These people failed to anticipate the pain and upheaval divorce leaves in its wake. I have heard countless divorced couples battle tenaciously over the very same issues they believed they were leaving behind when they walked out the door. They learned too late that the act of divorce does not free them from their ex-spouse's emotional grip; some ghosts live forever.

I have heard too many disillusioned individuals express regrets about their belief that their ex-spouse was the problem only to discover similar problems in their second marriages or, even more surprisingly, in their new single lives. They admit to re-creating the same unproductive patterns of interacting in new relationships, repeating old mistakes or discovering that they are still miserable.

Diagnosing one's spouse as the source of the problem, a common antecedent to divorce, doesn't take into account the roles both partners play in the deterioration of the relationship. The habits spouses developed over the years go with them when they end the marriage. This may partly account for the saddening statistic that 60 percent of second marriages also end in divorce.

And then there are the children, who are also victims in a divorce. Research shows that except in extreme cases of abuse children want their parents together. Children have no say in a decision that profoundly affects them for the rest of their lives. When parents decide to end their marriage, it means the death of the family. As the family disintegrates, a child's sense of comfort and security becomes shaken.

Carl Whitaker, a leader in the field of family therapy, once said, "When children are involved, there is no such thing as divorce." Battles over parenting issues don't end with divorce, they get played out even more vigorously with children as innocent by-standers or even pawns. Uncomfortable gatherings at future family weddings, bar mitzvahs, graduations, births and funerals provide never-ending reminders that divorce is forever.

I've met children of all ages who, even after both parents remarry, secretly hope their own parents will, someday, reunite. Many well-adjusted adults whose parents separated or divorced when they were children admit an emptiness that never goes away. Most parents recognize that divorce will impact on their children, they just don't anticipate the lasting effects. In regard to this, I've heard too many divorced parents say, "I wish I knew then what I know now." Gradually, I have come to the conclusion that divorce is not the answer. It doesn't necessarily solve the problems it purports to solve. Most marriages are worth saving.

MOST PROBLEMS ARE SOLVABLE

I have not arrived at this conclusion based on religious or moralistic views. From my perspective, divorce is not immoral or bad. In fact, in extreme cases, certain relationships are better off terminated for the health and well-being of everyone involved. This book will also address these exceptional situations. However, most people considering divorce do not fall into this extreme category.

For example, research shows that the primary complaints leading to divorce are not physical abuse or addiction but, rather, lack of communication, lack of affection and nagging (Hetherington, Cox, and Cox, 1981, p. 58). I've grown increasingly convinced that most marriages are worth saving simply because most problems are solvable. Or to put it another way, most unhappy marriages can be changed, and therefore are worth changing. In fact, I don't believe in "saving marriages," I believe in divorcing the old marriage and beginning a new one—with the same partner.

Believing that most problems are solvable is new for me. Although I never would have agreed with the therapist from my area who said that 90 percent of the marriages in his practice were dead on arrival, I did feel that many problems were insurmountable. I attributed therapeutic dead ends to dead marriages. "These people really don't want to change," I told myself, or "They aren't admitting they really want out," or "Their marriage is so pathological it can't be changed." These explanations freed me from responsibility for the lack of progress, but I never fully believed them. I knew instinctively there had to be a better way.

I recognized that I needed new tools to help couples. Rather than thinking stubborn marital problems were the result of incorrigible spouses, I began to scrutinize my therapy approach. This traditional approach, which was based on the appealing but naive assumption that understanding and expressing feelings will clear up problems, simply did not work. The couples I saw in my practice expressed their feelings, even understood their feelings, and yet their problems persisted.

Nor did I find useful the idea that couples can free themselves of their problems by gaining insight into their childhood traumas. Psychoanalytic theory has contributed the notion that people experience problems because of unresolved childhood traumas. In theory, once the root of the problem can be identified and worked through, the problem will disappear. While this approach works for some people, experience has taught me that insight of this sort simply takes too long for people in crisis. Couples on the brink of divorce require immediate evidence of light at the end of the tunnel to avoid the all-consuming pessimism that dissolves relationships.

Another detour on the road to problem solving was my belief that couples need to understand how their upbringing influences their behavior and attitudes as marital partners. While this particular route was often interesting and sometimes informative, my clients would frequently plead, "Now I see that we are reenacting our parents' marriages, but *what do we do about it?* We can't stop fighting." I learned that having explanations for problems doesn't necessarily solve them!

Furthermore, when I looked around I noticed that there was precious little agreement among professionals; each therapy approach had a different way of explaining how problems develop. TA (Transactional Analysis) therapists told their clients, "You are coming out of your Child instead of your Adult." Gestalt therapists said, "You aren't in the here and now." Family therapists told their clients, "Your son's behavior is a symptom of what is happening in the family." What was most confusing was that research failed to show any single explanation to be more valid or accurate than any other.

"So now what?" I wondered. "If no single underlying cause can ever be defined, or if explanations fail to change anything, where does that leave me?" That left me at the doorstep of Solution-Oriented Brief Therapy, an approach which emphasizes finding solutions rather than developing explanations for problems.

"I'D RATHER SWITCH THAN FIGHT"

Solution-Oriented Brief Therapy (SBT) is a new dynamic, results-oriented therapy approach. Based on assumptions that are radically different from traditional ones, the methods of SBT enable couples to make sudden shifts that transform their relationships. In my practice, divorce is the exception, not the rule. Even in extreme cases like Ann's, couples who initially appear indisputably divorce-bound often reverse their decision and remain in their marriages to work things out.

As its name implies, brief therapy is short-term, meaning that goals are usually accomplished in a limited number of sessions. Research indicates that the average length of treatment for practitioners of SBT is four to six sessions. Though brief therapy comes in many varieties, shapes and forms (in fact, there is much disagreement, even among brief therapists, as to the definition of brief), all brief therapists have at least one thing in common—they are task-oriented. Clients are asked to set goals early on so that progress can be closely monitored at each session. In contrast to long-term therapy where change is expected to be a difficult and long-drawn-out process, if little or no progress has been made since the previous session in brief therapy, a new strategy is planned.

How can brief therapy be so brief? In other words, how is it possible that goals can be achieved in such a short period of time? Chapter 3, which describes the theory and evolution of SBT in detail, discusses several explanations. One significant reason is that, as compared with psychoanalytical approaches, which begin the therapeutic journey with a trip to the past to uncover pertinent information about the nature and origin of the problem, brief therapists are more interested in the present and the future.

By identifying each person's role in the way the problem is being handled *today*, brief therapists obtain the raw data necessary to generate prescriptions for change. By so doing, lengthy reviews of personal histories are bypassed. More importantly though, SBT therapists focus on the future, helping couples envision what their lives will be like without the problems. Unlike psychodynamic or psychoanalytic approaches which emphasize how problems develop, SBT asks: "What do you want to become?" and "What are the necessary steps to get there?" Therapy becomes less explanation-oriented and more solution-oriented, a process which takes considerably less time.

SOLUTIONS RATHER THAN EXPLANATIONS

SBT's emphasis on finding solutions to marital problems rather than exploring the problem and developing explanations is based on a fairly simple formula: doing more of what works and less of what doesn't. Couples learn to identify what they do differently when they are getting along so that they can do more of it, and to identify unproductive patterns of interactions so that they can eliminate or do less of that.

Once couples can see what they need to build on and what to eliminate, they have specific parameters to guide them. The most common complaint from clients who have had disappointing therapy experiences is: "We talked a lot about feelings but my therapist never gave me a clue about how to change my situation. It was really frustrating." SBT clients don't have this complaint since this approach emphasizes "less talk and more action." People know what to do differently when they leave the session; they go home with a plan.

"YES, BUT IT SOUNDS TOO SIMPLE"

At first, it appeared incredible that problems could be solved without an in-depth understanding of the problem; it seemed too simple. I struggled with this phenomenon for a long time because it contradicted everything I had ever read or been taught about how people change. Most people, including most therapists, believe the change process has to be complicated and arduous. "No pain, no gain" is the general rule of thumb.

I was having an impossible time explaining to myself why, in case after case, my clients reported significant changes after the first few sessions without exploring the past. Try as I might, the old theories about change simply did not apply. I needed to reorganize my thoughts to come to terms with what at first seemed like psychotherapeutic sleight-of-hand. Finally, in the midst of a golf lesson, an explanation became obvious to me.

I had been terribly frustrated by the lack of progress in my golf game. Friends advised me to take a lesson from a golf pro. Ready to drop the game entirely, I agreed, thinking that the only thing that would cure my bad golfing habits was a major overhaul of my technique.

Imagine, if instead of just correcting my golf swing, my instructor espoused explanations about my problem. "You obviously have a fear of winning," he might have postulated. "Let's examine how you inherited your fear of success from your father." Or "The reason you're playing poorly is to make your golf partner look good. First we must explore where you learned that you must take care of others in this way."

These hypotheses, interesting though they may be, would have irritated me since what I really wanted was some concrete advice about swinging the club, not an explanation of what was preventing me from playing well. Luckily for me, the golf pro was not interested in developing theories about my ineptitude. I certainly had enough of those of my own.

Instead, the instructor closely observed my golf swing. At one point he held out his arm and asked me to squeeze it with the same strength that I gripped the club. I nearly stopped the flow of blood in his arm. Then he asked me to extend my arm so that he could demonstrate the correct relaxed grip. I was amazed at the difference between our grasps, and thanked him for this tidbit of information. The lesson continued without the major overhaul in my technique for which I had hoped.

It wasn't until I got on the course later that week that I realized how this seemingly small, seemingly insignificant bit of information had radically transformed my game. My balls went further and straighter than ever before, cutting points off of my score. So much for small pointers.

Anyone who has ever had a golf lesson can probably attest to the fact that slight changes in the swing can have profound effects on the golfer's game. Loosening one's grip on the club, placing one's feet further apart or allowing one's torso to turn with the momentum of the swing might drastically reduce one's score.

Similarly, if you think about interactions in relationships as habits or reptitious patterns developed over the years, you can see how a minor change can make a major difference in the relationship. An unexpected peck on the cheek in the morning can have a ripple effect throughout the day, which in turn can engender good will throughout the week and so on.

This has certainly been true of the couples in my practice. After observing case after case where people talked about how minor shifts in their behavior led to major changes in relationships in relatively short periods of time, and that these positive changes occurred without investigations into the causes of the problems, I gradually realized that change doesn't have to be as complicated or as enervating as I once thought. In fact, frequently the best solutions are the simplest and the ones most easily overlooked.

Follow-up research on brief therapy is encouraging. It suggests that brief therapy is at least as effective as long-term therapy in terms of achieving lasting results. Given the cost and the time commitment involved with long-term therapy, brief therapy is an appealing alternative. It provides answers to people who want to *change* their lives, not just understand their marital merry-go-rounds.

FAREWELL, FREUD

My observations during this period reminded me that while psychoanalytic theory has made a major contribution to and has had a tremendous impact on the Western world, it is only a theory. Different theories provide different maps. Though road maps and relief maps are both useful at different times for different purposes, which one you require depends on what you are trying to accomplish. For the purpose of solving problems in marriages teetering on divorce, it may be time to look beyond psychoanalytic explanations of behavior. In fact, a growing number of therapists are doing just that.

THE PURPOSE OF THIS BOOK

Once I recognized the effectiveness of SBT, I became a devoted teacher, traveling extensively to spread the word to my colleagues. The response over the years has been overwhelming. Thousands of professionals seeking to become more effective in their work have attended workshops and other training events and have felt energized by the innovative ideas. When one considers how SBT challenges mainstream psychotherapeutic thought, the enormous reception to this model has been surprising.

While I have been extremely pleased about my impact in professional circles, it has become clear that my work has just begun in terms of spreading the word. "Since SBT works, is practical, teachable and doable, why not make it available to the public?" I asked myself. Given that one out of every two marriages ends in divorce, I felt the urgency to translate the principles and procedures of SBT into everyday English for couples. This book was written with the hope that it will help many of its readers rapidly get more out of their marriages so that considerations of divorcing vanish.

IT'S NEVER TOO LATE

Perhaps you have been thinking about getting divorced. We all do from time to time. Few people are exempt from having this fantasy. Maybe your spouse is the one who wants out. Maybe you are someone who has thought about divorce for so long that you are ready to take action. Or perhaps you have already seen an attorney or are separated. Why, if you are so convinced that divorce is inevitable, did you pick up this book? You are still hopeful that somehow, some way, something will happen so that you and your spouse will be loving and happy again.

This hope, however small, can be the beginning of a new relationship. I am not saying that if you passively sit around wishing and hoping things will get better, they will. They won't. *You* have to make changes; then the relationship will change. The purpose of this book is to tell you it is *not* too late to mend your broken marriage. If you have even the slightest interest in working things out, change is possible. Like Ann, even if you think you have tried everything, you probably haven't. I can't begin to tell you how many times I've heard "I tried everything and nothing works" from people who quickly discover they overlooked solutions.

"BUT MY SPOUSE DOESN'T WANT TO WORK ON THE RELATIONSHIP"

An all too common stumbling block to working out problems in marriage is the idea that both spouses need to commit to working on the relationship in order for the relationship to change. For example, prospective clients often ask, "My spouse won't come for therapy, so is there any point in my coming?" My answer is always, "Yes! Yes! Yes!" Relationships are such that if one person makes significant changes, the relationship must change. Too many marriages go down the drain because each spouse is waiting for the other to change first. The message throughout this book is clear—

change your marriage by changing yourself. The key is in discovering which particular behaviors to change since all changes are not created equal; some efforts are more cost-effective than others.

With this in mind, this book will help you identify problem-solving approaches that you can implement on your own. Techniques which require both partners to participate, such as experiential exercises, are impractical. Even in the best of marriages, it is often difficult for couples to coordinate time together. So (although it may be fun) you don't have to read this book together, you don't even have to conspicuously leave the book around the house hoping your spouse will notice the particularly relevant pages heavily highlighted by your magic marker. By changing yourself and how you respond to your spouse, *you* can change your marriage. I have seen it happen again and again and again.

THE BASIC STRUCTURE

This book consists of two major sections, the why to and the how to. The why-to section offers a rationale for couples staying together and working things out. There are lots of good reasons for people to forgo the temptation to leave the marriage in order to find peace of mind. This section outlines those reasons and describes the pitfalls of divorce.

The how-to section concretely describes marriage-enriching, divorce-preventing techniques based on brief therapy principles. Whether you are someone who is seriously considering divorce, or someone whose marriage is basically sound and want to keep it that way, this section will help you discover the shortcut to making marriages work. Generic marriage-saving advice like compromise, compassion and unquestioned commitment has no place in this book. Instead, you will find a step-by-step, nuts-and-bolts approach to getting unstuck and making your marriage loving again.

Over the last few years I have lost count of the many people I've worked with who were just about to give up on their spouses but turned things around instead. These individuals have taught me a great deal about the making of successful relationships. As you read about them, what they endured and how they changed, you will understand what David Ben-Gurion meant when he said, "Anyone who does not believe in miracles is not a realist."

PART ONE

CHAPTER 1

Divorce Is Not
the Answer

THE DECISION TO DIVORCE OR REMAIN TOGETHER TO WORK THINGS out is one of the most important decisions you will ever make. It is crucial for those considering divorce to anticipate what lies ahead in order to make informed decisions. Too often the fallout from divorce is far more devastating than many people realize when contemplating the move. This chapter outlines some of the common pitfalls of divorce to aid readers in decisions about their marriages.

The following is a letter written by a woman who read an article about my views on divorce in the *Los Angeles Times:*

Dear Ms. Weiner-Davis:

My age is sixty-seven, and after nineteen years of a marriage that was impossible in my opinion, I did seek a divorce. I sincerely believed that my children and I would be better off if I got out of the marriage, and this was confirmed and encouraged by therapists. I should have tried harder to make our lives better. I should have changed myself more. I wish I knew then all the things I know now. It takes so long to attain wisdom, when it is needed when one is young.

I was forty and attractive and wanted to "grow," and did not like the way my children were, emotionally, living with the type of person their father was. I did what I thought was the best thing to do, at that time. And yes, I did think I would spend a year or so alone, remarry, and everything would be fine.

My children, who did not like their father, were nevertheless adversely affected over the years because of the divorce. They are now grown and have learned to accept him as he is. But damage was done. I "went out into the world" for the first time in my life and I did grow, learn, experience fantastic fun and loneliness as well. I eventually remarried and my marriage at this time is fine. But it took a lot of work to make it this way.

The article stirred up lots of feelings and doubts about what I thought for so long was "the right thing" to do—divorce. Many years ago, a friend said to me that getting a divorce is like getting hit by a Mack truck. It is. For everyone involved.

My ex-husband has remarried and I believe his wife has difficulty coping with some of his idiosyncrasies but she accepts them and enjoys an otherwise good life with him. (I should have been wise enough to do the same.)

I am not thoroughly convinced that I did the wrong thing, but I am sorry that I did not get better counseling and give it more time before disrupting four lives (two children). Maybe the marriage could have been saved.

Mainly, I would like to applaud you and the other therapists on the new view of divorce. Divorce should only be done as a last resort, when all other efforts have been exhausted. For everyone's sake.

You should feel proud of the work you are doing. Congratulations.

Mary

I was very touched by this letter because it captured the feelings expressed by so many divorced people I've met over the years. In a desperate attempt to expand her own life and improve the quality of life for her children, she left her husband. Convinced this move would be best for all concerned, she made a decision that would change their lives. As she reflected on the outcome of her decision, she was not without regrets. Her second marriage taught her that all marriages require a commitment to work out differences since no partners are perfect; like any package deal, there are pluses and minuses. With painstaking honesty, she admitted the wisdom in accepting certain idiosyncrasies in one's spouse in order to enjoy "an otherwise good life with him" (as his new wife understands).

Her children taught her about the damaging effects of divorce despite her belief she was rescuing them from their unlikable father. Ironically, they eventually learned to "accept him as he is" anyway. Despite her personal gains from the divorce, she regretted not having given the marriage more time and gotten more support for staying married from the therapists she encountered along the way.

ARE WE FINALLY LEARNING?

Clearly, divorce supplied no magic solutions for Mary. It appears that more and more couples are beginning to take a skeptical view of divorce. In fact, something remarkable happened in 1982: For the first time in twenty-five years the divorce rate dropped, after having first leveled off for one year. The National Center for Health Statistics indicated that the 1989 rates were down 4 percent from 1988. This decline followed an unprecedented rise in the number of divorces in our country from 1960 through 1980.

Why the decrease; what's going on? There are many theories. Some say the growing threat of AIDS is keeping couples together or that more couples are separating but not divorcing to spare themselves legal costs. However, my explanation is different. I believe that people are beginning to realize how devastating divorce is—emotionally, financially and spiritually—for everyone involved. With enough time under our belts to have observed the results of rampant divorce, we are beginning to recognize the price we have paid for the freedom of disposable marriages.

My conclusion—that divorce is not the answer—is based on more than a decade of observation of clients, friends and family who have opted to divorce and on input from many of my colleagues who work with couples and families. In regard to divorce, this is what I have learned:

1. DIVORCE DOESN'T SOLVE THE PROBLEMS IT IS MEANT TO SOLVE

There are primarily two reasons people divorce. One is to escape a relationship that has been painful, loveless or destructive. The second is to seek a more satisfying life with a new partner or alone. As you will see in this chapter, these goals are not always accomplished through divorce. Some people do go on to enhance their lives, but the price they pay is often higher than anticipated.

Few adults anticipate accurately what lies ahead when they decide to divorce. Life is almost always more arduous and more complicated than they expect. It is often more depleting and more lonely for at least one member of the marriage. At the time of divorce, people are intent on getting rid of their unhappiness, and they find it difficult to conjure up understanding for something they have never experienced. It is hard for them to imagine the multiple changes that divorce will bring in its wake. Eventually they do learn, however, that the changes we make from divorce are hard-won. (Wallerstein and Blakeslee, 1989.)

"If It Weren't for You, I'd Be Happy"

Desperately unhappy people search for ways out of their unhappiness. They start by trying to determine the cause of their misery. As they look around, married people often see their spouse as the culprit. Blaming your spouse for your unhappiness is easy to do. Everyone does it, often supported in this kind of thinking by friends and relatives. "I would be happier if he were more attentive"; "If she didn't nag so much, I would enjoy my life"; "He's gone so much, of course I'm miserable" are some of the more common spousal complaints. Underlying each of these statements is the belief that the person's unhappiness is caused by his or her mate. Logic then dictates that divorce is the solution: "If I get rid of my spouse, I will get rid of this problem and then I will be happy."

Unfortunately, it doesn't work that way. People are shocked to discover that their difficulties continue to hound them in spite of their single status or their choice of a new partner. Some disillusioned divorced people tell me, "My spouse's habits really irritated me, but now I can't cope with this loneliness. The silence in the evenings is killing me." Or "The new guy I married seemed so sensitive and open, the qualities I missed in my first marriage, but as I've gotten to know him better he now seems more like a clone of my first husband." Or "I thought leaving my wife and all of her demands would make me happy, but oddly enough I am still unhappy."

As you will learn from this book, diagnosing your spouse as the problem means that your microscope lens may be too narrowly focused. You are failing to notice how the habits you *both* have developed and the roles you've *both* played have contributed to your unworkable marriage. Unfortunately, you take those habits with you when you go.

If getting rid of one's problematic spouse was a solution, why would 60 percent of second marriages end in divorce? If divorce were truly an answer, people would learn from the mistakes they made in their first marriage. Their second marriage would provide them with opportunities to apply what they learned. Sometimes this is the case, but more frequently, people are not prepared for the complexities of second marriages or blended families. Sometimes the trials and tribulations of the previous marriage with all its aggravation seem mild by comparison. But the results of this sort of comparison come too late. People discover that the grass isn't any greener on the other side after all. Then the decision to divorce a second time is often less agonizing since there's familiarity with the process.

"If It Weren't for You, There Would Be No More Arguments"

Many people leave their marriages expecting the arguments to stop. Divorce does offer a temporary reprieve from the tension and/or arguing, but when children are involved, marital debates frequently *do not* cease with the divorce decree. I have worked with divorced couples unable to resolve child-custody, visitation and child-rearing issues. They give new meaning to the words "hostile" and "angry." That these two human beings once shared a cordial or loving relationship is almost unthinkable because all that remains of their shared history is hatred.

What also continues to amaze me is how even many years of physical separation fail to free these couples from intense emotional bonds. Their inability to resolve certain child-rearing issues reflects their inability to let go of each other.

Debra and Thomas, a divorced couple, arrived in my office for divorce mediation since they were unable to resolve major disagreements over the visitation schedule. Like many couples needing mediation, Debra and Thomas's interactions were characterized by animosity and lack of respect. Even when addressing each other, they maintained eye contact with me. They frequently interrupted each other with accusations or alternative versions of the truth. When I requested that each person be allowed to speak uninterrupted, "loud" grimaces took the place of verbal attacks.

Although I kept them focused on the task at hand, finding solutions to the visitation problems, eventually the conversation turned to the disappointment they felt about unmet needs in the marriage. Debra wept as she told of her close relationship with her father and how Thomas failed to live up to the memories she had of her childhood with her dad. Thomas felt that Debra never really respected him due to their cultural and socioeconomic differences. He thought he was never good enough in the eyes of Debra's family. The sadness of their failed relationship was fresh for both of them though they had been divorced for five years.

What upset Debra the most was that, since the time of their divorce and Thomas's subsequent marriage to Sue, Thomas was taking a more active parenting role. Now each time Thomas sought more contact with the children, instead of feeling pleased for the children that they were important to their dad, she felt betrayed and manipulated. "Why, if the children are so important to you, didn't you make time for them when we were married?" she challenged him. His requests for increased visitation were often denied because of her resentment over thwarted dreams.

Thomas never took Debra's criticism about his priorities seriously when they were married because, according to him, Debra criticized him about everything. Debra's pleas for more involvement with the children were seen as just one more item on Debra's long laundry list of Thomas's inadequacies. So Thomas had resisted more involvement with the children, not because he didn't love them or want to be with them, but because of the tug-of-war with Debra. Once separated from her, he missed the children and saw that his relationship with them was important to him. This explained his recent desire to spend more time with them.

Although an agreement about visitation was reached during that session, Debra left crying. I believe she cried all the way home. Thomas also showed signs of feeling drained emotionally. They both had hoped that their divorce would free them from disappointment, arguments about the children and criticisms of each other, none of which happened. Clearly, their unresolved relationship issues kept them super-glued to each other, making it impossible for them to cooperate as parents.

If you have children and are considering divorce, you must remember that your spouse will *always* be your children's parent, no matter what you do. Unless he or she decides to sever ties entirely, you will continue to have contact with that person for the rest of your life! This contact serves as a constant reminder of the past. Children can also be ghosts of failed marriages when, because of their looks or personalities, they remind a parent of an estranged spouse. This can have deadly consequences for the parent-child relationship.

2. DIVORCE CREATES NEW PROBLEMS

When people divorce they have visions of better lives. Old problems will vanish, they hope, as new dreams take their place. These dreams usually include meeting candidates for more intimate relationships, more compatible sexual partners, improved financial status, more freedom to pursue personal goals and new opportunities to make independent choices. As explained above, these dreams frequently do not materialize, creating a whole new set of problems. Even when desired changes do occur, they are not without unintended or unexpected consequences. Let us take a look at some frequent but unexpected consequences of divorce.

Money Matters

If you are a woman, the statistics are bleak. Lenore Weitzman, a sociologist who conducted an extensive study of divorced families, wrote in her book *The Divorce Revolution* that one year after divorce, women's standard of living decreases by 73 percent while men's increases by 42 percent. Furthermore, alimony is a thing of the past. Women seldom are awarded it. Weitzman writes:

> These apparently simple statistics have far-reaching social and economic consequences. For most women and children, divorce means precipitous downward mobility—both economically and socially. The reduction in income brings residential moves and inferior housing, drastically diminished or nonexistent funds for recreation and leisure, and intense pressures due to inadequate time and money. (Quoted in Berman, 1991, p. 57.)

Unfortunately, all too often, effects of changing financial status are overlooked, minimized or denied.

Where Is Mr. Right?

There are other disadvantages to being a newly divorced woman. According to the Census Bureau, divorced women are far less likely to remarry than divorced men. Forty percent of the women who divorce after age thirty do not remarry. A portion of those who do not remarry may do so by choice, but many say that the pool of marriage-minded men available to these women has been shrinking. It seems that many men in similar age brackets are marrying younger women.

Imagine how shocking it is to the woman who leaves a marriage hoping to find intimacy and romance in the perfect new mate and finds herself alone instead. Loneliness is a frequent complaint in my therapy practice. "How do I meet someone if I can't stand the bar scene?" is the $64,000 question.

Being Single Again Isn't All That It's Cracked Up to Be

There is a line in a popular country and western song by K.T. Oslin that goes, "Don't kiss me like we're married, kiss me like we're lovers." The newly divorced often look forward to the excitement of playing the field. The routine and boredom of married life gives way to the titillation of being single again. What they do not anticipate and what many veterans of single life have discovered is that being single again isn't all that it's cracked up to be. Fear of rejection, fear of AIDS, learning about and adjusting to a new person's idiosyncrasies, struggling to trust again, all make single life a real challenge. Many people find themselves yearning for the very stability they left behind.

While most people do not naively assume that the adjustment period after divorce will be easy, they don't expect the intense loneliness and depression that often follows. Judith Wallerstein's long-term study of divorced couples revealed that even one decade after their divorce, many people still had not completely recovered:

> With typical optimism, we wanted to believe that time would mute feelings of hurt and anger, that time itself heals all wounds, and that time automatically diminishes feelings or memories; that hurt and depression are overcome; or that jealousy, anger, and outrage will vanish. Some experiences are just as painful ten years later; some memories haunt us for a lifetime. People go on living, but just because they have lived ten more years does not mean they have recovered from the hurt. (Wallerstein and Blakeslee, 1989.)

No matter how badly a person wants a divorce, there are usually feelings of remorse about the failed relationship—especially in cases where couples have been married for many years. Looking at photographs of memorable occasions and wonderful vacations together, rereading once-cherished love letters, glancing at sentimental memorabilia, all arouse feelings of sadness and loss.

Frequently, people in the throes of divorcing are too angry and antagonistic to acknowledge these emotions, which lay dormant until the divorce proceedings have ended and the dust has settled. Then even the most zealous divorce seekers often report a sense of failure and personal loss. Even when the decision to divorce is firm, there is no escaping the sadness.

3. DIVORCE HURTS CHILDREN OF ALL AGES

There is no optimum time to divorce when children are involved. People once comforted themselves by thinking only young children get hurt when parents split. Now we know better. We have learned that, regardless of children's ages at the time their parents divorce, children lose a great deal. I recently heard a story which vividly illustrates this point from a man I sat next to on a plane.

The man was in his late sixties and said he had been married for twenty-four years. "One day, my wife announced she needed to find herself and filed for divorce," he said. He went on to tell me, "My youngest son was thirteen at the time and was the only child of three still living at home. I must admit that although I was devastated by the divorce my career blossomed afterward. Although always financially comfortable, I had never been quite as successful professionally during my marriage as I was after my divorce.

"My wife also benefited from our divorce. She went to school and received two degrees and developed her own career. I am convinced she has made more of her life than would have been possible had she remained my wife. Still," he added, "the real losers in divorce are the children." He then told me about an incident involving his thirteen-year-old son in the period leading up to the divorce.

"I have had a lifelong habit of changing my clothes each night after work and placing the coins emptied from my pants pockets on my dresser. After several weeks, I noticed I was missing money. By the time I became aware of it, about eighty or ninety dollars had been taken. I confronted my son about the missing money and he admitted to taking it.

"Hurt, disappointed and puzzled, I asked him why he took the money. He lowered his head and replied, 'When you and Mom divorce, I will have to live with Mom and since she doesn't have a lot of money, we will need the money for food.'" These words were like daggers to his heart. Finishing his story he reiterated, "Children are the real losers in divorce," and quickly averted his eyes for fear I would see his tears.

Couples Don't Divorce, Families Divorce

There are many reasons that children lose out. What children lose when their parents split is their family. It is a fallacy to think of divorce as something that happens between a husband and wife. Couples don't divorce, families divorce. What was once the basis of security and protection for the children no longer exists. A child of divorce has his very foundation pulled from beneath him with no say in the matter. Parents move away, sometimes siblings get split up, intensely loyal family members take sides. The family structure disappears into thin air when a marriage dissolves. The unspoken rule—mom and dad will be together forever—has been broken.

Divorce Is Forever

In her book *Adult Children of Divorce Speak Out* Claire Berman recounts her extensive interviews with men and women ranging in age from twenty-four to sixty-seven who during their childhood experienced their parents' separation or divorce. The vast majority of these adults described their reactions to the divorce as a pain or emptiness that never goes away, a pain that continues to affect many aspects of their adult lives. "The divorce of my parents has left a hole in my heart. It is a hole that will never be filled," said one of the study's participants, and many others echoed this or a similar phrase. What is particularly striking is the freshness of the memories despite the distance time placed between those interviewed and their parents' divorce.

Berman tells her readers:

> The most striking impression one comes away with is that for children, *the divorce of the parents never goes away*. It may be welcomed. It may be understood. But even when it is a positive solution to a destructive family situation, divorce is a *critical experience* for its children. Although there may be relief that a painful situation has been ended, there is also regret that a healthy family could not have been created. (Berman, 1991, p. 18.)

Some say that death is easier for children to accept than divorce because death is a single event which passes, and for which there is usually a clear-cut cause. People mourn, grieve and have memories, but death is final. Divorce, on the other hand, lasts forever.

For the Sake of the Kids

We are now beginning to see that it doesn't necessarily follow that what's best for parents is best for children. Frank Pittman, author of *Private Lies: Infidelity and the Betrayal of Intimacy*, believes:

> Our experiment with abolishing marriage has not worked very well for either the adults or the children, but it's the adults who don't seem to realize it. I don't know anyone with divorced parents who doesn't see the divorce as the most central experience of their lives. Children who grow up seeing their parents run away from home have a different relationship with marriage than those who saw parents hang in there. Brutal marriages may be bad for children, but I'm not sure boring marriages are. (Quoted in Nord, 1989, p. 26.)

This raises the popular question: "Should couples stay together for the sake of the kids?" Implicit in this question is the assumption that people stay together for any single reason. Even successful long-term marriages are rarely held together by one bond, including love. Couples stay together for a multitude of reasons: financial and emotional security, sex, dislike of the singles scene, stability, companionship, status, fear of loneliness, feelings of love and commitment, religious mores, the children. There is nothing unusual or unhealthy about kids being one of the many ties inextricably connecting couples.

Another assumption implicit in the question "Should couples stay together for the sake of the kids?" is that these couples will always be miserable, that they must live in conflict for the rest of their lives. Couples *should not* remain in unhappy or lifeless marriages for the rest of their lives just for the sake of the kids. Research shows that whether their parents are married or divorced children suffer when there is conflict. Couples *should* do everything within their power to make their marriages work again so that their children's lives will not be adversely affected by conflict or divorce. In other words, couples should stay *happy* for the sake of the kids.

IS DIVORCE ALL BAD?

Research on the potential effects of divorce on childhood development is about two decades old, and the lasting effects are only beginning to be documented. The actual percentage of children adversely affected is still largely an unanswered question.

We do know that children are not necessarily doomed to a life of depression or delinquency simply because their parents have decided to divorce. In fact, many children do quite well. Some researchers believe that the parental conflict that often follows divorce, rather than the divorce itself, is the major cause of childhood behavior problems associated with divorce. Children whose parents strive to cooperate or co-parent after divorce experience fewer post-divorce difficulties.

So whether you decide to learn how to cooperate with your spouse within the context of your marriage or in the post-divorce period, if you want you, your spouse and your children to have a stable environment you will need to develop and practice problem-solving skills. The message of this book is: "Why not begin right now?"

You are probably saying to yourself, "Yes, but how?" This book was written to provide you with answers to this question. Based on my work with hundreds of couples, it has been my observation that a vast number of marital problems are caused by misconceptions about love and marriage. Unrealistic expectations about relationships are the viruses in unhealthy marriages. Chapter 2, "Illusions Leading to Dis-solutions," outlines these misconceptions so that you can see how faulty thinking may be underlying some of your difficulties.

Illusions Leading
to Dis-solutions

WHEN I WAS PREGNANT WITH MY FIRST CHILD, MY HUSBAND AND I attended a series of Lamaze classes. In preparation for parenthood, one of the last classes was devoted to life with children. I distinctly remember my instructor's solution to the fatigue she felt from the never-ending demands of her three children. She confessed that she would lock herself in her room for five minutes, telling her children that her room was off-limits. She would then fall into a Zen-like meditative state and reappear downstairs refreshed.

My reaction to her parenting tip was so extreme, I couldn't wait for the class to end to hear my husband's response. I almost laughed out loud when she told us that five minutes did the trick for her. "Here is a woman who is obviously satisfied with very little," I thought to myself. "She thinks that stealing away for five short minutes is a major accomplishment. She's either a martyr or some extreme version of Supermom." As we walked to our car (or should I say waddled), my husband said he agreed with me completely. We shook our heads and laughed all the way home.

We are not laughing anymore. Now, some ten parenting years and two children later, our eyes have been opened. What I wouldn't give for five (even three) minutes of solitude on our many frenzied days. We obviously had a great deal to learn about children and being parents. Needless to say, our many erroneous and idealistic expectations about raising children made the transition into parenthood a challenging one.

There have been a fair number of times when our naive expectations have clashed loudly with the lessons of reality. These occasions left us feeling depressed, disillusioned and nostalgic about our childless days. In the midst of these rough spots, I found it curious that most parents do not question their lifelong commitment to their children. Divorcing our children is not an option even when they thwart our goals and plans, even when they behave in ways we never would have dreamed of. Imagine an overwhelmed parent announcing, "I'm divorcing my son on the grounds of extreme mental cruelty," or "I'm leaving—my daughter and I are simply incompatible." Sounds absurd, doesn't it?

Instead, we learn to readjust, to modify our expectations and roll with the punches. We become grateful for the good times and learn to expect the hard times. "My son is in the terrible twos, no wonder I'm a basket case," reasons the harried parent. We enroll in courses entitled "Surviving Adolescence" to make life tolerable when their hormones are raging. But where are the courses entitled "Survival After the Honeymoon Period" or "Dealing with His Midlife Crisis" when he loses twenty pounds and buys a red sports car?

Parents often quip, "Too bad babies don't come with instructions." Not knowing what to expect makes parenting a nerve-racking business. But babies aren't the only things that arrive without instructions. Marriage vows are also taken without marriage manuals. Entering marriage with unrealistic expectations can eventually kill the relationship, and often does. Unlike the committed, all-forgiving attitude we have toward our children, when our mates fail to live up to our expectations we consider divorce as an option. Without any manuals to guide us, how do we learn what to expect from our spouses?

"BUT THAT'S HOW MY PARENTS WERE"

Our own parents' marriage is one source of information. Children are like sponges, soaking up images of marital and family life as they grow. Growing up provides children with detailed maps of how spouses interact. Grown children then take these maps into their own marriages, influencing how they behave as marital partners and how they expect to be treated by their mates. These preconceptions present problems to couples when, as is often the case, their expectations fail to coincide.

Harville Hendrix, marital therapist and author of *Getting the Love You Want: A Guide for Couples*, writes:

> As soon as they start living together, most people assume that their mates will conform to a very specific but rarely expressed set of behaviors. For example, a man may expect his new bride to do the housework, cook the meals, shop for groceries, wash the clothes, arrange the social events, take on the role of family nurse, and buy everyday household items. In addition to these traditional role expectations, he has a long list of expectations that are peculiar to his own upbringing. On Sundays, for example, he may expect his wife to cook a special breakfast while he reads the Sunday paper, and then join him for a leisurely stroll in the park. This is the way his parents spent their Sundays together, and the day wouldn't feel "right" unless it echoed these dominant chords.
>
> Meanwhile, his wife has an equally long, and perhaps conflicting, set of expectations. In addition to wanting her husband to be responsible for the "manly" chores, such as taking care of the car, paying the bills, figuring the taxes, mowing the lawn, and overseeing minor and major repairs, she may expect him to help with the cooking, shopping, and laundry as well. Then, she, too, has expectations that reflect her particular upbringing. An ideal Sunday for her may include going to church, going out to a restaurant for brunch, and spending the afternoon visiting relatives. Since neither of them shared expectations before getting married, these could develop into a significant source of tension. (Hendrix, 1988, pp. 54–55.)

Recently, couples are learning that their parents' relationships are not necessarily the best prototypes for today's marriages. Our parents had it easier in some ways; their roles were clearly defined while ours are not. The women's movement has greatly changed the roles men and women play within marriages and families. Granted, we—both men and women—have more freedom to choose, but with this freedom comes uncertainty. No wonder we are confused.

MEDIA MARRIAGES

Our upbringing isn't the only thing shaping our ideas about love and marriage. The media and what other people tell us about their nuptial lives influence us as well. Television and movie marriages are usually shallow, exaggerated, and caricatural. Remember Ozzie and Harriet and the Honeymooners? The media's job is to entertain, not necessarily inform. The more entertaining, the higher the ratings. I can recall one movie that seemed realistic in its portrayal of the trials and tribulations of marriage—Ingmar Bergman's *Scenes From a Marriage*. I also distinctly remember many people, men in particular, saying the movie was boring.

MY HAPPILY MARRIED FRIENDS WHO JUST GOT DIVORCED . . .

Another source of information that shapes our views of marriage is the marriages of our neighbors, friends and family. We look around us to see how the "average" married couple lives. As you will see, there are major drawbacks to drawing conclusions this way.

A friend of mine named John told me a story which illustrates how little we really know about our friends' marriages. Several years ago John's lifelong friend, a writer, was doing a feature story on successful long-term marriages. Since the writer had known John and his wife for many years and thought they were the ideal couple, he wanted to interview them to learn the secret of their success.

For months, John kept putting off the interview and his friend couldn't figure out why. Finally, when he confronted John, John admitted that he could not be interviewed on successful marriages because he and his wife had just decided to divorce. His friend was absolutely shocked. Despite the many years they had been friends, despite the fact that the men and their wives socialized with one another constantly, John's friend had absolutely no clue that John's marriage was on the rocks.

That's not atypical of the outsider's view. I can't count the number of times I have heard people say, "I just can't believe that Brenda and John are getting divorced, they seemed so perfect together." What we observe about our friends' or acquaintances' marriages doesn't teach us much since we don't really know what goes on behind closed doors.

SO NOW WHAT?

Some say that the changes in our culture over the last two or three decades have taken marriage into uncharted territory. We have few concepts about what makes marriages work that still apply. As we embark into the nineties we need to investigate and experiment with new models. We need new language to describe the recent emphasis on making marriages work instead of getting out. We have a term for what couples do at the beginning of the nuptial union—marrying—and for the end of the union—divorcing—but we have no term for what happily married couples do to *stay* married. Perhaps "marriaging" is just the word we need. Marriaging is what couples do to make their marriages work. We don't know enough about successful marriaging in the nineties.

DIVORCING YOUR ILLUSIONS

But we do know some things. We have become experts on what doesn't work. Having unreasonable expectations about marriage is high on the list of things that destroy otherwise reasonably sound relationships. This chapter looks at common illusions about love and marriage that lead people to divorce. Once you see how unrealistic expectations about marriage may have been contributing to your marital problems, you can better understand your situation. Without this understanding, you are likely to blame your spouse, yourself or your relationship for the destructive effect of these illusions.

Once each illusion is identified and understood, solutions start to emerge. However, this chapter does not explore solutions to the illusions in depth. That's what the rest of the book is about—SBT and its specific application to marital problem solving. For now, the first step to improving your marriage is to identify your marital misconceptions because what might need to be discarded are these ideas, not your spouse.

The following list of illusions leading to dis-solutions is by no means comprehensive. There are many other unrealistic ideas that have damaging results. However, these six illusions are the ones I hear about most often from distressed couples.

ILLUSION #1: "OUR PROBLEMS HAVE LASTED SO LONG, IT'S TOO LATE TO CHANGE"

Going Back to the Future

Sometimes people think that long-lasting problems are unsolvable. They say, "We have had this problem for ten years, we (he, she) can never really be different." Most unhappy couples have at least one thing in common: a myopia about the future. They are fixated on the past, primarily on relationship failures over the years, or they are lost in a labyrinth of blame and counterblame about the present. They fail to remember that there *is* such a thing as the future, and fail to imagine how the future can be anything but a miserable extension of the past and present.

Franklin D. Roosevelt once said, "Some people see things as they are and ask, 'Why?' Others see things as they could be and ask, 'Why not?'" Why do people lose sight of the fact that relationships and people *can* change no matter how entrenched problems seem to be? One reason is that most people attribute their marital problems to some deeply ingrained personality characteristics of their spouse. They think of their spouse's difficult behavior as static, fixed and unchangeable.

"My Husband Is Just Like That—He's an Angry Person. He'll Never Change"

For example, if your husband gets angry every time you raise a financial concern, you may overgeneralize and think of him as an angry person or as a disrespectful person. You probably think of his responses in those specific situations as being representative of who he is as a person. Anger, the overt behavior, is apparently just an expression of the real person inside.

So far, so good. However, now things get a bit more complicated. What is puzzling about all this is that when you talk to your husband about a different topic, he does not respond with anger, or if someone else raises the subject of finances with him, he remains calm. How do we explain this to ourselves? Do we contradict our previous conclusion by saying, "My husband is a reasonable person"? Generally not. Typically, we fail to notice these exceptions or, if we do notice, we attribute the reasonableness to some other negative personality trait. "My husband is two-faced" may be the preferred explanation. Rather than seeing a person's action as being a response to a specific situation, we are blinded by our labels.

If, in your view, your marital problems stem from the fact that your husband is an angry person, there may be little that can be done to fix things short of his undergoing a personality overhaul. If, on the other hand, you believe that your husband becomes angry in response to certain stimuli, you can experiment with different approaches. Although these alternate approaches will be addressed thoroughly in later chapters, a few examples here might be useful.

In the above situation, a wife with financial concerns might try varying her strategy to elicit a reasonable response from her husband. She might raise the issue in a different environment (during a walk together outside), or at a different time (timing is everything, they say) or with a new slant (including some recent updated information). Any of these different strategies may work, but if she believes her spouse needs a personality overhaul, she'll be less inclined to try them. Clearly, seeing our mate's actions as responses to specific situations and not deeply ingrained personality traits is a much more optimistic perspective.

A Case of Faulty Genes

When I met Kim and Glen, it was clear they both thought their marital problems were due to a fixed, undesirable trait of Glen's personality. Kim was prepared to leave the marriage because she believed that Glen was incapable of developing a close relationship with Todd, her son from a previous marriage. This hurt Kim greatly because part of the reason she remarried after the death of her last husband was that she wanted a father for Todd. For ten years, Kim yearned for Glen to nurture Todd and show interest in him, but Glen kept his distance. Glen thought that Todd was a nice kid, but felt incapable of showing affection to a male child.

Over the years he told Kim about this self-imposed limitation frequently enough that eventually she grew to believe it too. They spoke of Glen's "lack of ability to bond with a male child" in the same way people talk about physical traits, such as whether you have brown eyes. As I listened to them, it became apparent they were convinced that Glen missed out on the gene responsible for adept father-son relationships. Something went wrong with his DNA.

Kim finally came to the conclusion that Glen could never

change. When Kim admitted to herself that Glen's "disability" was going to last forever, she decided to give up on her marriage. "He's been this way for our entire married life. He can't change now," she told me. Rather than disagree, I chose to meet alone with Glen.

During our meeting it became evident that, in contrast to Kim's portrayal of Glen, he *had* tried to reach out to Todd in various ways over the years, but Kim never noticed the attempts he made. She had grown to expect the same old thing from Glen in regard to Todd, and failed to notice any behavior that deviated from her expectations. Glen received no positive feedback from Kim for his efforts, reinforcing his own idea that he was inept.

Glen made the mistake of thinking that because he felt awkward and unsure interacting with Todd that their relationship wasn't meant to be. He thought that his dealings with Todd should have felt more natural. But through our discussion Glen saw that feeling comfortable takes time. We talked about the awkwardness of doing anything new, like riding a bike or driving a car for the first time. He recalled those uncertain feelings and admitted that, as a child, he did not give up bicycling when he fell off his bike. By the end of the session he agreed to work on his relationship with Todd.

Much to Kim's amazement, Glen started spending more time with Todd. He initiated conversations, they watched TV together, they even shared some household chores. Kim was flabbergasted! In retrospect, I'm not sure who was more surprised by the sudden change—Kim, Todd or Glen. Delighted by the changes, Kim reversed her decision to leave the marriage and Glen and Kim began to enjoy each other again.

You Can If You Think You Can

As I reflected on my experience with Kim and Glen I realized that what worked for them was my refusal to accept their shared definition of the problem, that is, Glen's parental ineptitude. Instead I helped open the door to other possibilities by seeing Glen as capable of change. When Glen told me he couldn't bond with a male child, I asked him incredulously, "Where did you get that idea?" Exploring Glen's background for clues about his apparent dysfunction might have been the approach I would have taken prior to SBT. The results of that exploration only would have reinforced Glen's negative self-concept.

Kim and Glen's success is not an isolated incident. The rapid changes in their marriage were not a fluke. When you think about your spouse's patterns of behavior in terms of habits rather than as an outcome of personality quirks, change is more likely. Anyone can break a habit or replace a bad habit with a good habit.

A woman told me that her husband had the habit of leaving bottle caps off of carbonated beverages such as seltzer, which resulted in the beverage losing its effervescence. This annoyed her since she didn't like the taste of flat seltzer. She took repeated steps to help him remember to use the bottle cap and, although forgetting had been a lifelong habit, he eventually started to use the cap regularly.

Imagine how different the results might have been had she thought about her husband's bottle cap habit as a personality characteristic: "My husband is sloppy," or "My husband is absent-minded," or "My husband is spiteful." Describing his behavior as a personality characteristic would make his putting the bottle cap on properly seem less likely. Other, more serious personal and relationship habits can be kicked in the same way—cold turkey.

The Self-Fulfilling Prophecy

If you have spent the last few months or even years trying to improve your marriage to no avail, it is easy to see why you would eventually think change was impossible. It hurts to be in a seemingly unescapable rut. You console yourself daily with your mantra, "You can lead a horse to water, but you can't make it drink." This perspective shields you from the pain and disappointment of trying unsuccessfully to find happiness again. You tell yourself, "If I expect the worst, I won't be disappointed." Right? No, wrong!

Norman Cousins said, "We fear the worst, we expect the worst, we invite the worst." Simply, if you expect the worst, you'll get it. This is not a superstitious suggestion that you will be jinxed if you think negatively. What it means is that self-fulfilling prophecy is the overriding dynamic in most social interactions. Here is an example.

The Rosenthal Effect

In the sixties, a social psychologist, Robert Rosenthal, and his associates spent many years studying a phenomenon called "experimenter bias." Rosenthal was interested in knowing whether an experimenter's expectations about an experiment's outcome influence the outcome. In other words, does an experimenter's bias affect how he approaches and performs the experiment, and if so, does that in turn affect the results?

Although he performed numerous experiments and wrote prolifically on the subject, one particular experiment with children received considerable attention. Rosenthal and a colleague went to an elementary school and gave the children a standardized test measuring IQ. Twenty percent of the children were then randomly selected and labeled as having superior intelligence. The teachers were told that they could expect superior academic performance and unusual intellectual gains from this group of students during the school year. In other words, the teachers were falsely led to believe that the randomly selected group was superior intellectually to other students.

At the end of the school year the test was readministered to all the children. They found that the students who were *expected* to achieve more showed a significantly greater gain than the children in the average group. The teachers' expectations were communicated to the students—students believed to be brighter were handled differently from students believed to be average—and the children lived up to the respective expectations.

What relevance does the Rosenthal Effect have for you? Perhaps now you can see that if you expect failure, you are communicating this expectation to your spouse through your actions. You may or may not be conscious of it. You may be subtle or overt in your message. Nevertheless, if you believe the illusion "Our problems have lasted so long, it's too late to change" you have been broadcasting loudly and clearly: "HONEY, YOU CAN NEVER AND WILL NEVER CHANGE!" (or some variation on that theme).

This message is hardly a welcome mat for good will or domestic tranquility. In fact, like the students in the Rosenthal experiment, your spouse may simply be living up to your expectations. This is important for you to know because you may have been inadvertently sabotaging your own problem-solving efforts by visualizing unhappiness, boredom or doom for your marriage.

The Proof Is in the Pudding

I have worked with hundreds of people who had serious, chronic relationship problems that got resolved. Research on the SBT approach shows no correlation whatsoever between the duration of difficulties and successful treatment. It is understandable that you might think, "We've had this problem for so long, it's unsolvable," but it is inaccurate. People change all the time. No matter how bad things have been, regardless of how long problems have existed, people *can* and *do* change.

If you have been overwhelmed with the feeling of hopelessness, it might not go away overnight. Be patient. As you read about the success stories in this book, remember that many of the people whose lives are depicted in the stories were as discouraged as you before they discovered their solutions.

ILLUSION #2: "MY HUSBAND CAN'T COMMUNICATE"

This is the most frequent complaint women voice about their husbands. Musician John Prine spoke for many women when he sang: "How the hell can a person go to work in the morning, come home in the evening and have nothin' to say?" Women complain that their husbands seldom talk but when they do talk it's about superficial, meaningless topics. Women also feel that their spouses rarely verbalize feelings and, when confronted on this matter, they just clam up. Feeling cheated, isolated and lonely, women often look to divorce as a solution.

People Cannot "Not Communicate"

Although women frequently say, "My husband and I do not communicate," in reality this is impossible. Even not talking at the breakfast table is a form of communication:

> Communication in marriage is a constant exchange of information—of messages—between the two spouses by speech, letter writing, talking on the telephone, the exhibition of bodily or facial expressions, and other methods as well. The information may be straightforward and factual, conveyed by words ("I want coffee"; "It is raining"; "Here is five dollars"), or it may indicate, by tone of voice and by gesture, the nature of the relationship between the parties involved. Receiving a message is not a matter of understanding spoken words alone: the rattling of pots in the kitchen or the slamming of a door may telegraph the mood of a spouse." (Lederer and Jackson, 1966, p. 98.)

If all behavior is communicative, then why do women feel there is no communication? There are several reasons. In her book *You*

Just Don't Understand: Women and Men in Conversation, Deborah Tannen, a professor of linguistics, offers answers to this age-old question.

According to Tannen, there are many major differences in conversational styles between men and women which lead to gross misunderstandings. She writes, "There are gender differences in ways of speaking, and we need to identify and understand them. Without such understanding, we are doomed to blame others or ourselves—or the relationship—for the otherwise mystifying and damaging effects of our contrasting conversational styles" (Tannen, 1990, p. 17).

The Gender Gap

What are the differences in conversational styles? Tannen feels that many of the problems in male-female communication can be traced back to the disparate needs of men and women concerning intimacy and independence:

> *Intimacy* is key in a world of connection where individuals negotiate complex networks of friendship, minimize differences, try to reach consensus, and avoid the appearance of superiority, which would highlight differences. In a world of status, *independence* is key, because a primary means of establishing status is to tell others what to do, and taking orders is a marker of low status. Though all humans need both intimacy and independence, women tend to focus on the first and men on the second. (Tannen, 1990, p. 26.)

Tannen contends that conversation is a way of achieving intimacy or connections for women and independence or status for men. Since men and women have different focuses in conversations, they are often disappointed when their expectations are not met.

The phenomena regarding gender differences in communication that Tannen so deftly describes in her book can also be observed in couples I have worked with. For example, women tell me that they communicate with their spouses as a way of getting close or connecting with them. They thrive on the intimacy derived from sharing feelings, talking about personal issues and having in-depth conversations. Men, on the other hand, don't use conversation as a way of getting close. *Doing* things together— participating in activities such as team sports—breeds connections for them.

It is no surprise, then, that men and women often have trouble understanding each other's way of achieving closeness. In my work with couples, lack of understanding of differences in conversational styles as portrayed by Tannen, has been apparent and oftentimes at the root of many serious marital problems. Failing to see that there is no single correct way to converse, spouses doggedly defend their idiosyncratic styles, resulting in hurt feelings and conversations that go nowhere.

Wives complain that their husbands rarely talk, but when they do, the focus is on masculine subjects such as business, sports, cars and politics. Since women find masculine topics to be superficial or boring, they consequently feel isolated, unsatisfied and determined to "work on the relationship" by talking about the problem. Frequently, this sort of discussion results in husbands withdrawing, which women view as the ultimate rejection.

Another difference I've observed in male and female conversational styles which coincides with Tannen's observations is that when talking about personal problems, women say that they want to feel understood. In contrast to women's desire for empathy when talking about personal problems, men feel the need to fix things, and do so by offering solutions. These solutions are usually not well accepted because they give the message "So, do something about it," rather than "I know what you mean." Women then attack men for not listening, not caring and being insensitive. Men recoil from this attack, confused by their partner's response to their helping efforts.

Men admit that sharing feelings is a low priority for them. For them, the old adage "actions speak louder than words" is axiomatic. Trouble begins when a man feels he is showing his love and his concern through his actions but his wife is waiting patiently for those three little words. I hear many women say, "Yes, he brings me roses, but he doesn't *tell* me often enough that he loves me." Clearly, as Tannen contends, women define communication by the female standard of verbalizing, not through action. They want their spouses to *talk* to them in their familiar "female" style. They overlook, discredit or misinterpret "masculine" forms of communication.

Nature Versus Nurture

What accounts for the misunderstanding about conversational style differences between men and women? During the forties and the fifties women didn't complain about their husbands not being able to communicate. Men weren't expected to talk; talking was considered a woman's domain.

However, the last two to three decades have seen a blurring of traditional gender roles in our society. The optimistic message of the sixties and the seventies was that human behavior is culturally learned, not biologically determined. Men joined sensitivity or rap groups while women took assertiveness training.

While this easing of sex role distinctions has been mostly beneficial, it has also been confusing. Although many women have come to expect men to display more feminine behavior, men have failed to live up to their expectations; gender differences live on. This has been a disappointment for the women who believed men can and should change their conversational style. Perhaps this minimizing of gender differences has done a disservice to the couples whose lives are tormented by them.

If fact, recent research suggests that the major differences in the communication styles between men and women may be physiologically based. In his book *Male and Female Realities: Understanding the Opposite Sex*, Joe Tanenbaum cites brain research which suggests that differences in the structure of male and female brains might account for differences in verbal abilities.

The human brain consists of two hemispheres, the right and the left. Each hemisphere is responsible for different functions. Males predominantly use the left hemisphere, which is responsible for reasoning, rational thought and logic. The right side of the brain is responsible for such functions as abstract thinking, communication and spatial perception. Brain researchers have found that male and female brains are anatomically different. The corpus callosum, the mass of tiny fibers connecting the left side of the brain to the right side, is 40 percent larger in women than men.

This means that women's brains are better able to send messages back and forth between the right and left hemispheres. As a result, right-brain functions, such as verbal fluency, comprehension and other language abilities, come more naturally to women. Although men excel in areas requiring logic and rational thought, they are simply not as good at expressing themselves. Period.

These gender differences have been observed in young children. Male children vastly outnumber female children in communication disorder classes. Girls speak at an earlier age and their language is more sophisticated than boys'. A study done with preschool-age children revealed that little girls spend the majority of their time either talking to themselves or their peers, whereas little boys spend the majority of their time making guttural sounds that mimic trucks, cars and guns.

Biologically Based Gender Differences in Dealing with Conflict

Another area where females take the verbal lead is in confronting relationship problems. Women are much more likely than men to confront their spouses with their dissatisfaction about the marriage, whereas husbands frequently respond with avoidance and withdrawal. Withdrawal of this sort leaves most women feeling enraged and even more determined to get a reaction, which leads to more withdrawal, and so on. Psychologists John Gottman and Robert Levenson have published some fascinating evidence that offers a physiological explanation for this classic pursuing-distancing pattern.

During interviews with couples, Gottman and Levenson asked them to identify, discuss and then reach some resolution on a major area of disagreement in their marriage. The researchers simultaneously videotaped and collected physiological data indicating physical arousal such as heart rate, blood velocity, skin conductance and gross motor movement. What did they find? They found that definite gender differences exist in response to conflict. More specifically, they observed:

> men rapidly become autonomically aroused when confronting conflict, whereas women experience relatively low levels of arousal over sustained conflict, which permits them to tolerate longer, escalating bouts of conflict. Men, therefore, need to shut off or diminish their arousal or they may be overwhelmed and lose control. Hence stonewalling is a kind of protective safety valve allowing men to dampen their own levels of arousal. (Quoted in Hetherington and Tryon, 1989, p. 58.)

Furthermore, it takes men longer than women to recover from physiological arousal.

Although knowing that men's tendency to avoid conflict may have a physiological basis does nothing to eliminate the original source of stress, it may, however, reduce women's feelings of rejection when stonewalling occurs. If a wife were to feel less rejection, she might act in ways less likely to escalate the dissension. For example, knowing that men don't do well with sustained periods of conflict, a couple could build in a time-out period to prevent arguments from escalating, thereby making solutions more accessible.

Reconcilable Differences

It is clear that there *are* gender differences the question is what to do about them. Some say that the differences between men and women make satisfying communication unattainable. The late Virginia Satir, a pioneer in her work with families, once said, "In our differences we grow, in our sameness we connect." Once we acknowledge and respect gender differences, no-fault—or blameless—communication is possible.

ILLUSION #3: "MY WIFE NAGS ALL THE TIME"

Men sometimes say that their wives don't appreciate them and are always demanding something of them. From their perspective, they work hard to support their families only to be bombarded by constant demands: "Do something about these rotten kids." "We don't go out anymore." "I've asked you three times to fix the leaky faucet." "How come we don't talk anymore." "All you ever want to do is watch TV." When men don't immediately comply with these requests women respond by asking again. Men get annoyed by the reminder and now avoid honoring the request because they are angry about being nagged. This dynamic raises two obvious questions: "Why do women pursue men in this way?" and "Why are men so uncooperative?"

Why Women Nag

Women are usually the emotional and intimacy regulators in relationships; when the marriage becomes lifeless, women take steps to rejuvenate it, actively pursuing their mates to keep their relationships stimulating and meaningful. Frequently, when women make requests of their husbands, they are trying, to the best of their ability, to get a response—more emotional closeness. A man usually experiences his wife's requests as a personal attack, seldom recognizing the stabilizing effect her actions may have on the relationship.

For example, when a woman feels that she and her husband have been two ships passing in the night, she might announce, "We don't spend time together anymore." Her husband might regard her comment as an accusation and withdraw. When she notices him withdrawing, she might complain further, "We spend so little time together, and when we *are* together, you're always watching TV," and so he withdraws even more. Angered by this, she confronts him about all of his neglected responsibilities and his tendency toward couch potatoism, which provokes a screaming match (hardly the intimate response she had hoped for).

However, this screaming match frequently clears the air, which then allows for closeness. After a couple of hours (or days) they make up. They hug, they kiss or they make love. Over time this pattern repeats itself. Some experts theorize that wives provoke their husbands to vent anger as a way of completing this cycle.

Why Men Resist

To reiterate Deborah Tannen's research: Many of the problems in male-female communication can be traced back to the disparate expectations of men and women concerning intimacy and independence. When women request more intimacy, men feel their independence is jeopardized:

> That women have been labeled "nags" may result from the interplay of men's and women's styles, whereby many women are inclined to do what is asked of them and many men are inclined to resist even the slightest hint that anyone, especially a woman, is telling them what to do. A woman will be inclined to repeat a request that doesn't get a response because she is convinced that her husband would do what she asks, if he only understood that she really wants him to do it. But a man who wants to avoid feeling that he is following orders may instinctively wait before doing what she asked, in order to imagine that he is doing it of his own free will. Nagging is the result, because each time she repeats the request, he again puts off fulfilling it. (Tannen, 1990, p. 31.)

I will illustrate this dynamic by altering an example Tannen gives to illustrate a different point. Although the following example was suggested by one Tannen presents, the details have been changed and the dialogue is fabricated. A wife gets a request for a social engagement and responds by saying she will have to check with her husband regarding his plans since she assumes that partners behave interdependently. Conversely, the husband gets asked to do something after work, calls his wife to announce his plans and she gets insulted. "Why don't you first ask me if we have plans," she complains. He cannot believe that she expects him to ask her permission to do something. Her expectation that he check with her first feels like an intrusion on his independence, and he tells her, "You are such a nag. All you do is bitch, bitch, bitch."

If the husband in this case understood his wife's needs for connectedness, he might not view her request as unreasonable, and would not feel controlled. If the wife understood her husband's need for independence, she might not feel insulted when he made plans without consultation. Either alternative would result in the wife not being viewed as a nag.

What Do You Want?

Another reason women are perceived as nagging when they make requests for more closeness, more time together, more involvement and so on, is that the requests are frequently couched in criticisms and complaints. When spouses feel unhappy or dissatisfied, rather than specifying what they would like to *change,* they criticize and complain. Both men and women are guilty of the tendency to complain rather than suggest what they would like to have happen, but since women initiate more discussions about relationship issues, they appear to be the naggers. Here is an example.

Mary wanted to spend more time with Tom. Instead of saying, "I miss you since we haven't been spending time together lately. Let's get tickets for the theater Saturday night or plan something fun to do. I'll arrange for a babysitter," she said, "You're never around anymore. You don't spend time with me or the kids. Work is more important to you. You don't even notice me anymore." As a result, Tom felt attacked and offered a counterattack, resulting in Mary feeling even more hurt and rejected.

The Calm Before the Storm

Men should worry when their wives *stop* complaining. Research shows that a man's continued withdrawal leads to a woman's continued pursuit—but only initially. Eventually, his wife stops trying; she surrenders. From the male perspective, she stops nagging. Unless the husband compensates by assuming the emotional regulator role, both partners begin to lead parallel but separate lives. When this happens, the marriage enters the danger zone. As long as someone is trying to correct relationship ailments, there is caring, even if the caring feels like nagging. When the caring stops, the marriage is at risk of dying.

ILLUSION #4: "WE'VE GROWN APART"

Many couples say that they no longer share common interests or that each person has changed so much over the years that it is almost like living with a stranger. "When we were newlyweds, we were so alike and we liked doing the same things. We were practically clones," spouses explain. But time has changed all that. Now he hates shopping and she hates sporting events. He loves going out with his male friends, but all she cares about is the children. They used to love to go dancing, but not anymore.

While it may be true that couples develop divergent interests over the years, other variables contribute to the perception of growing apart. It is important to understand why you may be feeling estranged from your spouse because, oddly enough, you both probably haven't changed as much as you think. Consider Wendy's relationship with Mark.

Is Different Really Different?

Wendy met Mark when she completed a two-year associate degree in fine arts at a local community college. She was twenty-one at the time. Mark was a bookkeeper at the college with some background in accounting. He was twenty-three.

Wendy thought her prayers had been answered when Mark walked into her life. She was uncertain of her career goals and felt a little lost. Few jobs were available that would allow her to utilize her talent in fine arts. Normally, uncertainty didn't unbalance Wendy because she fancied herself a free spirit. However, after two months of unsuccessful job-hunting, she felt discouraged and disillusioned. Then Mark entered the scene.

Their mutual physical attraction was immediate. Wendy briefly forgot all about her job search as she devoted her attention to Mark. Although Mark needed to report to work daily, they spent every free moment together. She was impressed with his ambition and his sense of responsibility since her previous boyfriends were not as settled as Mark. Wendy found his stability appealing, the very thing she needed in her life.

Mark was also very supportive of Wendy. He actively involved himself in her efforts to find work and she admired his practical task-oriented approach to her dilemma. Eventually Wendy found a job at a small craft gallery and she and Mark were delighted, even though their schedules did not always coincide and they were forced to spend less time together.

Mark was wild about Wendy. He found her artsy appearance and outlandishness irresistible since he was raised in a reserved, conservative family. Wendy always seemed relaxed and comfortable with herself, qualities Mark felt he lacked, being methodical and detail-oriented, but which he greatly admired. He felt Wendy brought out undeveloped aspects of his personality. Mark found himself laughing more and not taking life so seriously. Wendy also seemed to appreciate his efforts to help her get her life back on track, which made Mark feel good about himself.

They especially enjoyed trying new activities together. Wendy would arrange for outings to museums and art exhibits and Mark convinced Wendy to take up playing tennis. They felt their different interests broadened their experiences. Convinced they were fated to be lovers, six months later they married. At first things were blissful, but shortly thereafter the very traits that pulled them together with a force like gravity were now causing them to seriously consider splitting.

As time passed, Wendy became more involved with her job at the gallery. Mark resented her time away from him because he had gotten so accustomed to their spending time together. He felt threatened by her relationships with her co-workers and disliked that she got along so well with them. The gallery had frequent shows and social gatherings which they both initially attended. Wendy started to feel that Mark was too stiff and didn't fit in with her artistic friends. Eventually, she became embarrassed and stopped inviting him to the openings.

When Wendy noticed that they weren't enjoying each other anymore, she quickly arranged for a weekend getaway, but Mark didn't feel comfortable making spur-of-the-moment plans. He liked to have all the details worked out far in advance. Wendy's spontaneity had become a nuisance for Mark. He saw her last-minute invitations as insincere attempts to work things out.

Mark had his own way of working things out. After considerable thought, he compiled a written list of the changes he thought were necessary in order to recapture what they once had. As might be expected from Mark, his plan was highly organized and specific. He showed it to Wendy expecting her to express gratitude as she did in the past when he helped her develop her job-hunting strategy.

Much to his surprise, she was appalled. Since he hadn't consulted her, Wendy thought he was controlling and insensitive. She didn't want that sort of help and discredited Mark when he told her of his benevolent intentions.

To make matters worse, when Wendy went to work, she appeared relaxed and eager to start her day, which Mark interpreted as her leaving the marital problems behind. When Mark visited her at work, she would smile and joke around with customers, acting as if everything was okay between the two of them. This further rankled Mark, who thought she was frivolous and shallow.

So what changed? If you reread Wendy and Mark's love story, you will see that the couple's behaviors remained fairly constant over time. What did change was each spouse's perception or evaluation of the other. Wendy's spontaneity during their courting period was now viewed by Mark as flightiness. Mark's stability and helpfulness were now perceived as his need to control Wendy. As their relationship unfolded and the predictable challenges of married life emerged, they blamed each other for feeling uncomfortable. In particular, they criticized the very qualities they had adored in each other when they met.

If you have said to yourself, "We have grown apart," take another look. Maybe you haven't really changed as much as you thought. In all likelihood, your spouse is basically the same person you once fell in love with. You're just looking at him or her through different eyes now. It is important to remember that today's negative view is not any more realistic than yesterday's positive one. Unless you were hallucinating when you met, your loving perspective of your spouse during the early part of your relationship was as equally valid as your present critical one. You weren't fooling yourself back then, you were just seeing things differently. The loving feelings you shared were the result of pleasant interactions. Chapters 4–6 will help you "bring back that loving feeling."

Is the Same Really the Same?

There is another reason some people think they have grown apart from their spouses. At the beginning of a relationship, when the attraction is intense, couples focus on their similarities, not their differences. Differences go by unnoticed, they're ignored or minimized. The expression "Love is blind" makes sense in this context.

Later, when the relationship matures and people settle down to a daily mundane existence, the differences become noticeable, sometimes glaring. Many couples go through a rocky transitional period as they slowly readjust their expectations. Although this process isn't always easy, the end result, a workable marriage, is worth it. Less fortunate couples believe that their differences are unique and insurmountable. This belief often results in marital breakdown and a search for partners who are more compatible. But not surprisingly, the new partner eventually appears less compatible too.

Is Different Bad?

There is a misconception that healthy relationships consist of two people with many mutual likes and dislikes, but this is not necessarily true. Spouses can have very diverse interests and still have a satisfying marriage. There needs to be *some* common ground, but not a lot. Divergent interests do not have to destroy a marriage. On the contrary, they can enhance one.

Paula, a woman in her thirties, was having difficulty resolving a marital issue. She began by telling me, "My husband always wants to go out and do things but I'm a homebody. He is very athletic and I love to read. He loves entertaining people in our home but I prefer to be alone. He loves to laugh but I am more serious." As she spoke I thought she was building a case for divorce. I was convinced she was about to say, "There are too many irreconcilable differences." Instead, she concluded her soliloquy with, "We are different as day and night—we're perfect complements." Her conclusion illustrates a very important point. Our lives are shaped less by what actually happens to us than by the meaning we ascribe to these events.

Is Different Forever?

Sometimes the separateness couples feel pertains not only to their transformed views of each other. These couples lead such separate lives that they lose touch with each other. If couples become passive about their marriage, allowing it to take a back seat in their lives, it becomes empty and boring. Excitement and fire are not qualities inherent to relationships, they are what happens when two people make marriage the number one priority.

If you and your spouse have been leading separate lives, you can make a conscious decision to put the spark back into your marriage. Your distance didn't just happen, each of you made decisions that allowed your marriage to go flat. The same process that wedged miles between you can be reversed to rekindle the old flame. In later chapters, you'll see how planned spontaneity can revitalize lifeless marriages.

ILLUSION #5: "MY SPOUSE HAD AN AFFAIR, THE MARRIAGE CAN'T WORK"

Some say that nothing compares with the devastation and shock of discovering that one's spouse has been unfaithful. Infidelity leads to feelings of betrayal, mistrust, anger and hurt. Sometimes these feelings are so intense that they seem overwhelming and insurmountable. Desperate words are spoken: "I don't trust you anymore, how can we stay married?" or "How could you do this to me if you loved me?" Difficult questions, difficult answers.

If you have recently discovered that your spouse has been unfaithful, it is perfectly understandable that you would doubt the viability of your marriage. You probably have been on an emotional roller-coaster; one minute feeling rage, the next minute excruciating hurt, or just when you think you have gotten over it, something reminds you of the affair and you feel destroyed anew.

This emotional turbulence is natural after the discovery of an affair, but it is not conducive to making clearheaded decisions about the future of your marriage and your family. You can't accurately judge the viability of your marriage when you vacillate between feeling revengeful, hurt and vulnerable. You may be tempted to walk out the door simply to try to relieve the pain. But the pain will follow. If you and your spouse go through the pain together, you can get to the other side.

But What Went Wrong?

Most people assume that affairs signal something lacking in the marriage. Sometimes this is true. When spouses grow very accustomed to each other, they can take each other for granted. They stop flirting, stop giving compliments and stop taking notice. Paramours, on the other hand, are good at doing these things. They make spouses feel attractive, sexual and understood again.

Once the affair is out in the open and each spouse is willing to share honestly about unmet needs, the couple can begin to identify areas needing improvement. Frequently, the affair is the jolt the marriage needed to get it out of automatic drive.

Other times, affairs are not the result of bad marriages, just bad judgment. A one-night fling after too many drinks or an unmeditated hop in the sack while on a business trip, while inexcusable, may not indicate a malady in the marriage. However, in either case, trust is destroyed and it must be rebuilt. The marriage contract needs to be renegotiated.

Crisis = Opportunity

Although infidelity causes a crisis in the marriage, it doesn't necessarily lead to divorce. I have worked with countless couples who were able to restore stability and trust in their relationships. In fact, many people say that as a result of working through the crisis, their marriage emerged even stronger than before the affair.

The word "crisis" has its etymological roots in the Greek verb *krinein,* "to judge, to choose." Therefore, a crisis is a moment when one must choose among various perspectives and opportunities which present themselves. Enhancing a marriage after an affair is a choice many couples are making. The facts speak in favor of marriages surviving infidelity. Research shows that two-thirds of couples who seek therapy after an affair are able to resolve the crisis.

If you or your spouse is having or has had an affair, the bottom line is that you don't have to assume your marriage is over. You *can* rebuild the trust. You *can* revitalize your marriage. It doesn't happen overnight, it isn't always easy, but many couples renew their commitment to each other as a result of going through the pain, learning and growing. You can do it too.

ILLUSION #6: "I DON'T LOVE HIM (HER) ANYMORE"

"The magic is gone," say many people who seriously consider divorce. I can't count the number of people I've heard say, "I just don't love him (her) anymore. The marriage is over." People who talk about falling out of love seem to be longing for the romantic love or the infatuation of the old days. People reminisce about the giddiness of seeing their lovers walk through the door. Many spouses are not prepared for the reality of marriage once life settles into a routine. Ecstasy is replaced with a certain calm that, instead of being prized for the level of comfort it offers, is scorned for the emptiness it supposedly creates:

> The high pitch of excitement and mutual gratification during the early stage of infatuation often serves as a kind of standard by which couples judge the later stages of their marriage. The hurts, quarrels, and petty frustrations stand in stark contrast to the euphoria of the courtship period. Many people are unwilling or unable to relinquish their early image of what marriage should be like—which promotes later disillusionment with both the spouse and the relationship itself. Of course, we know couples who still feel the magic of the relationship for years after their marriage. Their fantasies appear to be realized, but they are in the minority. (Beck, 1988, p. 45.)

Failing to recognize that few couples experience continuous feelings of romantic love can lead people to incorrectly think there is something wrong with their marriage. Real-life relationships get compared to relationships in romantic novels, movies and television and pale by comparison. The routine of waking up day after day with the same person next to you, seeing him or her in the morning before hair and teeth get brushed, being privy to bad moods, is a far cry from the days when every hair, article of clothing and thought had to be in place before that special someone was welcomed through the door.

"I'll Find Some New Magic"

Believing something is wrong with a marriage because the romance has died often sends people searching outside the marriage to fill the void. The newness of an affair is likely to offer the kind of excitement that has been missing. This misleads the searcher into thinking that his or her spouse *was* the source of the problem after all. However, the real disillusionment comes when the fire of the affair inevitably fizzles out, a realization which often comes too late for the marriage. Then, unless the searcher realizes that the fire always diminishes in long-term relationships, he or she will be doomed to serial affairs to keep the fire burning rather than committing to the primary relationship.

Mature Magic

Magic doesn't last forever. Happily married couples say magic visits from time to time, but by no means is omnipresent. When speaking of their mates these couples talk more of mutual respect, companionship, friendship and practical concerns like the sharing of financial and family responsibilities and having someone to grow old with than they do of magic and quivers-up-the-spine, butterflies-in-the-stomach responses.

One gets the impression that a good marriage is in many ways more like a good business partnership than the pairing of Mr. with Ms. Right. Failing to recognize the transience of magic in all relationships results in the gnawing feeling that something is wrong. *Believing* something is wrong with your marriage because intense feelings aren't sustained may be what's wrong with your marriage.

"I Never Loved Him (Her) to Begin With"

A twist to the illusion "I don't love him (her) anymore" is "I never loved him (her) to begin with." These people say that they got married for the wrong reasons—unexpected pregnancy, pressure from family and/or lover, escaping home and parents. "I should never have gotten married in the first place," they say.

Perhaps love was missing from these relationships. Sometimes people do marry for reasons other than love. However, the conclusion "I never loved him (her) to begin with" is often the result of selective memory. Research shows that individuals preferentially remember those past events and experiences which are congruent with their current moods and attitudes. For example, when depressed people are asked to reminisce about their lives, what they recall are depressing events. When elated individuals are asked to reminisce about their lives, happy experiences are recalled (Synder and White, 1982, pp. 149–67).

The reconstruction of one's past involves this kind of filtering process. If I think I don't love my spouse anymore, I recall all those experiences consistent with that feeling and forget contradictory experiences. Our memories play nasty tricks on us.

Nothing Magical About Magic

When I ask people who say that love has left their marriage what they have done or are doing to prevent it, most say, "Nothing, what can I do? Either the feeling is there or it isn't." These people see themselves as passive recipients of feelings. Feelings have a life of their own, they just happen.

The very same people who bemoan the loss of romance or intensity in their marriages do little to rekindle the spark. They either leave it up to their spouse, give up quickly if their initial efforts fail or assume the absence of warm feelings is indicative of an irreparable relationship. They fail to understand that, like anything else in life, you get out of something what you put into it.

Parents often say that their love for their children grows commensurate with the amount of involvement and energy devoted to parenting. Sleepless nights spent comforting a crying infant and mad dashes to the doctor's office for stitches arouse feelings of commitment and love for our children. Similarly, investment of time and energy in our spouses helps us feel commitment and love in our marriage. Love flows more freely from what we give than what we get from others—the more we put in, the more we get out. It may be useful to ask yourself the question "In what ways have I been showing or giving love lately?"

The Past Holds the Clues

Some couples say that they don't even know where to begin jump-starting their marriage. But that is really fairly easy. The past holds all the necessary clues for resurrecting the magic. For example, when I ask couples, "What was different about the time in your relationship when there was magic, when you felt excitement about being together?" I hear, "He would ask me to go out to dinner with him. He would initiate our going out and doing things together. It didn't always have to be my idea." Or "She would invest more energy in our sexual relationship, a candlelight dinner or an unsolicited kiss or pat on the behind."

People *do* know what they need to do to rediscover the excitement; they have to reach into the past and *intentionally* do those things they once considered romantic. People make the mistake of waiting around for the romantic feelings to emerge before they initiate romantic activities. But it works the other way around! Once people start doing the activities that they define as romantic, even if they're a bit rusty at first, it will trigger romantic feelings. Later chapters will offer a recipe for rekindling lost magic.

Faulty thinking isn't the only pitfall to relationship problem solving; not having a plan is another major stumbling block. The chapters that follow will help you design a strategy for making your marriage work. However, in order to design a blueprint for change, you first have to understand how SBT works. The next chapter offers a brief look at the evolution and theory of SBT and lays the foundation upon which the techniques and methods outlined in the remaining chapters are built.

CHAPTER 3

What Solution-Oriented Brief Therapy Is and How It Can Help You—Fast

THE FOXES AND THE RABBITS

Several years ago something mysterious happened in Canada. The rabbit population had diminished drastically. Intrigued by this, scientists searched for an explanation. Although they thought the drop in the number of rabbits must have been caused by an illness, they could not identify any. A few years later, scientists again noticed something unexplainable: The rabbit population increased. Adding to their perplexity, shortly thereafter it decreased once again. Still, scientists discovered no explanation for these variations in the rabbit population. Additionally, at approximately the same time, population fluctuations of foxes were noticed. As before, scientists investigated illnesses which might have accounted for these fluctuations but, again, none were discovered.

By coincidence, reports about the cycles in the rabbit and fox populations were read by another scientist who then put together the pieces of the puzzle. He noticed that as the number of foxes grew, the number of rabbits diminished, and when the number of rabbits grew, the number of foxes diminished. He figured that as the rabbit population multiplied, they provided an ample food source for the foxes, which resulted in larger numbers of foxes.

When the increased number of foxes ate the rabbits, the food supply vanished, which eventually resulted in the foxes dying off. When the fox population declined, the rabbit population increased, creating a new food supply for the foxes. This cycle was self-perpetuating (Lederer and Jackson, 1968, p. 88).

The rabbit and fox story illustrates an important point. If one's microscope is too narrowly focused, the meaning of an event may remain a mystery. This principle also applies to marriages. A wife's behavior may seem as mysterious as the unexplained rise and fall of the rabbit population until viewed together with her husband's actions. In order to understand her behavior, thoughts and feelings, it is necessary to study his to see how the parts fit together. For example, let's go back to Ann and Steve, the couple briefly described in the introduction.

Ann called me to set up an appointment after reading in the newspaper about my approach to marital problems. Ann had asked Steve to move out several weeks prior and, although she hoped things could be worked out between them, she worried that it might be too late. The rejection she felt from Steve was more than she could bear. She requested coming in alone for the first session. Based solely on Ann's description of their marriage and Steve's actions during the last several years, one might have prematurely concluded that Steve's behavior was insensitive, erratic and selfish and that she was lacking in good judgment when she married this immature man.

However, when Steve came in by himself for the second session, he seemed a far cry from the man Ann had described. In contrast to Ann's version of their life together, Steve thought *he* was the one who was rejected by Ann. As he talked about the marriage and how their relationship unfolded, his actions took on new meaning. The picture Ann had painted of Steve as an insensitive lout slowly melted as their marital interactions became evident. Steve and Ann's dilemma made perfect sense once the complex interplay between them was brought to light.

ANN AND STEVE: THE FOX AND THE RABBIT

Ann's Point of View

Ann, a professional woman in her early thirties, looked tired when she walked through my door the first time, the strain of the two-week separation from her husband showing on her face. She tearfully explained that it was probably too late to save her marriage but, wanting to leave no stone unturned, she set up her meeting with me.

Ann told me that Steve was never big on communicating, but there had been virtually no communication at all for the past five years of their fifteen-year marriage. I sensed Ann's desperation and extreme loneliness as she reflected on what went wrong. The marriage started going downhill when Melissa, their oldest of three, was born:

> Steve was a doting father; no one could have been prouder. We loved showing off Melissa to the world and we were getting along really well. But then everything changed. Steve joined a softball team two months after Melissa was born and he was gone a lot. When he wasn't playing baseball, he was practicing. That would have been fine with me but he also stopped for a couple of beers after the games with his buddies. It seemed like he was never home.
>
> At first I tried asking him to spend more time at home but he didn't seem interested in the least. I even tried attending his softball games, but it wasn't always so easy with the baby. To say that I was lonely is an understatement. My only outlet for human contact other than Melissa was my co-workers. We talked a lot about our husbands at work and they all seemed the same. Men!
>
> From that point on, the situation only deteriorated. When the softball season ended, he started playing football. In between team sports, he joined a health club and worked out what seemed like eight days a week. Then, as if all that weren't enough, he took up golf.
>
> I'm not exactly sure why we had two more kids knowing that our marriage was lousy. Maybe I was hoping that having a baby would bring us closer like it did with Melissa in the beginning. But, it didn't—just the opposite. Now we hardly speak to each other. I stopped trying to spend time together years ago. I think I stopped caring then too. I have so much resentment about having to raise these three kids by myself, I'm not sure I can ever get past it.

Ann's firm conviction that their problems were due to Steve's actions was matched by Steve's unwavering certainty that Ann was to blame for the deterioration of their marriage.

Steve's Point of View

Steve willingly came in for a session and, just as willingly, shared his views on their marriage. He immediately admitted that he was a quiet kind of guy, but added that Ann was not particularly open about her feelings either. He recalled many times when, instead of telling him she was hurt or angry, she would just stew about something he had done. Periodically, she would blow up and then things would be okay for a while. During the last few years, Ann's outbursts had ceased completely. Now when he tried to ask her "What's wrong?" or "Can I do something to help you feel better?" she always rejected his advances. Eventually, like Ann, he also stopped trying.

Steve and Ann agreed on at least one thing: Melissa's birth marked a turning point in their marriage. But Steve's perspective about this era was considerably different from Ann's:

> Melissa was a real joy to me. I felt really close to Ann after we had a baby; we had a great marriage. I knew our lives would change tremendously with this new responsibility but I had no idea that I would lose Ann in the process. All she cared about was Melissa. Melissa this, Melissa that. She didn't even notice when I came home from work at night. Many times I suggested that we get a babysitter and go out alone, but she would never let anyone but family watch the baby. Our friends got babysitters for their kids, so I couldn't see why she was being so picky. I think she just didn't want to be alone with me for some reason.
>
> As time passed, things got worse. Even though it wasn't logical, I started resenting Melissa. Being home was a drag. Ann wasn't fun anymore. My buddies asked me to play ball or go out with them and I was happy that at least someone wanted to be with me. Occasionally, Ann would make some nasty comment about my playing ball, but I think she was just jealous. Her life was dull and mine wasn't.
>
> Gradually we became more like roommates. She was not interested in sex anymore and it's a real miracle we had two more kids. It must have been the immaculate conception. Each time I would try to be affectionate in order to feel close to her, she would recoil. She accused me of just wanting to get laid, but she didn't understand that I really wanted to feel connected. The harder I tried, the further she pushed me away. A guy can just take so much rejection. I figured the next move was up to her, but the next move never happened.
>
> Instead, out of the blue, she told me to move out. She said she wanted some time to think, that it was only a separation, not a divorce. In my book, moving out *is* the start of a divorce. I didn't want to move out, but I also don't want to be in a marriage with someone who doesn't love me.
>
> I know I haven't been easy to live with and I probably haven't spent as much time with the family as I should. I'm willing to make changes for our marriage and our family. But she has to let go of the past and tell me what she wants from me rather than holding everything in. I'm sure we can work things out if she just gives it a chance.

The Circular Connection

If one were to ask Ann how their problems developed, she would point a finger at Steve. She would say that Steve started the problem by withdrawing from her. But if Steve were asked the same question, he would say that Ann caused their problem by shutting him out of her life. Perhaps now, after reading both Ann's and Steve's perspectives, you can see how the pieces of the puzzle fit together. Steve's absences from home make sense in light of his feeling rejected by Ann, and Ann's resentment of Steve makes sense in light of the distance he placed between him and his family. Each person's behavior is a response to an action or event which preceded it, while at the same time a trigger for that which follows it.

Rather than thinking about actions and reactions as being causally related (A causes B), for example, "If Steve spent more time at home, Ann would feel like having sex more often," SB therapists think about actions being related in a circular fashion (A leads to B leads to A and so on), for example, "She is less interested in sex because he's not part of her life *and* he is not part of her life because she isn't interested in sex." Clearly, it is not an either/or proposition, it is both. According to this view, it is impossible to determine blame or fault because there is no beginning or end to interactions. Attempting to assign blame results in the ultimate chicken-and-egg debate.

Think about the countless number of times you and your spouse have angrily tried to figure out who started a fight or who's to blame for a particular problem. "You started it" are words echoed throughout living rooms everywhere. The process of determining blame rarely yields a consensus because although we are aware of our partner's impact on our own thinking, feeling and behavior, we are not conscious of how we impact on our partner. Ann was acutely sensitive to the ways in which Steve's detachment affected her, but hadn't a clue that Steve felt a similar sense of rejection because of her lack of attention toward him.

Conversely, Steve felt hurt that Ann seemed disinterested in him, but had no idea that his athletic pursuits left Ann feeling rejected. Furthermore, neither of them recognized that their giving up by no longer pursuing each other was viewed by both of them as the ultimate sign of not caring. Steve and Ann's myopia was the result of too narrowly focused observations. They missed the bigger picture—how their interactions meshed into an interlocking grid.

LOOKING AT THE LARGER PICTURE

The idea that spouses function like a system is an outgrowth of research done in the early fifties. A research team headed by Gregory Bateson, a renowned anthropologist, discovered something interesting about the behavior of schizophrenic patients. As with the scientists searching for an illness *within* the separate groups of foxes and rabbits, schizophrenia was considered a disturbance *inside* the patient characterized by the individual's disjointed and distorted thinking. The schizophrenic was viewed as sick, and disconnected from the outside world.

However, the researchers noticed that hospitalized schizophrenics often relapsed for several days following a visit from their mothers. This surprised the researchers since they assumed that the patients were not really tuned in to their external environment. As they explored further, they discovered disturbances in mother-child communication patterns. Researchers also felt that many of the patients' mothers were overinvolved with their children.

Because of this observation, mothers were viewed as "crazy-makers," that is, until the researchers shifted their attention to the patients' fathers. What they found was that for every seemingly overinvolved mother, there was a distant and underinvolved father. A father's withdrawal from the family made it possible for the mother to dominate the household and its members. Conversely, the mother's overinvolvement with the children made it possible for the father to have little contact with the family.

The researchers observed something else about the families which changed their thinking about schizophrenia in particular and human behavior in general. In almost every family they studied, they noticed that the parents had chronic marital problems. Furthermore, episodes of acute psychosis followed intensely conflictual marital interactions. In other words, it appeared that the child got sick when things got heated between the husband and wife. This psychotic episode demanded the full attention of both parents, thereby diffusing the marital battles and forcing the parents to pull together to handle the crisis.

The researchers reasoned that family members act systemically in highly predictable patterns in order to achieve an equilibrium or maintain balance. In the families described above, the mother's overinvolvement is balanced by the father's distance and vice versa. From this perspective, the family's tolerance for conflict is closely monitored by the son or daughter, who lapses into crazy behavior when things get too intense in order to cool things down. Once the immediate crisis is handled, he or she improves and the parents return to their arguments. When the arguments reach an uncomfortable level the child relapses again. The researchers concluded that the behavior of the individual family members could best be understood when associated with the actions of other family members.

This research group was not alone in their observation that individual family members behave in ways to preserve the family's status quo. During that same period of time many other prominent therapists reported similar findings. As a result of seeing families functioning as a unit, these groundbreaking therapists began seeing whole families in sessions rather than individuals. In fact, Murray Bowen, a leader in the family therapy field, hospitalized the entire family of disturbed individuals rather than hospitalizing only the disturbed individuals.

However, these early attempts to understand psychotic behavior from a systemic perspective failed to fully take into account the circular connections within these families. For example, while they noticed chronic marital discord in the families studied, suggesting that the marital conflict was *causing* the schizophrenia, it is equally plausible that the discord was a *result* of the stress felt by parents raising a psychotic child. (In fact, we now know that there is also a genetic or biological component to the illness.) It took family theorists a long time to stop blaming the parents, particularly the mother, for the increase in the child's symptoms. Fortunately, contemporary systems thinking avoids making causal connections.

Despite the fact that this early research failed to fully appreciate the circular nature of family interactions, the beginnings of a systemic understanding of family functioning as presented by these researchers was definitely a major breakthrough. This systemic view provided a new and totally different way to understand human behavior: Problems stem from problematic interactions *between* people, and it is insufficient to look *within* individuals for causes or explanations of problems. In the story of the foxes and the rabbits, scientists trailed a red herring as they searched for the causes of the fluctuations in the populations *within* each animal group by searching for some fatal illness within each group alone.

Similarly, in the case of Ann and Steve, if one were to look no further than Ann to explain her lowered sex drive, one might conclude she is simply experiencing biochemical changes or depression. And if one were to look *within* Steve to explain his detachment, one might conclude he is selfish, has a fear of intimacy or is a passive-aggressive personality. While any of these explanations might fit the facts, a more complete understanding of Ann and Steve's situation is achieved by observing the problems *between* them: how her response influences and highlights his response and vice versa. This systemic perspective is the basis for family therapy and SB therapy.

SBT AND HOW IT EVOLVED

Solution-Oriented Brief Therapy is part of an exciting trend emerging in the psychotherapy field which departs from traditional, or psychoanalytic, therapy. Although psychoanalytic approaches have enjoyed wide public acceptance, serious criticisms began to surface in the fifties and the sixties. There was a growing discontent over the length and cost of treatment. Furthermore, many practitioners were convinced that such therapy, which is based on interpretations of a person's past and internal conscious states, is entirely too speculative and unscientific.

Disillusionment with the effectiveness of psychoanalytic approaches was a major impetus to the development of present-oriented models such as behavior therapy, gestalt therapy, cognitive therapy and family therapy. Convinced that one's past was unverifiable and unchangeable, proponents of these approaches were concerned with how problems are developed or maintained in the present.

PRESENT ORIENTATION

For example, behavior therapy is based on the idea that all behavior, both desirable and problematic, is maintained in the present by powerful reinforcers in the environment. When a particular behavior is reinforced, it persists. When it is not reinforced, it eventually ceases to exist or is extinguished.

Here are a few everyday examples that illustrate behavior therapy at work. Praising your mate for desirable behavior is likely to increase the behavior, whereas failing to notice good deeds will reduce the likelihood of his or her continuing to perform good deeds. Consistently ignoring a child's temper tantrums will reduce their frequency, whereas commenting, threatening and punishing, all forms of attention, will increase the tantrums. Some common powerful reinforcers in marital relationships are attention, sex, money and praise.

Instead of viewing Ann's lack of assertiveness to get her needs met with Steve as a disturbance in her personality or a symptom of an underlying childhood conflict, a behaviorist might examine what current factors or reinforcers might inadvertently be prolonging or reinforcing her lack of assertiveness.

For instance, over the years, when Ann requested that Steve change his behavior, he was unresponsive. Since she received no positive reinforcement when she verbalized her needs, she eventually stopped being open with Steve. Since Steve expressed discomfort with her lack of openness, a behavior therapist might suggest that Steve behave in ways that would reinforce any attempt Ann made to share her feelings. He could do this by being attentive and responsive to her requests. Hopefully, this would result in more communication between them.

As you can see, these therapeutic suggestions can be made without gathering lengthy personal histories. Although there are many other techniques used by behavioral therapists, they all are based on the following principle: *All the necessary clues to solving the immediate problem, that is, changing behavior, are available in the present situation.*

Cognitive therapy, another present-oriented model which emerged during this period of time, is based on the premise that problems develop when we misjudge or misinterpret what others say or do. These errors in judgment or misunderstandings cause us to act in ways that seem irrational to those around us, and they, in turn, respond defensively. The role of the cognitive therapist is to help people correct their thinking and their communication to prevent future misunderstandings.

For example, a cognitive therapist might teach Ann and Steve a set of communication rules designed to help them understand each other better. By improving their communication, Ann and Steve would be less likely to misinterpret the meaning of each other's statements and they could discuss differences in a more productive manner. Additionally, a cognitive therapist would help Ann to see that Steve withdrew from her, not because he didn't want to be with her, but because he felt rejected and hurt. Steve would learn that Ann's investment in the children came as a result of her feeling rejected by him and not because she lost interest in their relationship. In other words, a cognitive therapist would attempt to correct Ann and Steve's distorted thinking.

Clearly, what cognitive therapy, behavior therapy and SBT have in common is the notion that understanding the past to solve current problems is unnecessary. A by-product of this contemporary focus is a change in the length of treatment. The present-oriented models are, by and large, considerably briefer than the psychoanalytic approaches which preceded them. Any complete explanation of the similarities and differences between SBT and these present-oriented therapy approaches lies beyond the scope of this book. However, two of the primary theoretical differences rest on SBT's orientation to the future and emphasis on people's strengths, both hallmarks of Milton Erickson's work.

During the same period of time that family therapy, behavior therapy and other present-oriented models were being developed, the psychiatrist Milton Erickson was busily practicing his own brand of therapy from the late twenties through the late seventies. Although he was trained as a psychiatrist, his dissatisfaction with traditional, psychoanalytic methods led him to develop new methods which were remarkably effective. Therapists from all over visited Erickson hoping to decipher his unusual way of thinking about how people change. His unique work was undoubtedly the greatest influence on the development of SBT. One outstanding characteristic of his work was its orientation to the future:

> Perhaps Erickson was not the first therapist to bring a more here-and-now, present orientation to psychotherapy, in contradistinction to the historical orientation of analytic and psychodynamic orientations. But he almost certainly was the first to bring a future orientation to psychotherapy. He was not interested in "psychological archeology" and attempted to orient people away from the past into the present and the future, where they could deal with difficulties more adequately. (O'Hanlon, 1987, pp. 12–13.)

SBT, which is primarily based on this future orientation, helps clients identify their hopes, dreams and aspirations and the shortest route for getting there.

Another outstanding characteristic of Erickson's work was his focus on solutions rather than problems. A genius at helping people change, he had little interest in understanding how they became stuck. Erickson's interest in solutions is illustrated in the hundreds of success stories depicting his work with clients. One example of his approach is illustrated by a meeting he had with an elderly woman who had been extremely depressed for nine months. Fearful that she might be suicidal, her nephew, a client of Erickson's, requested that he visit her in her home in Milwaukee.

When he arrived, he found a sickly woman in a wheelchair living in a dirty, dismal house. He discovered she had no contact with the outside world other than her gardener and regular visits to church, since she was a very religious woman. However, she told Erickson that she came late to the service and left immediately at its conclusion in order to avoid contact with people in her congregation. The picture she painted of her life was overwhelmingly bleak.

Rather than plunge into the intricacies of her depression, Erickson requested a tour of her house. Much to his surprise, he discovered several African violets of different colors. Knowing how sensitive these plants are, Erickson surmised that she invested much time and effort growing them. This discovery provided him with the small ray of hope he needed to help the woman beyond her depression.

He used his authority as a medical doctor and announced that he had strict orders for her. Knowing that she was a devout Christian, he reprimanded her for being remiss in her Christian duty. He instructed her to go and purchase every type of African violet she could find, take cuttings from them, plant the cuttings and nourish them until they grew into mature plants. Then she was instructed to get a church announcement of every birth, death, christening, engagement and wedding that took place in her congregation. She was to send a violet to every family whose name appeared on the announcement.

This woman followed Erickson's instructions and soon had a room full of beautiful African violets which she faithfully sent out on joyous and mournful occasions. When she died, a headline in the *Milwaukee Journal* read, "African Violet Queen Dies, She Will Be Missed by Thousands."

Erickson enabled this woman to end her isolation and interact with others in a meaningful way, thus giving her life new meaning. Rather than living as a recluse, she became an important member of her congregation before her death, which gave her great joy. This case is characteristic of Erickson's work in focusing on people's strengths. He searched for any resource to be built upon and nurtured it until the problem disappeared. Therapy based on this premise is less painful, less time consuming and, oftentimes, more humane than trying to find the causes of a problem. The key is in assessing what works and identifying how to build on it, topics to be addressed in the following chapters. Perhaps this assumption represents the most radical departure from traditional psychotherapeutic practice. Many therapists have followed in Erickson's footsteps by incorporating this idea of "building on what works" into their practices. However, it was the Brief Family Therapy Center in Milwaukee, headed by Steve de Shazer, that recognized the effectiveness of implementing "building on what works" as *the* primary focus of therapy.

Let's take a closer look at how SBT differs from psychoanalytically influenced approaches.

PSYCHOANALYTIC THEORY

If the systemic perspective described in the fox and rabbit story or in Ann and Steve's story is new to you, you have probably been influenced by psychoanalytic theory which was developed by Sigmund Freud. You don't have to be a psychologist, psychiatrist or counselor to have been influenced by Freud's ideas. Most people, whether they know it or not, have a fairly sophisticated working knowledge of Freudian thinking. So deeply ingrained in our culture are Freud's ideas that psychotherapy and psychodynamic therapy (which is based on Freudian concepts) have become almost synonymous. As you read through the major concepts associated with this approach, you will become aware of how many of your assumptions about how people change are directly related to the work of Freud.

Iceberg Theory

According to psychoanalytic theory, a person's problem, such as depression, is just a symptom of some deeper underlying conflict, not readily perceivable to the untrained eye, stemming from an unresolved childhood trauma. Due to the upsetting nature of the trauma, the memory of it gets repressed into the unconscious. Therefore a symptom, like depression, represents a manifestation of these repressed feelings and memories and is merely the "tip of the iceberg."

Elimination of the depression can only occur when that which is repressed is brought into the person's consciousness or awareness. In other words, insight or understanding of the events in one's past is a prerequisite for change to occur.

In Ann and Steve's case, a psychodynamic therapist might have each of them discuss how they were raised, exploring in detail their relationships with each parent, their parents' relationships with each other, and all significant childhood experiences. Out of this extensive exploration of the past, a greater understanding about themselves would be derived. Once this understanding or insight is achieved, a fundamental change in their personalities would be possible. Psychodynamic therapists believe that for *real* change to occur, *personalities* must change, not merely behaviors.

For example, according to this theory, if Ann and Steve are distant because of mutual feelings of rejection, it would not help in the long run to resolve the immediate problem, that is, suggest ways for them to get along better and feel closer. According to psychodynamic theory, first Ann and Steve must understand that the rejection they feel is composed of misplaced feelings based on negative childhood experiences (for example, times when they felt rejected by a parent or some other significant person). Not until insights such as this are achieved can personalities change. And, according to this theory, without personality changes, improvement won't last.

Focusing on the Past Is Unnecessary

In contrast to the idea that people must understand how their background has contributed to the present problem, SB therapists have found this delving into the past unnecessary and frequently ineffective in changing things. We do not require extensive personal and social histories to solve problems. Instead, as I've mentioned and as you will see, we focus on the present and the future to help couples generate solutions to the current problems they are experiencing.

Why do SB therapists bypass an introspective look at the past? For one thing, we have found that the insight gained from the past frequently offers no clues about what to change. Couples say, "We know why we are fighting, we don't know how to stop!" In fact, rather than liberating people from the shackles of the past, identifying past causes for current problems often results in blame and bitterness. A growing number of professionals are expressing concern about a particular kind of blame, parent bashing, which frequently results from looking for causes of maladaptive behavior, and how it may actually divert people's energies from making changes in their own lives. Furthermore, research indicates that "attempts to help others understand and cope with their moods (in particular, their depressed moods) by encouraging them to talk about relevant [past] events in their lives also may serve unintentionally to consolidate and perpetuate their [current] mood states" (Synder, 1982, p. 282).

And finally, even when the journey into the past is productive, it undoubtedly takes considerable time, time which many couples whose marriages dangle by a thread simply do not have. SBT works so rapidly because the process of reviewing the past to seek explanations is bypassed.

Symptom Substitution

Solving the immediate problem couples bring to therapy is not the goal of psychodynamic therapists because they believe that eliminating a symptom without understanding its cause or meaning would result in symptom substitution: A new symptom would replace the old one or the original symptom would recur at some later date. In other words, if the underlying causes of the difficulties don't get addressed in the therapy process, although the present difficulties might be eliminated, the causes still lie dormant like lava in an inactive volcano.

Based on this theory, if Ann and Steve were given tools to overcome their alienation from each other without understanding the events in the past which supposedly caused their current predicament, they may temporarily feel closer, but some new symptom, such as one of them having an affair, would inevitably manifest itself. A "superficial" treatment of Ann and Steve's marital problems would result in recycled problems at some future time. A common analogy would be the line of thought that one shouldn't take too many painkillers: The pain may subside, but the actual illness is still there, only masked by the drug.

There Is No Evidence for Symptom Substitution

Although belief in symptom substitution is widespread, SBT is not based on this assumption. SB therapists assume that resolving present complaints restores a spirit of cooperation, feelings of love and optimism. In fact, we assume that when present complaints are resolved, couples stop fighting and blaming each other long enough for the healing to begin.

From our perspective, Ann and Steve's complaints about each other and their marriage are seen as the real problems and a legitimate focus for therapy. No deeper meaning is sought after. They would not be directed to embark on introspective journeys of self-examination. We assume they came to therapy to have something repaired. The goal of therapy for Ann and Steve would be to decrease or eliminate hurtful and destructive interactions and to increase pleasant times together and to do so as quickly and painlessly as possible.

Why don't SB therapists worry about symptom substitution? To begin with, we simply do not observe this phenomenon in our work with clients. By helping people find solutions to their present difficulties, SB therapists report a decrease in tension, marriages that blossom and children who rejoice, not additional problems. Furthermore, there is considerable research supporting SB therapists' observations:

> It has never been empirically demonstrated that elimination of symptoms must inevitably lead to family disruption or new symptoms in other family members. It certainly was not the case in the 300 or so case records that I examined at MRI [Mental Research Institute]. The most typical reaction of families to the improvement of a member is relief." (Coyne, 1985, pp. 60–61.)

Contrary to the psychoanalytic cautioning about symptom substitution, additional research indicates that there is scant evidence for it: "Investigators of this area have reported estimates of such occurrence as ranging from zero to (at most) 5 percent" (Rachman, 1963, pp. 133–37). "It appears clear, then, that symptom substitution is the exception and not the rule" (Ullmann and Krasner, 1969, p. 158).

The Strength Underlying the Symptom

Another reason SB therapists don't worry about symptom substitution is that, in contrast to psychodynamic therapists who believe that pathology underlies symptoms and that this pathology will emerge in another form if the symptom is eliminated, SB therapists believe that skills and resources can be discovered beneath symptomatic behavior.

For example, Steve would not be viewed as being *incapable* of intimacy with Ann due to unresolved childhood traumas or as having to gain insight into his supposed fear of intimacy before he could achieve closeness with her. Steve would be viewed as having within him all the necessary skills to be intimate, but as not using them temporarily because he is employing alternative responses. Following Milton Erickson's work, the goal of therapy, then, would be to access and increase behaviors that enable Steve to attain closeness, thereby decreasing his behaviors of detachment.

With this in mind, SBT therapists believe that couples don't need to go to skill-building classes; they don't need to be "fixed" or "cured." By redirecting people's attention to their innate strengths and abilities, many problems can be resolved easily.

For example, a woman in her late thirties sought therapy because she thought time was running out for her in regard to her finding a suitable mate. She was an extremely successful career woman in a business that required excellent people skills. When asked what she wanted to change in her life, she said, "I want to understand why I always get involved with men who can't give me what I need. I must have a fear of intimacy. I'm attracted to the wrong kind of guy. I'm incredibly shy when it comes to meeting men. I feel like I fall apart in social situations."

We talked for a while and I discovered that although she had no current relationship, over the past eight to twelve months she had actually been involved with two men. I then realized that, contrary to what she initially said, she had the skills to meet men and get involved to some extent. She had given me a negative image of herself that I could have reinforced by discussing it further, or I could have looked beyond her pessimism to find a way to work with her based on her obvious strengths.

With this in mind, rather than talk about her "fear of intimacy" or what she "does wrong in social situations or intimate relationships," I asked her, "If one of your clients came to you with the same problem you are discussing here, how would you advise him or her?" She thought for a moment and an embarrassed look appeared on her face. Coyly, she said, "Well, I have actually been thinking about that." Eager to hear further, I encouraged her to tell me more.

I was thinking back to what I did when I was trying to get my business off the ground. I knew I needed lots of contacts. It's a numbers game. So what I did at that time was to join lots of groups, all different kinds of groups, just to meet people. It worked—my business started to skyrocket. So I thought that's what I need to do, join groups, and I've already started.

As she listed for me the five or six groups in which she had already gotten involved (this is pretreatment change, which I'll describe shortly) she explained:

> Well, in order to be more marketable, you need to increase your visibility. And, like in sales, "cold-calling" [the process of randomly contacting prospective buyers as opposed to getting leads of potentially interested buyers] seldom works. Going into bars is like cold-calling. So I thought I needed to join groups with people who share similar interests.

She was hesitant to admit that she had a "marketing strategy" for meeting men or that she viewed finding a mate as a "marketing objective," but, as I delighted in what she was telling me, her mood changed markedly and she enthusiastically set out to implement her plan. (She soon met the man of her dreams and they now have "closed the deal" [Weiner-Davis, 1990, pp. 42–48].)

Clearly, this woman had all the necessary skills to improve her situation, she just didn't know where to look. SB therapists have noticed that occupations, hobbies or avocations are often fertile ground from which many marital problem-solving skills can be reached. Later chapters will suggest other ways to rediscover other forgotten capabilities.

Then why, if people *can* find their innate strengths, do so many spouses feel void of resources and at the end of their marital ropes? Couples' strengths and problem-solving skills are often camouflaged by the hurtful knee-jerk reactions which characterize intense marital embroilments. Partners respond to each other without thinking and persist in their patterned behavior without achieving the desired results. SBT reminds people of their problem-solving skills which, when put to use, enable them to break the vicious problem cycle and develop long-lasting solutions.

Now that you are beginning to understand some of the differences between Freudian-influenced therapy approaches and SBT, let's go back to Ann and Steve.

BALANCE

As you read about Ann and Steve, you probably noticed something else about their relationship. In addition to Ann and Steve's actions being related in a circular manner (what Ann does affects what Steve does, which, in turn, affects what Ann does and so on), their actions and reactions are delicately balanced. Although Ann and Steve shared parenting responsibilities initially, as she became more responsible for the children, Steve grew more carefree. The more she dedicated her energies to the children, the less involved Steve had to be since he knew Ann was handling things. Or it can be stated in another way: The less interactive and responsible Steve was at home, the more responsible Ann had to become to insure the health and well-being of the family.

Like all couples, Ann and Steve carved out roles for themselves which, over the years, had become increasingly rigid. Ann became the "involved parent" and Steve the "distant father." Other inflexible roles were also tacitly negotiated throughout their marriage: Steve was the "initiator of sexual contact" and Ann the "reluctant or unwilling partner." In the recent weeks of their deteriorating marriage, Ann was the "pessimist," calling an end to their marriage, and Steve the "unfaltering optimist," convinced that solutions to their seemingly endless problems were imminent.

Although the specifics vary from situation to situation, from couple to couple, the dynamics remain constant: The more responsibility person A accepts for something, the less person B does. Period. This equation applies to most relationship activities. Perpetual social planners are inevitably married to people who sit back waiting for Saturday nights to take shape. For every sex-starved husband, there is a wife with low sex drive. Every compulsive cleaner is paired with a hopeless slob. Calm, rational men are married to deeply emotional wives.

Are we simply gluttons for punishment? Hardly. Is it that opposites attract? Perhaps. But much more likely—opposites are created. Remember, the more you do of something, the less your spouse does. Imagine that two people are riding a tandem bicycle. If person A stops pedaling, person B must do all the work or the bicycle stops. If, after realizing that he is doing all the work, person B stops pedaling, person A must take over. With this in mind, SB therapists help people stop blaming or diagnosing themselves or their spouses and, instead, suggest ways to alter unproductive patterns and achieve a better balance.

Since marital interactions are circularly connected, when one person changes his or her behavior, the other person cannot continue to respond in the same old way. It doesn't matter who's "right" or who's "wrong." When someone takes the initiative to start the ball rolling by doing something different, the relationship changes. Let's look at what happened between Ann and Steve when they decided to act.

ANN AND STEVE'S SOLUTIONS

After an individual session with each of them, Ann and Steve came to a session together. Since it was too soon to discuss Steve's moving back home, I began the session by saying, "Since I've met with each of you separately, I have a pretty good idea about your individual perspectives. Now I'd like to know more about you as a couple. Tell me what's different about the times in your marriage when the two of you get along. What are each of you doing differently? In what ways is your relationship different?" Since they had been separated for several weeks and since things had been tense between them for several months leading up to the separation, they initially had a difficult time answering my questions.

I reminded them that although things were strained currently, they had been married for fifteen years. In fact, I recalled that, in a previous session, Ann said that severe problems in communication surfaced only five years ago. As I encouraged them to focus on problem-free times, Ann began to speak. "We used to spend more time together. We loved being together. It didn't matter what we did; as long as we were together, we had fun." Steve glanced at her, appearing surprised by Ann's pleasant memory.

Steve continued the discussion. "Before the kids, Ann made me feel really important. She paid a lot of attention to me. If I played ball, she came along and cheered me on from the sidelines. I loved that about her." As Steve reflected on their marriage he added, "We used to talk more. I would talk about my dad and so would she. Or we'd talk about what was going on in the world. Now we don't talk a lot and if we do it's about the kids. We got along better when we had interests outside of the children."

Although Ann agreed with Steve's observations, she also felt that they got along better during the times Steve was more involved with the children. Despite the fact that his involvement with the children was minimal, Steve also noticed that Ann seemed friendlier when he spent time with them.

As a result of this discussion, it became clear as to what each of them needed to do to get their marriage back on track. They needed to spend more time together as a couple and as a family. They needed to share outside interests and communicate more.

Later in the session, the conversation focused on Ann's reluctance to believe that Steve would really change and her hesitancy to ask him to return. Rather than move too fast, I suggested that they go out on a couple of dates. Additionally, I suggested the following homework task: "Between now and the next time we meet, I'd like you to notice what's happening that you want to continue to happen" (de Shazer, 1985, p. 137).

Two Weeks Later

Their second session together occurred two weeks later. When I asked, "What's happening that you want to continue to happen?" Ann said, "We actually went out on two dates, out to dinner and to a movie. It was a bit tense at first, but then we relaxed. It felt good to be together for a change. We even laughed a little, something we haven't done for months."

Steve also enjoyed their dates and particularly enjoyed Ann's undivided attention. He said it felt like old times. Although he had hoped Ann would ask him to come home, she didn't. This upset him but he decided not to discuss it because he wanted to have a pleasant evening. Besides, he felt that their going out and enjoying each other was a good first step.

Furthermore, Ann noted that Steve visited the children and helped around the house when he was there, which she greatly appreciated. Steve knew she appreciated it because Ann was more physical with him. She hugged him when he left.

Although their pleasant feelings about each other were still tentative, I could tell that they were moving in the right direction. In fact, after three more sessions, Ann asked Steve to come home. She felt satisfied that he was eager to change and to keep the changes going. Steve was pleased that Ann was so responsive to his changes and, contrary to what he expected, she wasn't holding a grudge about the past.

Clearly, Ann and Steve had gotten over a major hurdle and they were becoming a family again. I cautioned them about the importance of continuing to do what was working or they would find themselves back in their lonely corners. They understood my admonition and planned what each of them might do if they noticed any sign of relapse. I haven't heard from them since.

What Happened?

Let me summarize my approach with Ann and Steve. Instead of dissecting their relationship problems or finding explanations for how their problems developed, I asked them to recall what they had done differently in the past that worked for them. Then I suggested that over the next week they "notice what's happening that they want to continue to happen." I was asking them to pay attention to positive actions in order to increase their expectations that, as compared to the tension of the previous months, something different was about to occur.

Expecting good things to happen contrasted sharply with their previous predictions that each would feel a generous daily dose of rejection and alienation. Armed with these increased expectations of mutual good will and a new awareness about what it takes to make their marriage work, Ann and Steve had the necessary tools to begin changing their relationship. These methods are part of the backbone of SBT, the details of which will be discussed throughout the rest of this book.

By now you have probably noticed that this approach is extremely different from what most people envision when they think about therapy. I've already mentioned some of these dissimilarities: Focusing on the past is unnecessary since therapy goals are more readily accomplished by maintaining a present and future orientation, and eliminating symptoms does not result in symptom substitution. Here are some other differences. SB therapists believe that:

THE DISCUSSION OF FEELINGS SHOULD NOT BE THE MAIN FOCUS OF THERAPY

Most people think that therapy is a place to get out your feelings, and it is surprising to some when they come to SB therapy for the first time and they are not asked, "How do you *feel* when she acts in this way?" or told, "Let your anger out." This expectation is based on psychoanalytic theory. Originally, Freud believed that the goal of treatment was the release of emotions that had been stifled at some point in the person's development. The person was encouraged to have a catharsis—to vent feelings in order to clean out or purge oneself of negative emotions. The therapist would help exorcise unproductive feelings. Crying, screaming and pounding fists signaled the venting of undesirable emotions.

Contrary to such approaches, in SBT the discussion and exploration of feelings is not essential to the problem-solving process. SB therapists believe that most couples have discussed their negative feelings at length prior to coming for therapy. Most people know how they feel and how their spouses feel, they just don't know how to resolve the differences between them.

For example, before starting therapy, based on hundreds of discussions, dirty looks or snide comments, a husband knows his wife feels shortchanged when he brings his work home instead of relating to her, just as his wife knows that he feels neglected when she shows little interest in sex. The question which interests SB therapists is not "How do you feel when he brings his work home?" or "How do you feel when she busies herself to avoid sex?" The question which interests SB therapists is "What needs to happen for both people to feel satisfied?" The focus is on the changes that need to occur, not the feelings involved in creating or maintaining the problems. Although most people spontaneously discuss feelings and are not discouraged to do so, SB therapists gently redirect the conversation to the actions people will need to undertake to make their lives more satisfying.

Interestingly, contrary to what has been believed for decades, research indicates that the expression of rage, aggression and anger, rather than diminishing the effects of these emotions, actually increases them (Kahn, 1966, pp. 278–98). In other words, the more you talk about being angry, the more angry you feel. Traditional therapy approaches may have the unintentional effect of exacerbating rather than eliminating problems!

UNDERSTANDING FOLLOWS BEHAVIOR CHANGE

As stated earlier, the psychoanalytic dictum is that behavior change follows insight or changes in perception. *Real* change is not possible without insight. SB therapists have a completely different view about how people change. We've noticed that once a person changes his or her behavior and acts in new and productive ways, there are corresponding changes in perception and increased awareness about oneself. In other words, changes in perception *follow* changes in behavior.

For example, when Ann and Steve began therapy, they were regretful about how little time they spent together doing enjoyable activities. In times past they were considerably more involved with a variety of social events like going out for dinner together, playing bridge, trips to the city with their gourmet group and so on. For a multitude of reasons, they no longer participated in these things.

When I asked them, "Since you both enjoyed these things, why not just start doing them again?" Ann replied, "Lately, I have been feeling so bad about the relationship, I haven't felt like spending time with Steve. So I never suggest that we go out." I reassured her that I understood what she meant but was still puzzled by one thing. "Ann," I asked, "is it possible that *not* doing fun things together with Steve, which you used to love to do, has contributed to your bad feelings about the marriage?" She responded, "I guess so."

Ann was sitting around, waiting for her thoughts and her feelings about Steve to change before she could take action (do fun things). I was suggesting that it might be possible for her to push herself out the door with Steve (even if she didn't feel like it at first), do something enjoyable, and that this action might result in her feeling better about their relationship. I imagined that when she and Steve did the things they once enjoyed, it would trigger positive memories and positive feelings.

Quite simply, I was suggesting that her thoughts and feelings about Steve would change as a *result* of an immediate behavior change. A step out the door with her husband was a step closer to feeling better about the marriage. Taking action would effect a change in their perception, which would generate even more time spent together. The expediency of taking action rather than waiting for loving feelings to emerge is evident in Ann and Steve's example.

PEOPLE DEFINE THEIR GOALS FOR THERAPY

Psychodynamic therapy is based on the idea that only a trained eye can perceive the so-called *real* problem. Therefore, as a lay person describes the symptom, the supposed expert ascertains the goal of treatment.

SBT is not founded on this premise. We believe that people know themselves best and that *they* are the experts on what needs to change, not the therapist. So when therapy begins, clients are asked, "What is it that you would like to change?" and this is the starting point in therapy. If couples complain of fighting about how free time is spent, solutions to this complaint are sought. No underlying problem is assumed, no complicated meaning is attributed to the fighting. The goal as it is defined by the client is the goal for therapy. As Carl Rogers, the father of humanistic psychology, said, "Begin where the client is," and we agree.

BUILDING ON STRENGTHS IS MORE EXPEDIENT THAN DISSECTING WEAKNESSES

Traditional therapy is often described as a "corrective experience," a place where people can analyze and correct their shortcomings. SB therapists find it both inefficient and somewhat paradoxical to have clients reflect on their failures in order to build skills. Instead, we have found that if we ask people about their strengths, they inevitably show up as more capable and creative, and have renewed energy to find solutions.

I clearly remember the night many years ago when my colleagues at the Brief Family Therapy Center (BFTC) in Milwaukee and I discussed a session we had observed which illustrated this theory. A mother brought her twelve-year-old son to the center because of his deteriorating school performance. For thirty minutes she angrily discussed his misbehavior and her embarrassment at having to go to school to talk with his teachers. Five minutes before the end of the session, the mother casually mentioned that for the last two or three days prior to the appointment, her son had been trying in school.

The therapist stopped for a moment, turned to the boy, expressed great surprise and asked him why he decided to turn over a new leaf. The boy initially appeared perplexed but then agreed that he had changed his behavior—because he was tired of getting in trouble in school. The therapist concluded the session by asking the boy what he needed to do to stick to his resolution. The boy concretely described to him his step-by-step plan to keep the changes going.

As we discussed this situation, I recalled many other clients (as did my colleagues) who reported improvements between the call for a therapy appointment and the first session. In other words, we noticed that many people start to solve their problems on their own once they make the therapy appointment.

We also noticed that, consistent with the mother's response in the above situation, when people mention the changes they initiate between the phone call and the appointment, they attach little significance to them. They saw these changes as flukes or accidents. We suspected that since people discredit or minimize the importance of their pretreatment changes, the actual incidence of these changes was higher than our client reports indicated. We decided to test our theory by designing an informal survey where we asked people attending first sessions three questions:

1. Many times people notice in between the time they make the appointment for therapy and the first session that things already seem different. What have you noticed about your situation?
2. (If yes to No. 1): Do these changes relate to the reason you came for therapy?
3. (If yes to No. 1): Are these the kinds of changes you would like to continue to have happen? (Weiner-Davis, et al., 1987, p. 360.)

Two-thirds of the clients who were asked these questions reported specific positive changes they had made prior to the first appointment. Two-thirds! Our study confirmed what we had believed all along: that people do have the resources to solve problems—once they decide to use them.

As I travel across the country speaking about these results to therapists of various theoretical orientations, the overwhelming response I receive is emphatic nods and knowing smiles. Most therapists acknowledge that many people start solving their problems before they start therapy. I have a sign posted in my office that reads, "Please solve your problems in advance so I can help you more."

PROBLEMS HAVE NO PAYOFFS

If people do have the resources to solve problems, why would a couple like Ann and Steve push each other further and further away for five years rather than solve their problems? Were they getting something out of being distant? Were there some benefits for each of them by avoiding intimacy?

As we've seen, most people, including most therapists, believe that symptoms serve functions. In other words, there is some payoff to having a particular problem. People may not always be consciously aware of the benefits they are deriving from the problem, but the problem would not exist if it weren't serving some function in the person's life. From a psychodynamic perspective, Ann's failure to achieve intimacy with Steve might be directly related to her relationship with her father. If her father was a cool and distant man, Ann would unconsciously re-create distance between Steve and her as a way of making their interactions feel familiar. In theory, since she never experienced closeness with her father, the main male figure in her life, she would unwittingly perpetuate similar dynamics with other males in her present life.

Similarly, based on research mentioned earlier, family therapists believe that a symptom serves a function within the family system. For example, family therapists might suggest that since both Ann and Steve are overly dependent on their parents, the distance in their own marriage is a way of remaining loyal to their respective families of origin. Both family and psychodynamic therapists believe that once the function of the difficulty is addressed, the problem can be resolved.

Unlike our predecessors, SB therapists do not think that problems persevere because they serve a function. We explain persistent problems in another way:

> In the theoretical model used at the Brief Therapy Center of the Mental Research Institute (MRI) in Palo Alto, problems are thought of as the unintended side effects of (usually) well-meant efforts to resolve life's ordinary difficulties. Some solutions have the effect of reinforcing, rather than dampening, problem behavior. This occurs because people frequently do not realize the connection between their efforts to help and the evolution and maintenance of the problem. (Bogdan, 1986, p. 35.)

As will be explained in greater detail in Chapter 4, the way in which people go about solving a problem sometimes prolongs it. However, rarely do people recognize this dynamic since their solution makes perfect sense given their analysis of the problem.

Rather than attributing some conscious or unconscious motivation to keeping problems alive, we believe that people really don't *need* problems at all. Conflictual couples don't *need* to fight constantly in order to maintain intensity in the marriage, just as a woman in an unhealthy relationship doesn't have a *need* to punish herself. SB therapists find that most people happily and readily rid themselves of problems once they see alternatives to the habitual responses which have kept them going in circles.

PEOPLE RESIST CHANGE

Regardless of their orientation, most therapists believe that people are ambivalent about change and that they will resist their therapist's efforts to help them. Psychoanalytic therapists believe that people resist change when looking back becomes too painful. Family therapists believe that people resist change to maintain an equilibrium among family members.

SB therapists believe that most people really do want to change, they just aren't quite sure how to go about it. Although we would agree that those who initiate changes may receive "change back" messages from friends and family members, we do not assume that others are *trying* to thwart the change process, or that they have an investment in not changing. We assume that unproductive ways of behaving become habits and that these habits can be broken. We do not attribute malice or negative intent to others; we assume they are not yet aware of alternative responses to change.

SB therapists have noted with interest that the less resistance we have come to expect from our clients and their family members, the less we have observed. We can't help but wonder once again about the workings of self-fulfilling prophecies! Thousands of clients have taught SB therapists an important lesson: Change does *not* have to be a laborious, painful or lengthy process.

RAPID RESOLUTION OF PROBLEMS IS POSSIBLE

Erickson taught us that change can occur quickly. He reasoned that since people can get sick suddenly, so too can they heal suddenly. He postulated that lengthy treatment is less the result of intractable problems, and more the outcome of the therapist's self-imposed belief that rapid resolution of problems is impossible.

Today we know for a fact that people can solve problems much more quickly than had been suspected by our predecessors. The average length of treatment for SB therapists varies, but it is generally under ten sessions, typically four to six. Although the research on this approach is relatively new, some of the preliminary findings indicate that approximately 75 to 80 percent of the people attending solution-oriented therapy sessions report improvement or having accomplished their goals completely. Follow-up research at six-, twelve- and eighteen-month intervals indicates that these changes are lasting (Kiser, 1990, p. 34).

Because SB therapists have seen so many people make long-lasting changes quickly, we expect problems to be resolved rapidly. While this doesn't happen in every case, we nevertheless begin with the assumption that problems are readily resolvable until proven otherwise. We do not assume that long-standing problems are impervious to change. In fact, SB therapists make no distinction between recent and long-standing problems in regard to their solvability. One explanation for people being able to solve problems so quickly is the Butterfly Effect—a process whereby small changes rapidly build on each other.

THE BUTTERFLY EFFECT: A SMALL CHANGE LEADS TO BIGGER CHANGES

Noted meteorologist Edward Lorenz was attempting to analyze the effects a small change would have on global weather patterns. He discovered that even the most minute changes have profound effects on complex systems like weather. Lorenz described the dynamic of nearly imperceptible changes resulting in enormous changes as the Butterfly Effect because, as he put it, a butterfly flapping its wings in Brazil might create a tornado in Texas.

Proponents of SBT are convinced that the Butterfly Effect is alive and well in relationships. Small but significant changes in a troubled marriage can, without a doubt, turn things around dramatically. Take for example Paula and George, married for eight years. They sought therapy because, according to Paula, they had been fighting and unhappy for two of their eight years together.

After a couple of weeks Paula made an offhanded comment that she knew things were getting better when, instead of beginning her day by fighting with George, he surprised her with a kiss one morning. Although in the words of a well-known song "a kiss is just a kiss," in matters of marital problem solving, a kiss is much more than a kiss. Let's trace what happened in Paula and George's household following the morning kiss.

I asked Paula, "After George kissed you, what difference did that make to how the rest of your day went?" She replied, "I was so surprised, it caught me off-guard, but it was a pleasant surprise. After my shower I went downstairs and, hoping he would come and join me, I made a pot of coffee. We used to drink coffee together often, but lately the tradition has fallen by the wayside."

Interested in further implications of the Butterfly Effect I asked, "And then what happened?" George filled me in, saying, "I smelled the coffee, got dressed and came down for a cup. We actually had a pleasant conversation, something really different for us recently." I then inquired, "In what ways did this make your day at work more pleasant?" They both reported being more relaxed and lighthearted. I asked if co-workers noticed the difference and Paula confirmed that they had. Reminiscing about the evening, the couple remarked that even the children seemed more relaxed and less argumentative with each other. This pleased them both, adding to their positive feelings about the day.

Prior to my tracing the Butterfly Effect initiated by George's kiss (or was it initiated by something Paula did before they went to sleep that night?), Paula might have thought that a kiss was just a kiss. However, after noticing how one good turn deserved another and another and another, she might have agreed with Edward Lorenz.

When one partner makes a conciliatory gesture, it gets noticed by the other partner, who then reciprocates by offering some other conciliatory gesture and so on, until the changes begin to snowball. Furthermore, when couples make changes in their relationship, the changes mushroom into other aspects of their life as well.

Understanding that changes in relationships grow in this manner can be a godsend for spouses who, rather than taking the initiative to change, are stuck debating who is right or wrong or who should change first.

Ann and Steve's story also illustrates the impact of the Butterfly Effect. When Ann called for an appointment, Steve reciprocated by agreeing to join her in therapy. When Steve agreed to go out with her as if on a date, Ann reciprocated by being receptive to his overtures. He listened more carefully and she talked more. He was attentive to their children and helpful at home and she responded by being more physical. In respect for her feelings, Steve restrained himself from pushing her to allow him to return home. She recognized and appreciated his patience, which influenced her to ask him back, and so on. You can see from Ann and Steve's example how small gestures create big changes in relationships.

The Butterfly Effect also offers hope for marriages where only one spouse is committed to working on the relationship. The theory is, if one partner makes any significant change, the relationship must change. Spouses' interactions over the years become habitual and these highly patterned actions and reactions can be thought of in many ways—for example, two people playing a game of tennis. If one person puts a new spin on an old serve, then the return shot will inevitably be different.

Based on the mechanics of the Butterfly Effect, SB therapists frequently work with only one spouse—the spouse willing to come for therapy—to help him or her identify which actions to change in order to have the most impact on the marriage. I have even seen positive results in seemingly last-ditch cases where one person had already moved out or filed for divorce. Chapter 6 will describe how to target specific areas to change to reverse the vicious circle into a beneficent circle in these near-divorce marriages.

NO MARRIAGE IS AN ISLAND

To fully understand the complexities of a marriage, it is sometimes necessary to look beyond the individuals in the relationship. Marital difficulties can be precipitated by factors outside the marriage. While it is a well-accepted fact that children go through varied developmental stages as they grow into young adults, we must remember that adults also continue to change throughout the life cycle. SB therapists believe that the family undergoes developmental changes in much the same way that individuals do and that these changes often put stress on the marriage.

For example, both Ann and Steve mentioned that problems between them began when their first child was born. Obviously, they had not anticipated the ways in which an infant would impact on their lives. Many other couples say the same thing, that their marriage went sour after the birth of their first child. When I hear this complaint, I sometimes cite research that suggests that marital satisfaction goes down with the birth of each child. This information often normalizes or depersonalizes negative feelings about the marriage.

Any change in the family system—the birth of a baby, the first child going to school, the last child leaving home, turning forty, an aging and sickly parent, the death of a loved one—challenges even the best of marriages. Other factors, such as losing one's job, a geographical move or an acting-out child, are also definite marital stressors. Recognizing that marital difficulties can arise due to external events frequently casts a troubled marriage in a more positive light, since the partners can remove themselves from the unhelpful cycle of blame and recrimination.

NOW WHAT?

If solving problems is as simple as it sounds, you may be asking yourself, "Why have I been going in circles?" Chapter 4 describes how problems originate and why they persist despite your best efforts to eliminate them.

PART TWO

It Takes One to Tango: Change Your Marriage by Changing Yourself

GETTING STARTED

Now that you understand some of the nuts and bolts of Solution-Oriented Brief Therapy, you are probably ready to roll up your sleeves and start making your marriage work. The good news is that the marriage-enriching techniques described in Chapters 4–8 do not require both partners' coordinated efforts. Your spouse doesn't have to read this book in order for the methods to be effective. In fact, your spouse doesn't even have to overtly agree to wanting to make the marriage work. Years of experience have taught me that both partners need not be present during therapy sessions for the marriage to change. In certain situations, both parties' presence hampers the change process. I have observed hundreds of people change their relationships without the presence of their spouse in therapy and without a formal agreement from their spouse to work on the marriage.

What does this mean for you? If *you* want your marriage to change, *you* can change it. If you want a better relationship with your spouse and are willing to make small but significant changes (remember the Butterfly Effect), you can turn things around by starting the ball rolling. By following the guidelines laid out in these chapters you will, single-handedly, be able to get your relationship back on track.

"Why Do I Always Have to Be the One to Put Effort into the Marriage?"

Let's face it, there is usually one person in a relationship that takes the initiative to iron out relationship kinks. Since you are reading this book, you're probably the one. This doesn't necessarily mean that your spouse is disinterested or less interested than you in working things out. It just means that you have gotten in the habit of taking charge in the relationship department and your spouse has gotten in the habit of expecting you to do so. Remember the tandem bicycle?

There's absolutely nothing wrong with this division of labor as long as you don't mind it. If, on the other hand, you do mind it, at some later point you might want to kick this habit and, after reading the technique section, you will know just how to do it. But for now it's up to you to tip over the first domino.

Perhaps you are saying to yourself, "I do want my marriage to work and I have been trying, but things don't seem to be improving. In fact, lately things seem to have deteriorated." That's because not all problem-solving efforts are created equal. Some solutions are more effective than others. If you have felt like you've been going in circles trying to straighten things out, perhaps the following section will shed some light on your dilemma.

THE SOLUTION IS THE PROBLEM—A FORMULA FOR DISASTER

Quicksand is known to envelop its victim more speedily if one struggles to escape. The more intense the efforts to free oneself from the pull of the quicksand, the faster one sinks. The very action taken to sustain life actually increases the danger. Clearly, some problem-solving efforts backfire. The harder you try, the worse things get.

Solving marital problems can be like freeing oneself from quicksand. The harder you try to make things better, the less things change, which leads to frustration and, frequently, the decision that the marriage is dead. But there is a good reason that marital problems stubbornly persist, especially in the face of intense problem-solving efforts. Problems in marriages are maintained and aggravated by the particular way that people go about solving them.

When something troubling happens in a marriage, the spouse most bothered by the situation usually tries to fix it. If that particular strategy works, life goes on. If it doesn't work, the fixer typically escalates his or her efforts or does more of the same. Spouse A reasons, "Perhaps I haven't gotten my message across," and, rather than trying a totally different strategy, employs the same ineffective strategy with greater intensity. Unfortnuately, more of the same behavior from spouse A yields more of the same undesirable behavior from spouse B. This more-of-the-same approach not only maintains the problem, it increases it. In other words, the attempted solution becomes the problem (Fisch, Weakland, and Segal, 1982, p. 13).

Larry and Joyce are caught in the "solution is the problem" vicious cycle. For the past two years Joyce has been feeling depressed; she hates her job, feels overwhelmed by their two children, has no friends and rarely wants to do anything other than stay at home. Their sexual relationship has become virtually nonexistent. Larry, a high-energy, life-is-what-you-make-it person, has little understanding for someone who is, in his eyes, immersed in self-pity.

Previously, when Joyce felt depressed, a little pep talk from Larry would boost her spirits and she would be up and running again. But this was no longer true. Recently, rather than lightening Joyce's load, Larry's reassurances only made matters worse. "You don't understand what I'm going through, just leave me alone," Joyce would protest.

But Larry didn't leave her alone. He loved Joyce too much to just sit back and watch life slowly drain from her. Instead, he became even more determined to offer a pick-yourself-up-by-your-bootstraps lecture. "Take an aerobics class, you'll feel better," he would tell her. "This is just a phase you are going through, things aren't so bad." Joyce couldn't have disagreed more. Now, instead of feeling supported by Larry, she felt betrayed, isolated and deeper in depression.

At a loss for what to do next, Larry tried to figure out what might be contributing to Joyce's mood. He thought about her childhood and remembered her father died when she was a teenager. "Could she be suffering from unresolved grief?" he wondered. He recalled that Joyce's sister was a very moody person and thought perhaps Joyce's depression was inherited. He wondered whether Joyce was simply a negative person, unable to change her doom-and-gloom perspective about life. Finally, having just watched a television program about PMS (Premenstrual Syndrome), he feared her hormones had run amuck.

What is noticeably absent from Larry's list of possible explanations for Joyce's low spirits is anything having to do with his handling of the situation. Ironically, how Larry reacts to Joyce is the only thing he truly can change. Perhaps if he had initially recognized that his optimism had a reverse effect on Joyce, he could have experimented with other responses.

For example, he might have acknowledged her feelings and said, "Based on your feelings about your job, the strain of dealing with two active children and no social outlet, no wonder you're depressed. I'm sorry things haven't worked out differently for you. I can really understand why you're feeling this way, and all I can say is, 'I love you.' " Or, since his enthusiasm made her feel worse, he might have talked with her about aspects of his life which bothered *him*. In other words, rather than being the helper all the time, he could show his vulnerable and dependent side, forcing her to be the helper for a change. This might have increased her self-confidence and improved her mood. However, Larry did none of these things. The problem was prolonged because Larry did what common sense dictated: "If at first you don't succeed, try, try again." Unfortunately, for solving problems in relationships this is very, very bad advice.

I once met a woman who had an overwhelming fear of losing her boyfriend. "Whenever I see him look at or talk to a woman, I convince myself that he is having a passionate affair with her," she said. Each time she felt vulnerable or threatened, she told him about it. She knew she was behaving irrationally, but she felt she couldn't help herself. She hoped that sharing her fears would elicit reassurances from him and that she would feel closer to him.

At first, when she expressed her fears he was reassuring, telling her about his love and commitment to her. However, after a while, he noticed that the comfort she felt from his assurances was extremely short-lived. He eventually got so frustrated by her jealousy and his inability to comfort her that he stopped trying. He grew to detest the constant accusations of infidelity since he had been completely monogamous. In fact, each time she talked about her jealousy, he got angry and withdrew, making her more suspicious and anxious.

As she grew increasingly insecure about his affection, she doubled her efforts to get him to respond, but it was too late—he had nothing left to give. He wanted to end their relationship. Her fear of losing him had brought about the very thing she didn't want to happen.

WHY DO WE DO MORE OF THE SAME?

If cheering up a depressed person makes her more depressed, if asking for more closeness from an aloof person makes him more withdrawn, if pleading for more reassurance about commitment leads to a breach of commitment, why do we persist in doing what doesn't work? Why don't we quit doing the same old thing and try something else, anything else? Since what separates human beings from other animals is our ability to reason, why do we act so unreasonably so often?

Moi?

There are a couple of simple answers to this curious question. First of all, although we are very much aware of the impact of our spouse's behavior on us, we are less aware of how we impact on our spouse. We fail to notice our own role in the persistence of the problem:

> Human nature is such that when we are angry, we tend to become so emotionally reactive to what the other person is doing to us that we lose our ability to observe our own part in the interaction. Self-observation is not at all the same as self-blame ... self-observation is the process of seeing the interaction of ourselves and others, and recognizing that the ways other people behave with us have something to do with the way we behave with them. We cannot *make* another person be different, but when we do something different ourselves, the old dance can no longer continue as usual. (Lerner, 1985, p. 45.)

I overheard a conversation between my husband, Jim, and my then four-year-old son, Zachary, which is a perfect illustration of how "we lose our ability to observe our own part in the interaction." They were looking through the kitchen cabinets because Zach wanted soup for lunch. The conversation proceeded as follows:

ZACH: Do we have any soup?

JIM: I don't see any.

ZACH: But, do we have any soup?

JIM   (in a louder tone): I don't see any.

ZACH   (matching Dad's volume): But, do we have any?

JIM   (now screaming): I don't see any!

Then Jim turned to me and shouted, "I can't believe he keeps asking the same question over and over," to which I responded, "I can't believe you keep giving him the same answer over and over!"

The problem in their interaction was obvious to me since I wasn't in the middle of it. In Zach's eyes, the fact that my husband couldn't *see* the soup didn't mean that we didn't have any, hence his persistence. Unfortunately, my husband didn't recognize this. My husband's statement, "I can't believe he keeps asking the same question over and over," indicating that he saw Zach as the problem, was very humorous to me in light of his rigid response to Zach.

Zach would have appeared more reasonable if Jim had altered in any way his approach during the soup hunt, and Jim would have seemed more responsive if Zach had phrased his question in a different manner. Given that my son was only four at the time, I was betting on Jim to transport them out of their muddle but he was only aware of how Zach's "stubbornness" impacted on him, not what *he* might do differently.

Logical but Ineffective

Another reason that we persist in "more of the same" behavior is that it makes perfect sense given our assessment of our situation. The way in which we size up our problem determines the kinds of remedies we need: Once the marital problem is diagnosed, it narrows the field of solutions considered appropriate or fitting.

For instance, Rita is upset because her husband, Roy, has lost interest in making love. She thoroughly enjoys sex with Roy and can't understand the sudden decrease in his sex drive. As she contemplates how to approach him with her concern, she first tries to guess what is causing him to behave so uncharacteristically.

Her first thought is that he is angry at her for something that happened between them two months ago. She reasons that he has withdrawn from her sexually as a way of punishing her. "He's doing this out of spite," she says to herself. "He knows how much this is bothering me and I bet that's exactly what he wants." Each time she makes sexual advances, his lack of interest serves as evidence that he is still holding a grudge.

As she thought about Roy in this way, she felt herself getting angry. Although she believed that Roy was entitled to his feelings about the misunderstanding that occurred two months ago, she thought it inappropriate to try to punish her by withholding sex. She was enraged that he was not being more direct with her.

Her anger colored her ideas about what her next step should be. "I'm just going to let him have it as he walks through the door tonight. We'll have it out. I'll let him know that I won't stand for his behavior any longer. I'll put an end to it." Then she thought she would give him the cold shoulder and stop talking to him. Rita and Roy often grew silent when they were angry at each other. Another response Rita considered was to leave town for the weekend without advance warning to Roy. She hoped that this would bother him in the same way his behavior was bothering her and he would become conciliatory. In looking at the alternatives Rita had entertained thus far, one might say she was planning to take a firm action that would serve as a negative consequence for his aloofness.

As she thought about it some more, her mind began to wander. "Perhaps he isn't angry at all," she conjectured. "He's been having a really hard time at work these days, his boss has been extremely critical. Maybe he's feeling depressed or badly about himself. Maybe I've been too quick to judge. It's entirely possible that his lack of interest in sex has nothing to do with me. He might be preoccupied because of all the stress in his life. If I start hassling him about sex, it might just add to his stress. I really haven't been very understanding lately."

With this new perspective of the situation, her strategy changed drastically. She was not going to let him have it when he walked through the door. Hardly! She was going to make his favorite dinner, open a bottle of wine and ask him how his life is going. She was planning on expressing her concern about his stress and offering her help to ease things for him in whatever way she could. Then she remembered that it had been a long time since she had told him how much she appreciated him and thought that tonight might be as good a time as any to express her gratitude.

Just before she started making the dinner, a different explanation for Roy's behavior occurred to her. "Could it be that he is experiencing a physiological problem?" She recalled that Roy had been taking prescription medication and wondered if it had adversely affected his sexual appetite. With this thought in mind she was ready to cancel her dinner plans and suggest that Roy schedule an appointment with their family doctor.

As you can see, depending on Rita's view, certain solutions seemed appropriate while others appeared inapplicable. When she thought Roy was being spiteful, Rita considered punishing him. Compassion was the furthest thing from her mind and the only reason she would have considered scheduling a doctor's appointment for Roy was to have his head examined.

When he was seen as overworked, sad or depressed, her reaction was compassion. She felt guilty that she even *thought* about being vengeful when Roy needed her to help him out of his doldrums. A therapist rather than a physician is the professional with whom she would have consulted within this frame of reference.

And finally, when she considered the possibility of a physiological problem, neither revenge nor compassion fit the bill. A visit to the doctor was the only logical alternative.

Unlike Rita, most people diagnose the root of their marital problems more hastily, and favor a particular explanation rather than entertaining several. Once an explanation is favored, it is viewed as the correct one. Then corresponding correct solutions become apparent. However, if these solutions fail to produce the desired results, rather than rethinking the nature of the problem, which would lead to alternative solutions, "more of the same" becomes the only logical choice.

People say there are two things we can count on with certainty— death and taxes—but I know there are at least three. When people continue doing the same old thing to solve a problem that doesn't work, the situation will never improve. In fact, as you already have seen, it is likely to get worse. That's guaranteed.

"AM I DOING MORE OF THE SAME?"

It is easy to spot when you are doing more of the same. Take a moment to recall the specific times you and your spouse routinely reach dead ends. Maybe discussions about money, sex or careers always end in a battle. Perhaps monthly visits from in-laws trigger arguments. Maybe struggles about time together versus time alone always end the same old unproductive way. It is evident that certain issues resurface continually and remain unresolved.

When these issues arise, you can't believe how stubbornly your spouse handles the situation. He refuses to understand or even acknowledge your point of view. You can predict with great accuracy the exact moment when her subtle facial expressions will display her disgust. You can even precisely anticipate when the discussion will turn into a full-fledged fight. Isn't it amazing how predictable our spouses are?

The funny thing is, though, the more predictable your spouse appears, or the more stubborn and unbending he seems, the more rigid you have become in your response to him. If I were to ask your spouse about your usual scuffles, he would say that *you* are the one who behaves predictably, not him!

Most people get so involved in their routines that they do not even realize that there is something else they can do. Our patterns of interactions become habits. When we behave habitually, our relationship is on automatic pilot. We stop paying attention to what we are doing or how our partners are responding to us and, therefore, fail to notice whether we are getting the results we want.

Once you recognize that *you* have been playing a role in keeping things the same, you can change. A change in your actions will interrupt the pattern and lead to a change in your partner's actions, since you will no longer (unintentionally) provoke him. I've seen too many couples spend years debating who's right and who's wrong while their marriage goes down the drain. Engaging in endless debates about culpability conceals the fact that neither party is doing anything to solve the problem. Once you change, regardless of who is to blame, relationship changes are inevitable.

"BUT WHERE DO I BEGIN?"—GOAL SETTING

An essential first step for anyone hoping to change something is goal setting and that's what the remainder of this chapter covers. Establishing goals is important for several reasons. It will help you clearly envision what you want to accomplish. This, in turn, will enable you to identify what you need to do differently to make that happen. Goals make dreams become realities. The very act of defining goals and taking a more organized look at your life makes your goals more achievable.

I am frequently called upon to consult with other therapists when they reach an impasse with their clients. Nine times out of ten, the reason therapists get stuck is that the goals for therapy are either nonexistent or vague. Therapy meanders when it is not goal-directed. Similarly, people get lost when they don't know where they're going.

You might be thinking, "Of course I know what my goals are, no more fighting and more love from my spouse," but that's not enough. As you will see in the following section, having vague goals is comparable to having no goals at all. In fact, it's probably worse because you think you know where you're headed when you really don't.

The Immaculate Assumption

Politicians are notorious for using vague phrases that evoke powerful images yet in reality say very little. We fight for "Truth, Justice and the American Way." We want to make the world "safe for democracy." Who knows what this means? The words give the illusion of being packed with meaning, meaning that we all share. Yet it is unlikely that any two people would define these words in exactly the same way. This ambiguity works favorably for the politician who wants to build enthusiastic support while deflecting critics who would have held him accountable had his promises or goals been quantifiable.

Unfortunately for couples, ambiguous marital goals can be deadly. Take, for example, the couple who, after months of fighting, finally agreed to "be more affectionate" without ever defining what that meant. Several weeks after their truce they were threatening divorce as they accused one another of not trying. Interestingly, each spouse believed that he or she *had* been trying and it was the other who had reneged on the agreement.

How did that happen? Because "being affectionate" had never been clearly defined, they were not aware that they had extremely different expectations from the outset. The wife defined "affectionate" as spending more time as a couple, doing thoughtful things like calling each other to say hello during the day, and giving and getting hugs. The husband defined "affectionate" as sexual foreplay or making love. When he approached her sexually, he felt he was trying, but she recoiled because he hadn't yet shown affection according to her definition. When she called him at work to let him know she was thinking about him, he seemed oblivious to her affection. They missed each other's attempts to improve their marriage because they could only spot signs of affection based on their own definitions.

Similarly, a woman expressed her disappointment to her husband when he failed to buy her flowers for her birthday. Defending himself he said, "You never told me you wanted flowers." Insisting that she had, she reminded him, "Don't you remember, last week I told you that you should be more thoughtful." It's amazing how often people think they have spelled things out when, in fact, they haven't.

What *Do* You Want?

When I ask couples about their goals I notice that they are experts on what they *don't* like about their marriage. They tell me, "She never wants to have fun. She takes life too seriously" or "He doesn't ever want to plan in advance, he expects me to be spontaneous all the time." Other people say, "I can't stand so much confrontation" or "She talks too much."

While these statements begin to paint a picture of the relationship, it is a negative one. Describing what you don't like, or complaining, is not the same as describing what you want. Complaints don't offer maps to guide people beyond their difficulties. In fact, when complaints are expressed to our partners, they are experienced as putdowns or criticisms even when they are not intended that way.

Goal-setting rule number one is:

DESCRIBE WHAT YOU WANT TO ACCOMPLISH RATHER THAN WHAT YOUR SPOUSE IS DOING WRONG

Similarly, when I ask people, "What will be the very first sign that things are starting to be on the right track?" they tell me what they want to eliminate or see *less* of. They say something like "less seriousness, less confrontation and less talk." Again, this is not as helpful as identifying what you want to see *more* of because it is hard to observe or quantify "less seriousness" or "less confrontation." It is easier to notice a positive deed than it is to notice a decrease in a negative one.

For example, when a person tells me, "I want my wife to be less serious," I ask, "When this happens, what will she be doing instead?" To this he might respond, "She will joke around with me. We will make plans to go out together and do something fun, like

going to the movies." An invitation to the movies or an unexpected laugh will be much more noticeable than a decrease in
seriousness.

Start by conceptualizing or stating your goals in terms of "what
will be happening" rather than "what will be happening less often." You will see how much clearer the goals are, which will, in
turn, make getting there easier.

Vague goals and requests lead to mind reading and misunderstanding. No matter how long you have been married or how
well you know your spouse, you cannot expect to achieve your
goal or have your requests honored unless they are concrete and
specific, and stated in an observable form. Goal-setting rule number two is:

GOALS SHOULD BE DESCRIBED IN BEHAVIORAL
OR ACTION TERMS

In response to my question, "What will be the first sign that things
are starting to be on the right track?" a husband told me that his
wife would have more self-esteem. Since self-esteem is a subjective
feeling and not readily observable, I asked for an outward mea-
sure. "When she has more self-esteem, what will she be *doing*
differently? If I were watching her, how would I be able to tell
that she is feeling better about herself?" He responded, "When
she has more self-esteem she doesn't interpret my comments as
criticisms and, therefore, responds more calmly to me. Then I
don't fly off the handle because she is being more reasonable." His
wife agreed.

The following week the couple reported getting along better,
offering each other more compliments and fewer criticisms and
having better communication. Based on this feedback, I predicted
that the wife would report feeling more self-esteem, which she
did.

Some common goals people strive for are more love, happiness,
freedom, intimacy, togetherness, security, respect, sensitivity, better communication. However, in regard to marital problem solving, these goals are meaningless until they are translated into
observable, behavioral terms. I call these concrete behaviors "action goals." The following examples will help you translate vague
goals into action goals.

Vague Goals	Action Goals
Be respectful.	You will ask me about my day.
	I will compliment you about your work.
Be more loving.	You will tell me you love me at least once a week.
	We will make love twice a week.
	I will volunteer to watch the kids so you can go out.
Be more sexual.	I will initiate sex once a week.
	I will suggest we try something different.
	You will be more verbal when we make love.
Be less selfish.	You will ask what I want to do on weekends.
	I will check with you before making plans.
	I will clean up if you cook dinner.

If your goals have been too global, you can adjust them by asking yourself, "What will the two of us be *doing* differently when _____ (fill in your goal)?" For example, if your goal is better communication, you might answer, "When we have better communication, my husband will ask me more questions about my day, tell me he understands my feelings even if he doesn't agree and allow me to finish speaking before he speaks." The more specific your goal, the more attainable it will be. As you ask yourself this question, envision what you, your spouse and the two of you (as a couple) will be doing differently when you reach your goals.

Less Is More

There is a wise Oriental saying, "A journey of a thousand miles begins with one step." Relationships change one step at a time. Goals must be broken into small steps to be achievable. The question "What will be the first sign that things are starting to be on the right track?" is a most useful one because it asks that you look for the first sign of change, not the end goal. Eager for improvements, people frequently expect too much too soon and fail to notice the steps along the way. If these steps go unrecognized, discouragement builds and efforts to rebuild the relationship get derailed.

I was working with a couple who, though separated for six months, had lingering hopes for reconciliation. Both spouses had

had affairs. There was a great deal of hurt, resentment and anger. When they got together, instead of enjoying each other, they fought continually about whose affair was a more serious breach of their marital vows. Yet they held on to the hope that they would be able to overcome their past.

At the end of our first session I asked them about the first sign of change. The husband said, "We will trust each other completely again." In light of the recent affairs, and the pervasiveness of the tension, I thought that the goal of complete trust was not only too global, it was unrealistic. Granted, in order for the marriage to work, trust would have to be restored eventually, but first some mutually enjoyable, peaceful times were necessary. Trust and hostility do not go hand in hand.

I reminded them that, in all likelihood, trust would follow gradually after they rebuilt the foundation of their marriage. I cautioned them about having unrealistic expectations and asked, "What will be the first sign that you are doing what's necessary to engender good feelings?" They talked about going out on dates together, spending pleasant time alone, touching each other again and saying, "I love you." Once they had identified these goals I felt more certain of a positive outcome.

The familiar adage that "Good things come in small packages" is applicable to setting goals. Whatever you want to change must be broken down into small components that serve as signposts that you are on the right road.

Looking Forward

Perhaps when you ask yourself the question "What will be the first sign that things are on the right track?" you are having difficulty envisioning what needs to change. In that case, it will help for you to imagine a picture of the end product first. You can do this by asking yourself future-oriented questions. See if the following questions help get you started:

> "When you go to sleep tonight, if a miracle happens, so that when you awake tomorrow the problems you and your spouse have been having completely disappear, what will you be doing differently tomorrow?" (Lipchik and de Shazer, 1988)

> "Imagine that a friend (your children, your relatives, your boss) is watching you. How will he or she (or they) know the miracle has happened?"

"Which person will be the first to notice the miracle has happened?"

Once you have envisioned the future without the problem, ask yourself:

"What would be one or two small things you could do immediately to begin making the miracle happen?"

"Are there small pieces of this miracle already happening? If so, what are they and what do you need to do to keep them going?"

Another way of getting a bird's-eye view of the future is to ask yourself:

"If, magically, you and your spouse start getting along all of a sudden, what will you do with the time and energy you've been spending on mending and worrying about your marriage? What will you do instead?"

If you are still having trouble identifying your goals, they should become more apparent once you get further into the process.

Never Nirvana

One final word about the importance of setting reasonable goals. We've looked at the problems associated with expecting too much too soon. Another roadblock to achieving satisfying results is expecting too much, period. In his book *Helping Couples Change*, Richard Stuart writes, "The couple who would strive for perfection in their marriage have taken their first steps toward divorce and despair" (Stuart, 1980, p. 148). Certain goals are not attainable, ever.

After you finish this book and are reaping the benefits of getting along better, don't assume things will always be rosy. They won't. All marriages have ups and downs. No matter how solution-oriented you become, you will occasionally have rough times. Most people say that their rough times become shorter in duration, less intense and less frequent, but they don't disappear entirely.

It's amazing to me how many people imagine utopia when they are asked about goals. "We won't fight anymore." "He will *like* doing the dishes." "She won't get angry." Suffice it to say that,

even in the best of marriages, people fight, get angry, resent doing housework and look lousy in the morning. That's life.

'TIS A GIFT TO BE SIMPLE

If, after reading this section, you realize that you have been too
vague, too negative or impractical when you've approached your
spouse in the past, you might try applying what you've learned
here about setting goals and try again. This is the simplest and
most direct way to solve relationship problems. You may find that
by being more concrete, your mate is more accommodating, and
if so, great!

However, vagueness may not be what's ailing your marriage. If
your concrete requests have been ignored or rebelled against,
leading to less of what you really want out of your marriage, you
are an honored member of the "more of the same" club. Your
spouse's reaction (or lack of reaction) may have less to do with the
actual nature of your request and more to do with the predictable
yet ineffective way you've been responding to him or her.

If you have already been clear, specific and concrete with minimal results, don't repeat what's not working. Remember, "If at
first you don't succeed, try, try again" is bad advice for solving
problems in marriages.

SO NOW WHAT?

By now it should be clear that *patterns of interaction* rather than
individuals create problems and solutions. If you are experiencing
a marital problem, it is not helpful to simply blame it on your mate
unless self-righteousness and martyrdom are your goals. The dis-
advantage of blaming someone else for causing the difficulty is
that the solution is out of your control. You can do nothing but sit
around and wait for the other person to change. Good luck! At
the risk of being repetitive, let it be said once more. If you change
your actions, your marriage will change.

How can you identify which actions to change? There is a very
simple answer to this question. I have always been amazed at the
plethora of diet books available to the would-be weight-loss candidate when the bottom line for weight reduction is "Eat less and

exercise more." Period. The majority of people in my practice who have weight loss as their goal already know what to eat and what to avoid. In fact, they're often experts on nutrition. Nevertheless, they purchase book after book hoping to discover the "secret" to becoming and staying thin. Well, there are no secrets. Eat less and exercise more, that's all.

There is a similar formula to building and maintaining successful relationships. *"If it works, don't fix it; and if it doesn't work, do something different."* This formula suggests that you must first figure out what you and your spouse do differently when your marriage works so that you can do more of it. Then, you must identify your "more of the same" patterns (the ones that reinforce negative responses) in order to determine what to do less of. The next two chapters will help you assess which aspects of your relationship need fixing and which don't.

How to Get the Most from the Following Chapters

Before you get into the technique chapters, you need to know a bit about how they are structured so that you can navigate your way around them. Although the next few chapters are chock-full of case examples to illustrate the techniques, you will not find your particular problem handily labeled so that you can scan through the text looking for it. The following chapters are organized around *solutions,* not problems. This was not an oversight, it was done by design. Let me explain.

If you and your spouse argue about housework, you would naturally scan through the next chapters looking for a heading about housework struggles. Then you would read the example and, in it, find the solution that worked for that couple. You might assume that you should try that particular solution. That's okay. However, you might also assume that solutions to other problems aren't applicable to your situation, and that's not okay.

SB therapists have long observed that solutions to one problem can often be generalized to other problem situations. For example, the solution to fights over housework responsibilities may also be applicable to resolving conflicts over affairs. The following metaphor illustrates how one solution can be useful in a variety of difficult situations:

> The complaints that clients bring to therapists are like locks in doors that open onto a more satisfactory life. The clients have tried everything they think is reasonable, right and good, *and* what they have done was

based on their true reality, *but* the door is still locked; therefore, they think their situation is beyond solution. Frequently, this leads to greater and greater efforts to find out why the lock is the way it is or why it does not open. However, it seems clear that solutions are arrived at through keys rather than through locks; and skeleton keys (of various sorts) work in many different kinds of locks. (de Shazer, 1985, p. xv.)

The techniques in the next chapter are like skeleton keys. They can be applied to many different kinds of situations. If you limit yourself to reading about people who share your particular problem, you will miss out on a great deal of practical information.

Not only do SB therapists believe that a variety of problems can be resolved with a single solution, we think the converse is also true. Namely, a particular problem can have an infinite variety of solutions. SB therapists do not believe that a certain problem (a lack of communication, say) necessitates a particular solution (learning communication skills). Although couple A's problems with communication may be identical to couple B's problems with communication, their solutions may be (and probably are) extremely dissimilar. This is another reason the book isn't organized around problem areas.

So the message is, regardless of the nature of your marital difficulty, read each story carefully. The solution for which you have been searching may be on the very next page.

CHAPTER 5

Making a Habit of It: Identifying Patterns That Work

"IF IT WORKS, DON'T FIX IT"
—A FORMULA FOR SUCCESS

"You never show me you love me." "I'm always the one to initiate sex." "We never talk anymore." When couples aren't getting along, they make sweeping generalizations. These accusations, based on black-and-white, all-or-nothing thinking, represent how people really experience their partners. Under the stress of cold wars or extended periods of fighting, a wife really believes that her husband never shows his love for her, a husband is convinced that he is always the one to initiate sex. But rarely are relationships so unbending.

In my practice, I have noticed that no matter how severe or long-standing the marital problems, there are problem-free times, times when, for a variety of reasons, things go more smoothly; combative couples have peaceful days, inconsiderate spouses show more sensitivity and emotionally distant mates feel more intimate. Most people, including most therapists, see these problem-free times, or exceptions, as flukes and therefore unrelated to the process of finding solutions to marital problems. Generally, no effort is made to analyze what went right or to decipher how to make it happen again.

This lack of interest in exceptions is unfortunate because the mystery to most marital problems can be unraveled by examining the differences between times when the problem occurs and times when it does not. People need to do more of what works until the positive times crowd out the negative ones.

This chapter will help you identify times in your relationship when things have gone more smoothly. Those problem-free times, or exceptions, vary in length (lasting for several hours, months or years) and are often difficult to recall at first since not much critical attention is paid to a relationship when things go well. However, once you determine what you do or have done differently when you've gotten the kind of results you want from your spouse, you will be able to turn these exceptional times into habits.

A woman in the following case illustration was able to get her marriage back on track by identifying what she does differently when her marriage works so she could do more of it. Paula was at the end of her rope when she started therapy. She wished her husband would have come with her to the session, but he insisted, "You're the one with the problem, you go." Although she disagreed with his assessment, she was so unhappy she had to do something.

An Australian by birth, Paula met her husband, Sam, while traveling in China. Theirs was a thrilling, romance-packed encounter at the end of which they decided to marry. Paula agreed to come to the States to be with Sam. After one year of settling into their new lives together, Paula got pregnant with their first child. Two years after that, their second child was born.

As Paula reflected on the last several years, she could not believe how much her life had changed. She had gone from a single, carefree tourist traveling around the world to a wife, mother, professional woman living in a small town far from the excitement of city lights. But the biggest change of all, the hardest one to accept, was the drastic way her relationship with Sam had changed. They spent little time together, and when they did it was clear that their friendship had faded. Not a day passed when they didn't fight. Far from friends and family, Paula was heartbroken.

Her major complaint was that Sam was nasty to her. He worked long hours, stayed out with friends after work, did little to help with the children when he was home and balked at any suggestion to change. Paula described Sam and herself as volatile people and noticed that they had been extremely reactive lately.

I asked Paula what she wanted to change. She said, "I just want Sam to be nice to me again." Since I thought it would be helpful to know more about problem-free times, I inquired, "What is different about your behavior when Sam is being nice to you?" She responded, "I don't nag him. He always says that I nag. When he is nicer to me, I am nicer to him." I asked what she meant by "nicer," and she said, "When he spends more time with us as a family, offers to do things around the house and goes out with me once in a while, I feel more giving. I don't nail him for every little thing that bothers me, I let some things slide. I know it's important to let things slide every now and then, but when I'm angry at him, which I have been lately, I call him on everything. That's probably why he says I bitch at him." Then she added, "He has a bad knee. When I have good feelings about him, I am much more understanding about his knee and cater to him a bit. When I am angry, I think he just wallows in self-pity and I tell him so."

To get more information about the differences in their relationship between problem-free times and problematic times I asked, "What do the two of you do as a couple when you are getting along well that you haven't been doing lately?" She immediately replied, "We go out more. It's been a long time since we've done anything fun together. He never suggests going out and the last time I got a babysitter, he came home an hour late saying he forgot about our plan. It ruined our evening because I was so mad at him I couldn't let go of it."

Although it was clear to me that there were distinct differences in the way they treated each other during getting-along times and hostile times, it wasn't until the end of the session that Paula saw the connection between her behavior and the treatment she received from Sam. Until that point, she thought Sam's behavior was a result of his feeling down about his job.

Eventually Paula recognized that although Sam's job influenced his feelings and how he acted when he came home, it was not the only catalyst for his behavior. Paula's actions also influenced him a great deal. This realization helped her feel more control over their situation. At the end of the session, I suggested that Paula keep track of what she was doing differently when Sam was nicer to her.

Ten days later, Paula returned appearing more relaxed and smiling. She reported that they had had a good week and a half. I asked, "What have you been doing differently lately?" to which she replied, "Nothing really. The day after I came here, he just started being nice again." Although it was possible that Paula's seeking therapy prompted different behavior from Sam, I persisted. "Think about it a moment, what did you do that preceded his being nicer?" She was quiet for a moment and replied, "You know, you're right. The day I was here, he called and said he would be home at seven but didn't get home until eight, but I never said a word about it. He came home and I asked him how his day went and we had a really great evening. He played with the kids and put them to bed."

Then Paula commented on other changes in Sam: "We went out twice in ten days. I got a babysitter and called him at work to remind him. He was home promptly. I couldn't believe it. We went out to dinner together and had a great time. We also went to a party together. He got up early on the weekend with the kids so I could sleep and he is being more affectionate." As she reflected on Sam's changes, she recalled that she was more calm during the week, which allowed her to be more affectionate to him, more complimentary, less reactive and more upbeat, changes that Sam appreciated.

During the ten days there had been only one blow-up, which was a vast improvement for them. Paula noted that the fight was shorter than usual and that they quickly got themselves back on track. Finally, Paula commented, "He even apologized to me once this week, something he *never* does."

If Paula and I had not met for the second session, she might have attributed the good ten days to an unexplainable shift in Sam's mood. However, after dissecting what actually happened, how Paula had changed her own behavior and how these changes contributed to their getting along, Paula realized that she had to continue her changes if she wanted these results to last. She left the second session saying, "I get it. I have to be nicer to him if I want him to be nicer to me. I have to keep it up." To which I replied, "You got it."

The idea of building on the positive exceptions is so simple that, at first glance, it seems too simple to work. But be assured that, although new in its application to solving problems in human relationships, studying success to learn about success is not a new, untested idea. Olympic athletes view videotapes of themselves during peak performances to understand, internalize and reproduce the results. Patients surviving life-threatening diseases have certain characteristics in common. Now medical professionals like Dr. Bernie Siegel are studying what he calls "exceptional patients" to learn more about the healing process. Siegel writes:

If a "miracle," such as permanent remission of cancer, happens once, it is valid and must not be dismissed as a fluke. If one patient can do it, there's no reason others can't. I realized that medicine has been studying its failures when it should have been learning from its successes. We should be paying more attention to the exceptional patients, those who get well unexpectedly, instead of staring bleakly at all those who die in the usual pattern. In the words of Rene Dubos, "Sometimes the more measureable drives out the most important."

. . . One problem with cancer statistics is that most self-induced cures don't get into the medical literature. A survey of the reports on colorectal cancer found only seven such cases described between 1900 and 1966, although there have certainly been many more than that. A person who gets well when he isn't supposed to doesn't go back to his doctor. If he does, many doctors automatically assume his case was an error in diagnosis. In addition, most physicians consider such cases too "mystical" to submit to a journal, or think they don't apply to the rest of their patients, the "hopeless" ones.

Since I've changed my approach to focus on these rarities, however, I hear about "miraculous" healings everywhere I go. Once people realize that I know such things happen, they feel it's safe to tell me about them. . . .

In such cases physicians must learn to rush to the patient's home and ask why he didn't die when he was supposed to. Otherwise, such self-cures will not appear in the medical literature, and we will never learn from them that these are not instances of good luck, diagnostic errors, slow-growing tumors, or well-behaved cancers. (Siegel, 1986, pp. 20–21.)

The business world has also long been aware of the expediency of focusing on what works. In the book *In Search of Excellence: Lessons from America's Best-Run Companies,* authors Thomas Peters and Robert Waterman researched the management styles of the top American companies. By making the basic principles of good management accessible to the public, managers do not have to reinvent the wheel. They can learn from the success of others.

Another example of the efficacy of studying success is offered in Anthony Robbins's book *Unlimited Power.* He tells his readers:

There are strategies for financial success, for creating and maintaining vibrant health, for feeling happy and loved throughout your life. If you find people who already have financial success or fulfilling relationships, you just need to discover their strategy and apply it to produce similar results and save tremendous amounts of time and effort. This is the power of modeling. You don't have to labor for years to do it. (Robbins, 1986, p. 112.)

Couples don't have to search very far to find the answers for which they have been searching. Once they identify successful patterns in their own relationships, answers to many of their difficulties become evident. For example, a woman complained that her husband *never* talked to her about his work. This caused her to feel left out and uncertain of his respect. Although it felt like he *never* talked to her, after a while, the woman did recall an exception. "When my husband and I go out together for dinner he is more likely to talk about his day than if he comes straight home. At home, the kids vie for his attention and interrupt us, so he doesn't even bother talking very much." Recognizing this, she took his behavior less personally. Now when she wants to know about his work, she gets a babysitter, and asks him out on a date. Usually he is so delighted with the invitation he talks her ear off.

Creating a situation where a spouse is more likely to talk about his day may seem trivial when compared to serious marital problems. However, regardless of the nature of the problem, the same problem-solving principle applies: If you're experiencing a problem, determine what's different about problem-free times and do that instead.

Eleanor and Jack started therapy because they were bickering all the time. Hostility and resentment filled the air as they described their marriage. Jack said, "She nitpicks constantly, which makes me angry and I snap at her to get her to stop. It's driving me crazy." Eleanor had been married twice before and for Jack, this was a second marriage. Married for two years, they had a fourteen-month-old daughter. Although they did not describe their problems as major, they thought the problems could become so if not resolved immediately.

I began the session by asking, "So how will you know that coming here was helpful? What do you want to change?" Jack's response was, "Well, there are a lot of things. Do you want the symptoms or the solutions?" I told him, "If you've thought about the solutions, I'd prefer starting there."

Despite their argumentativeness throughout the session, I was able to weed out their accusations to help them identify what was different about the times when they got along. They told me of their recent move to a small rural town. Although Jack kept his job in the suburbs, Eleanor was no longer employed, an agreement they made when their daughter was born. Eleanor had no friends and no adult companionship during the long hours that Jack was at work. Eleanor admitted to feeling isolated, since prior to their daughter's birth she had always worked. She felt that they got along better when she didn't feel so lonely. Since working was not an option, we discussed several other possibilities: becoming a member of a parent-child discussion group, joining a year-round snowmobile club, meeting neighbors and attending their ski club more regularly.

Additionally, they agreed that they needed to spend more time as a couple since that seemed to work better for them in the past. They believed that more time together would ease Eleanor's sense of isolation and, at the same time, be enjoyable for both of them. They admitted to allowing projects around their home to take precedence whenever they found themselves with free time.

Unfortunately, Jack and Eleanor had no babysitter and felt discouraged about finding qualified and trustworthy child care without knowing too many people. Nevertheless, they agreed it was possible once they put their minds to it.

Then there were housekeeping issues which prevented them from feeling close. Prior to their move, their household tasks were not nearly as demanding and they fought less. Now Eleanor felt that Jack wasn't holding up his end of the housework. Although the increased work load wasn't something they could change, Jack recalled that there was less fighting about housework when they did it together on the weekends and he was more than willing to try that again.

Finally, Jack identified another exception to their difficulties. "Eleanor is deathly afraid of getting pregnant again and so we have absolutely no sexuality whatsoever between us and that creates problems. We got along much better when the relationship was physical. We haven't had sex in three months." Eleanor agreed that the lack of sex in their marriage was a major problem and discussed her desire for them to agree on a permanent birth control solution. Prior to our discussion, Jack thought Eleanor would never want to have sex again. Now he was more clear on her reason and knew what they needed to do to become intimate again.

As a result of our discussion during the first session, several exceptions were identified. Jack and Eleanor determined that they get along better when:

1. Eleanor has friends.
2. Eleanor has interests in addition to her home and daughter.
3. They spend more time together as a couple.
4. Jack helps more around the house.
5. The relationship is more physical.

The second session occurred two weeks later. They were relaxed and lighthearted and told me that they didn't fight at all for two weeks. Eleanor happily reported that she got out more. She said that every morning before Jack left for work, she took a shower and went for a long walk, which she found exhilarating. The babysitting problem was solved when she looked in the classified section of her newspaper only to discover that her neighbor was advertising her services as a babysitter. Eleanor brought her daughter to the sitter several times between sessions one and two to go to an exercise class in her community. Plus, now that they had a babysitter they trusted, Jack and Eleanor went out to dinner alone twice. It reminded them of the old times. Finally, although they hadn't made love yet, they reached an agreement about birth control. Eleanor decided she wanted a tubal ligation and was pleased that Jack agreed despite his original plan of having more children.

As you read about Jack and Eleanor, you might think that they were extremely reasonable, cooperative and patient—they weren't. The exceptions listed above were extracted from a smorgasbord of blame, accusations and interruptions. I simply (but persistently) kept redirecting their attention to what has worked for them. Eventually, the important information about exceptions was clarified during the session. Once they examined what made their marriage work, Jack and Eleanor knew exactly what to do once they walked out my door.

WHY FOCUSING ON WHAT WORKS—WORKS

Over the years that I have emphasized my clients' problem-free times, I have been amazed at the effectiveness of the method. Initially, there is confusion because no one expects to discuss with a therapist what *has* been working. After all, "Therapy is a place to talk about problems." But my clients learn quickly that therapy is a place to *solve problems,* a process which may or may not include talking about problems. Following the initial surprise, most people *can* describe very specifically what each person does differently when they get along. As you are about to see, the benefits of doing so are many.

1. Exceptions Shrink Problems

Once a single exception is acknowledged, black-and-white, either/or thinking is eliminated. People realize that their problems aren't as all-encompassing as they thought. For example, imagine that the identified problem is "We just can't communicate," implying that there is absolutely no communication. As I ask about exceptions a couple might comment, "We have better discussions when I give him a half hour after work to unwind," "I'm more talkative when she doesn't start the discussion right before we go to sleep," "I am more reasonable in our discussions when she doesn't cry constantly," "When we go on vacation, we have the best communication."

After discussing exceptions for a while, the perception "We just can't communicate" changes to "Sometimes we have an easier time talking than other times," an infinitely more hopeful analysis. By emphasizing what works, problems no longer seem insurmountable and optimism swells.

2. Exceptions Demonstrate That People Are Changeable

Another interesting thing happens as a result of finding exceptions. People's seemingly fixed traits appear fluid. The wife who is saddened by the loss of romance in her marriage may think, "My husband is never romantic, he's just not that kind of guy." However, after identifying exceptions, she is likely to revise her perspective. "My husband is romantic when we go out for dinner or when the children aren't around," a realization that casts her spouse in a more flexible light. Exceptions demonstrate that behaviors are triggered by specific conditions or contexts rather than the result of deeply ingrained personality characteristics, clearly a much more hopeful view.

3. Exceptions Supply Solutions

In addition to reminding people that good times really do exist, another benefit of talking about what works is that it offers couples a blueprint describing exactly what they need to do next to make their relationship satisfying. In other words, exceptions supply specific solutions. People leave with a plan they can implement immediately. Furthermore, the devised plan is *their* plan. It's not some generic marriage enrichment program designed to work for every shaky marriage irrespective of the individuals involved or the nature of their marital problems.

4. Focusing on Strengths Strengthens

Last but not least, focusing on exceptions empowers people. They realize for the first time in months (or years) that, despite the mayhem, there *are* some things they have been doing right. This real-ization often comes as a complete surprise because most people feel they've tried everything and nothing works. They think they have depleted their resources. Once feelings of resourcefulness are re-stored, resolution of the marital problems seems more feasible.

WHY ARE WE BLIND TO EXCEPTIONS?

If focusing on what works is so effective, why do we fail to notice the good things that happen? As I've mentioned, people have a great deal of difficulty recalling problem-free times in their mar-riages. These people say, "There are no exceptions," "My hus-band never shows his love for me," "My wife never initiates sex." However, more likely, a wife feeling cheated of her husband's expressions of love may not notice the little things he does to please her. Her resentment and hurt blind her to his thoughtful gestures. Similarly, the husband convinced he is the initiator of all sexual encounters may miss the signal that his wife is feeling am-orous when she puts her arm around him. These blinders con-tribute to the perception that nothing is working in the marriage.

There are several reasons we have blinders. When a marriage has been on the rocks for some time, a *series* of positive experi-ences are required to convince a couple that the marriage is on safer ground. One mutually satisfying experience is often viewed as a fluke unless it is followed by several other satisfying experi-ences. In contrast to this, if two weeks of harmony are followed by a single antagonistic episode, it completely negates the two har-monious weeks which preceded it. It is as if the two good weeks never happened. Our "here-we-go-again" mind-set filters out the positive experiences.

But more fundamentally, one major reason we fail to notice our spouse's positive efforts in the midst of our turmoil may be di-rectly related to the limitations of our power of perception:

> To notice is to select, to regard some bits of perception, or some features of the world, as more noteworthy, more significant, than others. To these, we attend, and the rest we ignore—for which reason conscious attention is at the same time ignore-ance (i.e., ignorance) despite the fact that it gives us a vividly clear picture of whatever we choose to notice. Physically, we see, hear, smell, taste, and touch innumerable features that we never notice. You can drive thirty miles, talking all the time to a friend.

What you noticed, and remembered, was the conversation, but somehow you responded to the road, the other cars, the traffic lights, and heaven knows what else, without really noticing, or focussing your mental spotlight upon them. So too, you can talk to someone at a party without remembering, for immediate recall, what clothes he or she was wearing, because they were not noteworthy or significant to you. Yet certainly your eyes and nerves responded to those clothes. You saw, but did not really look. (Watts, 1966, p. 29.)

Why Do We See What We See?

What then governs what we notice or fail to notice? Although it isn't the only prerequisite, in order to notice something we must have a label for it. Eskimos have many words for different varieties of snow because it is vital to their survival. We, on the other hand, have only a few. We are not able to *see* many different types of snow because we don't have separate labels or words for them. We classify bits of perception into the categories for which we have labels.

When spouses are in conflict, they develop negative images or labels of each other ("He's insensitive"; "She's controlling") and scan their daily interactions for evidence which confirms these images. Even well-intended deeds are frequently misinterpreted to fit enemy classification. An angry wife may tell herself that the dozen roses sent by her husband are just a sign that he is feeling guilty. A husband who complains that his wife nags all the time might interpret her unusual show of support to do as he pleases as a sign that she must want something from him. Our prejudices color our perception.

DISCARDING THE BLINDERS BY FOCUSING ON EXCEPTIONS

If you are like most people, you haven't been asking yourself what you've been doing right to resolve the differences between you and your mate. You've probably been emphasizing your failures or, more likely, your spouse's failures. Unfortunately, you are probably no closer to finding solutions with that approach.

Although you may not know exactly how to do it yet, you have the power to provoke positive responses from your mate. By changing how you act when you're together, you can significantly alter your patterns of interaction. Once you identify what you do differently during good times, you just need to do more of it. Remember, if it works, don't fix it. The following nine guidelines will help you analyze what works in your marriage and give you information you need to get your marriage back on track.

1. Notice What Is Different About the Times the Two of You Are Getting Along

As you recall recent problem-free times or exceptions (there are almost always some of them), determine what *you* do differently during those times. For example, you might have noticed, "When I don't complain about his occasional late nights at work, he is more responsive to my needs," or "If I ask for her input on my plans, she is much more cooperative," or "When I spend more time with her, we get along better." List as many recent examples as you can think of. The more the better.

If you are having difficulty answering this question, the following suggestion might help. Identify a recent peaceful time. For example, "Last night we had a reasonable conversation." Think carefully about what you were doing immediately preceding the conversation. Maybe you asked about your spouse's day or made a delicious dinner. Sometimes what you did differently preceding a peaceful time is subtle, so take your time thinking about it.

Now, as a *result* of the "reasonable conversation," what were you more inclined to do that you hadn't been doing prior to it? In what ways did this conversation influence you to act differently? Perhaps you felt closer to your spouse and therefore initiated sex, or maybe, for the first time in weeks, you said good night as you went upstairs. Deciphering what you do immediately preceding and immediately following good times reveals what you must do to initiate and maintain desirable changes.

Perhaps as you are responding to the question "What is different about the times the two of you are getting along?" all you can think of are the things your *spouse* does differently when things go smoothly. For example, you may think, "I am happier when he gets off my back about spending money."

Since, for now, the assumption is that you are answering these questions by yourself and not as a couple, it is important to remember that the goal here is to figure out what *you* can change to get the kinds of results you want from your spouse. If you focus on your spouse's behavior rather than on what you can change in yourself, you are doing the same old thing and it won't work.

Redirect your attention to your own behavior by taking an inventory of how you are thinking, feeling and acting when the two of you get along well.

If you are having trouble staying focused on yourself, it may mean that you are still holding out for your spouse to change first. Perhaps you haven't been willing to give to your partner until you have first received. Unfortunately, this catch-22 perspective will keep you from taking the first step to break the vicious cycle. However, once you discipline yourself to identify your contribution to making your marriage work, you can immediately see how surprisingly small but well-meaning gestures can extricate you from the self-defeating waiting game.

Paula's story at the beginning of this chapter is a good example of someone who stopped playing the waiting game (even though it was tempting) and figured out what she could do to alter the course of her marriage. She noticed that on the rare occasions that they got along well she had been nicer to her husband. Once she translated this realization into behaviors her husband appreciated, her relationship improved dramatically.

2. If You Are Having Trouble Identifying Current Exceptions, Recall What You and Your Spouse Were Doing Differently in Years Past That Made Your Marriage More Satisfying

Sometimes people are so polarized they are unable to describe any recent respite from marital battles. However, when asked about times past (particularly when marriages have lasted many years) practically everyone can recall trouble-free times and what they were doing differently then. The advice here is the same— reinstitute those activities and behaviors that once worked. They're likely to work again.

When Brian began therapy, he couldn't describe recent problem-free times because he and his wife, Melanie, had been so distant. However, he was able to identify what once worked in the past, which helped him restore positive feelings in his marriage.

They had been married for seven years when Melanie told Brian that she was extremely unhappy and considering leaving. Although this was a first marriage for Melanie, it was a second one for Brian and he could not believe he might be headed for divorce again. He was devastated. I started the session by asking him what he wanted to change and he said, "I want Melanie to be happy and for us to be a family again. I don't want to become a part-time father. I want to raise my daughter."

My first task was to assess whether Melanie might still be open to the marriage working. Since she wasn't present, I asked Brian if he thought that she was *convinced* that the marriage was over. He said, "No, although she did say that she loves me but does not like me and that we're not friends anymore." As he told me about a note Melanie had written, he began to cry. "She says she wants to give the marriage a three-month trial period to see how things go."

Despite his fears of losing Melanie, I thought it a positive sign that she didn't ask for a separation and seemed to be giving their relationship a chance. My next step was to help Brian recall what once worked so that he could repeat it. I wondered how their relationship was different when they were first married. He said they used to spend more time together and go dancing a lot, but now they just worked all the time. It was difficult for him to think of any other differences.

"What does Melanie think you need to change for the marriage to work?" I asked. He replied:

> When she was pregnant with our baby, I used to go out a lot with the guys. I probably drank too much and I know that upset her. But since the baby was born, I've gone out much less. I don't know if the pressure of having a baby or having to provide for the family financially scared me, all I know is that I screwed up. But it's too late to change all that now. Besides, I quit drinking completely six weeks ago and I feel great. I thought it would be tough, and Friday nights were tough in the beginning, but not anymore. Now I drink near beers and they taste just as good to me. I've even lost some weight.

So far it was clear that Brian needed to stay sober and spend more time with Melanie and the family, as he had done in the past, if their marriage was to work. But I felt Brian needed more ideas about what once worked for them so that he could make the necessary changes. Therefore I asked, "What seemed to work in the past?" He responded, "She liked it when I paid more attention to her—didn't watch TV—when she talked to me. She wanted my undivided attention. She also seemed to enjoy when I talked about my day." I wanted to know what he had been doing right recently. He told me that he was communicating better by making eye contact and talking more. He also sent her flowers and a singing telegram. He left her both serious and humorous cards around the house such as in the microwave, the refrigerator and the medicine cabinet. I asked how she liked them and he felt fairly confident that she did. Melanie thanked him and gave him a kiss each time.

Although Brian was tentative at this point, I thought that he was basically on the right track. The fact that Melanie thanked and kissed him for his efforts was a good sign. I assured him that if he kept up his "new" behavior things might work out the way he planned.

Two weeks later was Brian's second session. He was more relaxed and seemed happier. The times he and Melanie had spent together were cordial and he was a little more confident that things might work out between them after all. Although she was still reserved, Melanie seemed pleased with Brian's changes.

Session three was held two weeks later. They had gone out to dinner together, which they both enjoyed. The next evening when Brian was taking a shower, Melanie came into the bathroom, sat down and asked, "If I stayed to work things out between us, what would our relationship be like?" He told her that he would keep paying attention to her, he wouldn't drink anymore and that they would do things together like going shopping or even doing the laundry. He commented that it didn't matter what they did as long as they did it together.

Brian reported that Melanie's question shocked him. He appeared extremely happy and said that he was tickled to death but he was still cautious. I told him that I didn't think Melanie's wanting to work things out was a coincidence and reminded him that he had made significant overtures to her. He agreed, adding that he had been more of a father and husband lately, that he was constantly with the baby, reading to her, as well as reading about child development and doing laundry. He said he felt like Mr. Mom and was loving it. Additionally, he was being more responsible, attentive and communicative with Melanie, which she apparently enjoyed.

Brian felt that he wanted to take a break from therapy but commented that he would schedule another appointment if things got rocky between Melanie and him. I contacted him for a follow-up five months later to find that they were still together and things were going well.

Comment

Brian is one of many people who, after giving his situation considerable thought, could not think of a single recent example of problem-free times. Because their relationship had grown so far apart, Brian had to draw on past experience to extract the information he needed about problem-free times to change his behavior and turn things around in his marriage. He recalled how he was different in years past when Melanie was more responsive. Having quickly established concrete goals—that he needed to remain sober and be more attentive and communicative—Brian was well on the way to winning back Melanie's confidence that the marriage could work, which was his ultimate goal.

In addition to identifying how each of you acted differently in times past in order to make your marriage work, there is another way to discover what has worked for you as a couple. Ask yourself, "During peaceful times, what did the two of us like to do that we haven't been doing lately?" Recall hobbies or forms of entertainment such as going out to eat, or to the theater, sporting events, ballet, dancing and so on and start doing these activities immediately. When couples start doing the things they once enjoyed together, the relationship often improves. Unfortunately, not enough couples know this.

Most people assume that spending more time together will be the logical result of *feeling* better about each other. Therefore, they wait for the hostile feelings to be replaced by positive feelings before doing those things that once gave them joy. However, the reverse appears to be true: When couples engage in pleasant activities together, it triggers pleasant feelings, which in turn breed a cooperative spirit.

3. You Don't Have to Like It, You Just Have to Do It

Sometimes when I ask a person what seems to work I hear, "I know my wife is more understanding about my absences when I call her every day when I'm on a business trip, but I don't think I should have to do that. She should just trust me." Or "My husband puts the kids to bed when I ask him to, but he should just think of it himself." She should and he should, but they don't! So don't sit back waiting for your mate to change when you already have the formula for success.

Several years ago my friend Denise told me how she resolved an ongoing marital struggle once she recognized what worked and let go of the idea that she shouldn't have to do it. As a saleswoman, she has to do a significant amount of traveling. Initially, her absences put a great deal of pressure on her husband, Cal, who then had to balance his high-pressure career with caring for their two children. Since Denise regularly balances motherhood and career she could empathize with his feelings, but nevertheless felt he should just grin and bear it and be grateful for the times he is not on duty.

Each time Denise prepared herself for a trip, she got tense, anticipating a negative response or complaints from Cal. Sure enough, when he complied, grousing about having to take their daughter to school the next day, she used to accuse him of being unreasonable, unfair or sexist. Needless to say, he didn't thank her for the feedback. Instead, he would defend his position and they would get into a huge fight, hardly the response Denise wanted as she packed to leave her family.

Then someone advised her, "Denise, Cal doesn't have to love your traveling, he just has to agree to manage things when you're gone." This, she was soon to discover, was very important advice. From that point on, every time Cal mumbled under his breath something about being left alone with the kids, she remained quiet. Remarkably, within minutes, Cal would turn to her and start a completely unrelated, amiable discussion. Apparently, Denise's silence did not provoke him to justify his position.

At first she thought, "I shouldn't have to control myself in this way. He should just be more reasonable." But now, after many years of peaceful and loving departures, she knows better. The lesson Denise learned? Do what works, even if "you shouldn't have to." Since that time Cal has become extremely supportive of her demanding career and she has been known to send him flowers to express her gratitude.

One reason people feel "I shouldn't have to do X" is that they don't agree with or understand their spouse's needs. "She wants me to plan our evenings a week in advance, but I never know what my schedule will be like. I don't know why it's so important to her to get a week's advance notice. I like to be more spontaneous." Then the arguments begin in an effort to ascertain whose approach to life is correct.

My work with couples has taught me that there is no such thing as a correct way to live one's life. Spontaneity and the ability to plan are both desirable attributes when properly balanced. It is a misconception to think that you must agree with or be like your spouse. Disparately different human beings can peacefully coexist. If you do what works for your mate, even if you think it's crazy, he or she will reciprocate by pleasing you, even if he or she thinks it unnecessary.

When I work with couples and both people are present, I ask the same question about exceptions. Although there is generally some overlap in couples' perceptions about what makes their marriages work, there are also differences. For example, he thinks things go well when the relationship is more physical whereas she thinks they get along better when they spend more time together. It becomes apparent through our discussion that is is not an either/or proposition, it is both. When he spends more time with her, she feels an increased desire for intimacy. When they are more physical, he feels more desire to spend time together. "You scratch my back and I'll scratch yours" is sound marital advice even when you think your spouse's back shouldn't be itchy.

4. Focus on What's Doable or Possible

Since life never holds still for very long, sometimes what once worked is no longer feasible. For example, although Eleanor said that she and Jack got along better when she was working, she quickly informed me that getting a job wasn't currently an option. Instead, we explored the needs that were met by her working to see if some other solution might satisfy those same needs. Work allowed Eleanor to be around people, a need she more recently met by joining an exercise class.

Similarly, when a couple tells me that they communicate better when on vacation, unless they can take a permanent vacation I ask, "What's different for the two of you about being on vacation?" They might respond, "We are away from the kids, our home environment and far from distracting phones and television sets." From their response, the couple could then re-create certain therapeutic features of vacations without actually getting on a plane. They could, for example, plan a trip to the city to try a new restaurant, which would, in effect, get them away from the kids, their home environment and far from distracting phones and television sets.

If the exceptions you are identifying seem outdated or unfeasible, ask yourself, "What could I do that might address the same needs?" Focus on what you can do, not what you can't.

5. A Problem That Recurs Doesn't Necessarily Require a New Solution

When I ask couples, "Have you ever had this difficulty in the past?" some say that they have. "How did you solve the problem at that time?" I ask and they describe their past solution. When I inquire, "Have you tried doing that again?" most say no. Although most people can recall how they solved a problem in the past, repeating that strategy seldom occurs to people. Why is that?

Erroneous analysis blinds people to this simple solution. If people successfully solve a problem at some point in their lives, but the same or similar problem surfaces at some later date, they incorrectly assume that the original solution didn't work, for if it had, the problem would not recur. As a result, the original solution is crossed off the list of potential solutions.

Another, more likely reason a problem recurs is that once the solution starts working, people typically relax and go back to their old habits. Shortly thereafter the problem returns. This in itself is not catastrophic, as long as people remember to return to their more effective ways of interacting.

Such was the case with Lisa and Gerard. They had been married for ten years, and although their marriage was basically intact, they argued a great deal about money. They both thought that their spouse spent money frivolously. Although Lisa and Gerard earned a good income, they begrudged each other's every expenditure. Lisa felt that Gerard shouldn't spend money on a second computer since she thought it was excessive. Gerard vetoed a plan for home improvement, Lisa's way of spending money.

The tension between them grew to include other aspects of their relationship as well. During the first session they argued a great deal about housework and child-rearing responsibilities. Lisa thought many of their disagreements about housework would be resolved if they would just get a housekeeper. Naturally, Gerard vehemently disagreed. That too would be considered a waste of money.

In the midst of their blaming each other, I asked if they had ever had financial disagreements in previous years of their marriage. They said they had. I asked how they resolved them at that time and there was silence. Finally, Lisa spoke. "I guess we just minded our own business. I bought what I wanted to buy and Gerard may have disapproved, but he never said anything. He spent money on different things and I just stayed out of it." I asked Gerard if he agreed with that assessment and he said he did.

I wanted to know whether they thought they could reinstitute a laissez-faire financial policy and they agreed. Since their salaries were considerably higher than in previous years, it increased the possibility of spending large sums of money. Therefore, they added an addendum. If either wanted to purchase an item over a thousand dollars, the spouse had to be consulted. They were extremely pleased with their new old plan.

If the problems you and your spouse have been experiencing make you feel like you are having déjà vu, recall what you once did to resolve them and go back to that.

6. Pay Attention to How Your Conflicts End

"You started it" is a common household battle cry. A husband accuses his wife of ruining their evening because of her cutting remark. She tells her husband that her remark was merely a response to the sarcastic comment he made earlier in the evening. He defensively points out that his comment followed her rude behavior of the previous evening, to which she responds . . . and so on. Who is right? This classic chicken-or-egg discussion is not very productive. It's clear that each person's behavior is triggered by what preceded it and influences what follows. But as has been noted before, the popular "who started it" debate takes energy from finding a solution.

Rather than debating about who started it, a more useful question is: "How do your arguments (cold wars, unpleasant interactions) end?" Experts on canine behavior tell us that dogs in the wild have very distinct ways of communicating that a fight is nearing its end. One dog rolls on its back and bares its neck, a signal to its opponent that the competition is over. The fight ends.

Although people also send similar highly patterned and predictable peacemaking signals to their mates, we are rarely conscious of them. Although the argument gets diffused following these truce triggers, we fail to see the connection between our actions and the resolution of the problem. Couples who shift their attention to the sequence of events at the *end* of their unpleasant times are able to unravel the mystery of what triggers them to get along.

For instance, Janice and Joe have frequent heated debates varying in length from one hour to three or four days. However, there are days, sometimes even weeks, when peace prevails. When asked, "How do your fights end?" they were perplexed since they hadn't thought about it. Finally, Janice said, "When Joe acknowledges he understands my point, even if he doesn't agree, I feel finished. All he has to say is, 'I see what you mean. I don't necessarily agree, but I understand.' Once I hear those words, I feel satisfied."

Joe responded differently. "I know to stop when Janice threatens to leave the room. At that point, she's not listening to me anymore. If I continue, it goes in one ear and out the other. When she tells me she's going to walk out, I usually drop the subject for a while, and approach her later, when she has had time to think things over. She's much more rational then."

Once Janice and Joe identified their truce triggers, they became more aware of how they affected each other. Now they can make conscious choices to short-circuit their fights by being responsive to the needs of their partner. For example, when Joe tires of fighting, rather than reiterating his point for the fiftieth time, he could decide to acknowledge Janice's feelings. He doesn't even have to agree. He simply has to tell her he understands. If Janice tires of the go-around, she could tell Joe that she needs time to be alone to sort things out. Joe would realize she had reached her fighting limit, and back off.

Joe and Janice's truce triggers are probably different from yours. Nevertheless, all couples send and receive these peace signs. Once you identify the patterns to how your fights end and what triggers the transition from fighting to getting along, you will be able to consciously implement this strategy.

7. If There Are No Exceptions, Identify the Best of the Worst

Occasionally, it seems impossible to recall any exceptions or problem-free times whatsoever. If you are not able to identify exceptions, ask yourself, "Under what circumstances is the problem less intense, less frequent or shorter in duration?" Frequently, re-creating these helpful circumstances decreases the problem.

One woman told me that she was having a horrendous time getting past her hurt feelings about her husband's affair. Although it ended seven months prior to our first session, she felt like it had happened yesterday. When I asked, "What's different about the times when you are not thinking about the affair, when you feel more relaxed?" she responded, "There is no such thing. I am always thinking about it," and no one could convince her otherwise.

I then asked, "What's different about the times when the memories are not quite so intense?" She responded, "I've noticed that when I'm at work and occupied with my job, the feelings and memories are somewhat faded." She then agreed that keeping busy was essential to her well-being. We discussed additional ways for her to keep herself active. As a result of our discussion, this woman felt relieved that she could consciously diminish her pain by keeping active.

8. Notice What's Different About the Times the Problem Occurs but Something Constructive Comes from It

A therapist was working with a woman who said, "The problem is, I'm angry all the time and you have to help me get rid of it." The therapist asked the woman, "What's different about the times that something good comes out of your being angry?" to which she replied, "I guess those are the times I force myself to do something constructive rather than just stew about it. I let someone know my feelings and we resolve whatever is bothering me."

"What percentage of the time would you say that your anger is constructive?" continued the therapist. After considerable thought and several minutes of silence the woman answered, "Sixty percent of the time." As I observed this session I found it remarkable how rapidly this woman had shifted her perception from being angry "all the time" and needing to rid herself of it, to her anger being constructive 60 percent of the time! The dialogue between this woman and her therapist left her with a significantly smaller problem to be resolved than she originally thought. Furthermore, she saw that anger is not all bad. When she handled her anger in a particular way, it was even productive.

You may feel your problems have nothing but negative consequences, but think about it again. There are probably times when the problem occurs, but something positive comes from it. Identify what both of you do differently at those times.

One couple told me that they fight all the time. I asked them this question: "What's different about the times when something constructive comes from your fights?" Their answer was very interesting. They made a distinction between what they called bad fights and good fights. Good fights were ones that eventually led to a resolution. The solution did not have to be immediate, but could follow within one or two days of the fight. Good fights also ended with their making love. Bad fights were hurtful and unproductive. Name calling and blaming each other characterized them. Silence and withdrawal followed bad fights, but they noted that they did not call each other names when they had good fights.

As they talked, it became clear that they could identify a good or bad fight when they were in the midst of it. As a result, they made a commitment to end bad fights abruptly as soon as either partner noticed things becoming unproductive.

9. Notice What's Different About the Times the Problem Situation Occurs but Doesn't Bother You

Even when nothing positive results from a problem, perhaps there are times when it doesn't bother you in the same way it usually does. For example, your spouse might have a particular habit that generally irritates you. However, perhaps there are occasions when, for some reason, it rolls off your back when he or she acts that way. What are you doing differently during those times? Are you involved in activities that demand your attention so that your spouse's potentially bothersome habit doesn't faze you? Determining how you keep yourself from getting upset is a good way to diffuse problems. As long as you are not upset, you will be able to respond to your spouse in a calm and effective manner.

Mary complained that her husband, Joe, often made plans with his friends and she was left with nothing to do. Her anger grew with each passing moment every time he was out socializing. When he finally returned home, she would bombard him with countless questions and accusations. Then Joe would get angry at her for attacking him. He believed she didn't want him to have any friends at all.

When I asked Mary, "What's different about the times when he goes out but it doesn't bother you?" her response was immediate. "When I make plans for myself, I don't care if he goes out. In fact, I like spending time on my own." Mary decided to fill in the blank spots on her social calendar; she was not going to sit around waiting for Joe to make plans with her. If she thought of something she wanted to do, she would just call a friend and do it. If Joe asked her to do something with him, she would do it if she were free.

Mary felt a lot better recognizing that she had some control over the way she responded to Joe's going out. As a result of her new plan, she rekindled some old friendships, which made her happy. An unexpected bonus to Mary's new plan was that she and Joe got along better, and they discovered that the time they spent together actually increased. Although this was not her original intention or goal, she was very pleased. However, she continued pursuing her friendships because she discovered how much she valued them.

Another woman felt distraught because her husband "didn't communicate" with her very much. When he was home from work, he preferred to watch television, read or tinker around the house with various projects. At first, his lack of attention only hurt her feelings, but as their marriage developed, his quietness infuriated her. The more she tried to get him to talk to her, the more he withdrew into himself and his activities.

I asked her, "What's different about the times he is quiet but, for some reason, it doesn't bother you so much?" She thought for a moment and replied, "When I have spent time with my women friends talking, I feel more satisfied. Connecting with my women friends is very important to me and sometimes this intimacy takes the pressure off my marriage. When my intimacy needs are met by my friends, I see my husband reading his paper and I can even joke with him about his aloofness. I don't get angry at him at those times."

Although she and I brainstormed other solutions to this communication problem, she recognized the importance of meeting her communication needs in a variety of ways, not just through her husband. She also realized that when she was able to see him reading his paper and not get angry, they had a better evening together and increased the chances that he would be more communicative with her when he was done reading.

To summarize, there are four basic steps you must take to make desirable behaviors grow. As you think about each of these steps, you might consider writing down your responses to help clarify your thoughts.

Step 1: Describe as clearly and specifically as possible what troubles you about your spouse and/or your marriage.

Step 2: Identify the exceptions—times when the problem *doesn't* occur, when it is less frequent, shorter in duration, less intense or not as annoying.

Step 3: Determine *your* role in making the exceptions happen.

Step 4: Repeat what has worked.

These guidelines will help you identify patterns of interaction that work in your marriage. Building on these patterns is a sure-fire way to get the results you want. However, sometimes solely building on what works isn't enough. You might find that you also need to do less of what doesn't work. The next chapter will help you figure out what *you* need to change in order to get your spouse to change.

CHAPTER 6

Breaking the Habit: Interrupting Destructive Patterns

IF IT DOESN'T WORK, DO SOMETHING DIFFERENT— UNCOMMON SENSE TECHNIQUES

Up until this point, all the techniques you have learned have helped you identify patterns that have worked in your marriage so you know what to build on. Now you are about to approach problem solving from a slightly different angle. The techniques outlined in this section will help you identify patterns of interaction that haven't been working and specific ways to block these unproductive patterns.

As you read through these strategies, it is important to remember that your situation is unique and no single method works for everybody. Contrary to what you may have read in other self-help books or heard in workshops, specific relationship-building approaches that are generic are not universally effective. You might have to adapt or modify the techniques slightly to fit your marriage, which shouldn't be difficult since you know yourselves the best.

Furthermore, it is essential that you approach solution finding with a researcher's mind: Experiment with something new and carefully note your mate's response. If it appears that the new approach is helping you reach your goal, keep it up. If not, try a different approach. Marriage enhancement (along with parenting or personal growth, for that matter) is a trial-and-error process. Don't be discouraged if one method doesn't work—try another one. I once heard it said, "There is no such thing as failure, just useful feedback about what to do next."

Heather began therapy because she loved her husband, Al, but his recent angry outbursts had her more than a little confused. They seemed to come out of the blue. She could not determine what triggered the anger and felt that she was a innocent victim to his unexplainable mood swings. Heather wondered whether Al was depressed about his work, which she knew he found unsatisfying.

In an effort to get a clear picture of their interactions in regard to the anger I asked Heather to give me a recent example of the problem and how she handled it.

Heather thought for a while and said:

> Practically every night when Al comes home he looks discouraged and unhappy. I always ask how his day went. He usually complains about his boss and how he was treated unfairly that day. I'm a take-charge kind of person and when something bothers me, I take action. It really frustrates me to hear him bitch about work and then not do anything about it.
>
> So I usually start giving him advice about how he should have dealt with the incident that day. He not only doesn't seem appreciative, he starts listing all of his objections to my suggestions, which frustrates me even more. I often whip out the newspaper, searching the classified section to show him other job alternatives, but he will have no part of it. By this point, I'm angry and he's even angrier. He starts screaming at me, which hurts my feelings because I'm only trying to help him. I can't understand why he would attack me for helping him. Usually, I try to show him how unreasonable he is, but that only gets him angrier.

Despite the fact that Heather's "helping" wasn't helping matters, she reported doing it almost every night. I asked her, "What's different about the nights he walks through the door and you don't ask him about his day?" Although this rarely happened, she did remember one or two times when she was so involved with her thoughts she forgot to ask. He started telling her anyway. And once he began telling her of his trials and tribulations, she responded with "helpful" advice and he with his usual anger.

I noted that Heather was successful in her career, a fact that made it hard for Al to believe she could be truly sympathetic with his problem. Each of Heather's suggestions served as a painful reminder to Al of the disparity between her competence and his helplessness.

I suggested that she try an experiment: "The next time Al comes home from work, regardless of the expression on his face, do not ask him about his day. If he starts telling you about work, do not respond or give advice, but let him know that you are listening to him by making appropriate listening sounds such as 'I see,' 'Uh-huh' and so on." I reminded her to make eye contact and seem interested but to not, under any circumstances, give advice. She agreed to try it.

The next session she reported the following:

I was in the kitchen preparing dinner when he came in from work. I forced myself to keep cooking when he sat down by the counter. I resisted the urge to ask him about his day, but he started telling me about it anyway. As he complained, I said, "Oh, really?" or "I see," but gave no advice whatsoever. It took a lot of self-control. He talked for a long time and I kept saying, "Uh-huh." All of a sudden he said, "And then I took a boat to Bermuda." I lifted my head and said, "What did *that* mean?" to which he responded, "I just wanted to see if you were listening. I couldn't tell if you've been hearing me." She reassured him that she had heard every word and they ended up having a very pleasant evening together. Furthermore, their week went unusually well.

As Heather described the kitchen scene that night, she was laughing. She could not believe the promptness of Al's response to her doing something different. He thought she could not possibly have heard him since she did not respond in her usual advice-giving manner. She hadn't realized how predictable she had become to Al. (And she thought Al was the automaton.)

Not only did Heather avoid an argument that evening, she learned a valuable lesson—she realized that she could change Al's behavior and the flow of the evening by changing her own response to him. She later saw the broad range of applicability of this approach to her marriage.

The lesson from Heather's example is that if you continue doing the same old thing, you will get the same old results. Spouses who stop themselves from doing "more of the same" and do something different, anything different, greatly increase their chances of achieving changes in their marriage. But before you read about the methods of introducing the unexpected into your previously predictable marital tiffs, it is important to understand why novelty works so well.

WHY DOES NOVELTY WORK?

Human beings are creatures of habit. We behave in highly ritualized patterns. We have certain routines we faithfully follow from the moment we open our eyes in the morning to when we go to sleep at night. We brush our teeth and hair in a certain way at a particular time each day, drive to work the same way every morning, watch the same television programs each week, sit in the same seat at the dining room table during each meal and sleep on the same side of the bed each night. We give little conscious thought to our daily habits until something unusual happens, like someone else sitting in "our chair" for dinner.

So too do we behave habitually in relationship to others. The majority of our daily interactions are on automatic pilot. "Hi, how are you?" "Fine, thanks, and you?" are the robot-like greetings we exchange without thinking. We feel surprised when we hear any *other* response such as, "Do you really want to know?" a response which commands our attention.

We are fortunate that we do not have to think about or be aware of the multitude of actions we must take each day because we would get overloaded if we did. Habitual responses are economical. Behaving habitually is only problematic when relationship difficulties arise. When spouses are on automatic pilot they behave like robots; each angry gesture triggers the next unreasonable response. Spouses' interactions are linked together in a sequential fashion: A→B→C→D→A→B and so on. When a wife does A (complains) she expects her husband to do B (get angry), who expects his wife to do C (defend herself), who then expects her husband to do D (get angrier), who then expects his wife to do A (complain) the way they have done so many times before.

Neither spouse is aware of how his or her behavior is the catalyst for the undesirable response that follows. Both spouses are blinded to the way in which their actions provide cues which elicit antagonism from their partner. These cues link one vindictive behavior to another in a powerful spellbinding manner. In the same way that smoky bars, satisfying sex, filling meals and tense moments trigger smokers to light up without thinking, certain spousal behaviors trigger marital partners to respond destructively and to do so without thinking. The sequence of events A→B→C→D becomes a habit which takes on a life of its own. Spouses act and react like clockwork because they forget that either of them can, at any time, do something different. But that's where novelty comes in.

When either spouse does something different, it interrupts the negative sequence of events and prevents the cycle from being completed. Novelty blocks unproductive patterns of interaction. For instance, if in response to a wife's doing A (complaining) the husband does M (starts crying), she is not likely to respond in the same old way (C) (defending herself) because M (crying) is not a contextual cue for the same old response C (defending herself). M (crying) requires that the wife can no longer respond automatically. She must respond in a new way, N, which leads to other new reactions, O and P.

Furthermore, since unpredictable actions require that we relinquish our machine-like responses, they force us to more consciously explore options. An analogy which illustrates this point is driving a car. The majority of the time you don't have to think about driving at all. You pay very little conscious attention to the act of driving. As you drive, you can carry on a conversation, sightsee, listen to the radio or yell at the kids—all at the same time. However, if something unexpected occurs, like someone pulling in front of you without signaling, you immediately become conscious of the road and of your driving technique once again. Unforeseen happenings on the road place us in an alert state, ready to take action. Similarly, unforeseen happenings in our marital interactions wake us up and shift us out of automatic pilot.

The following nine techniques are designed to help you analyze unsuccessful patterns of interaction so you can see what you need to do differently. As you read them, you will notice that they are all variations of the basic tenet *"If what you're doing doesn't work, do something different"* (de Shazer, 1985, pp. 122–23).

UNCOMMON SENSE TECHNIQUE #1: CHANGE *ANYTHING*

You and your spouse have probably become so predictable to each other that any small change might be noticeable. In a way, the more inflexible you've become, the more perceptible any small shift in your behavior might be. What should you change? There is a fascinating story about Gregory Bateson, renowned anthropologist and husband to equally renowned anthropologist Margaret Mead, which might answer the question "What should I change?"

Bateson was once asked to observe some otters at a zoo. The zoo officials were concerned about the otters' listlessness, since otters are by nature extremely playful animals. Zoo officials hoped that Bateson could shed some light on the animals' uncharacteristic behavior.

As Bateson observed the otters he noticed that, indeed, they appeared lethargic and inactive. There was virtually no interaction among the animals and very little noticeable movement. At the risk of anthropomorphizing, one might have concluded that the otters were depressed.

After several days of observing the inactive otters, Bateson had an idea. He took a piece of paper, attached a long string to the end of it and dangled the paper in the area where the otters were resting. After a while, one of the otters spotted the paper and began pawing it, setting the paper in motion. Another curious otter came over and started reaching for the swinging paper but got intercepted by the first otter. Before long, the two otters were playfully attacking each other. Shortly thereafter, the remainder of the otters joined in the play. Intrigued by these results, Bateson retrieved the piece of paper. The otters continued playing. In fact, the otters never returned to their listless behavior.

Few people could have predicted that a dangling piece of paper would mobilize listless otters, since, on the surface, a dangling paper seems totally unconnected to otter behavior of any sort. The results of Bateson's experiment appeared to be magical. But they weren't. What happened? Why the sudden change in the otters' behavior? Bateson was certain of one thing. As long as nothing new was introduced into the environment, nothing new or different would happen. Conversely, he hypothesized that if something novel or unfamiliar was introduced into the environment, different results were, at least, more likely. This is not to say that the dangling paper was the only intervention that would have energized the otters. Bateson believed that any number of new or different alternatives might have worked equally well.

The dangling paper provides an important lesson to people who are trying to resolve marital problems. Rather than hesitate trying a new approach because the outcome is uncertain, Bateson's story demonstrates the utility of randomness in problem solving.

A couple's problems generally unfold in the same way, at the same time, in the same location much of the time. Arguments become highly patterned and once these patterns are discernible, any minor change might yield different results. To help you identify what to change, pay attention to the pattern the problem takes by asking yourself the following four "what, where, when, who" questions. As you respond to these questions, you will see that problems can be resolved by altering the way the problem is handled (who, what) or by changing the context (where, when) in which the problem regularly occurs.

1. *What* Have You Been Doing to Try to Make Things Better? *What* Are Your "More of the Same" Behaviors?

From your spouse's perspective, exactly what have you been doing to make things better? It is essential that you identify how your spouse sees you because your behavior has been triggering him or her to react in ways you dislike. Would your spouse say that you have been nagging a lot lately? Or would he say that you have been withdrawn? Would she say that you're outspoken or that you keep your thoughts to yourself? Does your spouse use a pet phrase to describe your way of handling things? If so, what is it?

Think critically about yourself. Imagine what your spouse has thought and felt about your problem-solving efforts. Ask yourself: "What would I have to do differently for my spouse to think I'm changing?" Or, if you were not present in the room and your spouse was asked, "How has he or she been acting lately in regard to the problems the two of you have been experiencing?" what would he or she say? For example, a man told me that if his wife were asked about his annoying behavior, she would say that he is lazy and never helps around the house. While he disagreed, saying that he worked hard on outside chores, he knew he would have to do more inside tasks in order for *her* to feel that he was changing. Keep in mind that like the man in this example, you probably won't agree with your spouse's assessment of your behavior, and that's okay.

Whatever pigeonhole your spouse has placed you into, this is the behavior you must change. You must surprise your spouse by handling the situation differently the next time. Any change might do as long as it is different enough for your spouse to notice. Be creative, use your imagination. The single guideline is: *The next time you get into the situation where you feel tempted to do the same old thing, do something different. No matter how weird or crazy it might seem, do something you have never done before.*

As you might recall from an earlier example, when Heather decided to do something different in regard to her husband's complaining about work, the results were immediate. It is often surprising how quickly and effectively novelty interrupts unproductive patterns of interactions.

However, despite its effectiveness, it is important to point out that doing something different usually requires a good deal of self-control. When provoked, it's tempting to respond in the same old way because that usual way of handling the situation has become a habit, a habit now needing to be broken. Several years ago I wrote about my own struggle with the seductiveness of "more of the same even though it doesn't work" ways of dealing with my husband, Jim:

Knowing that a particular approach is entirely ineffective has no impact whatsoever on my choice of actions during subsequent crises. I find this to be a truly curious phenomenon. Consider what happened one evening at my house during dinnertime.

Since I rarely prepare a homemade meal for dinner (my husband is the gourmet cook), I expect punctuality (and appreciation) when I do. Although my husband is generally considerate about informing me of his schedule, he occasionally "forgets," returning home later than usual without a phone call to advise me of his plans. There seems to be an uncanny correlation between the extremely infrequent occasions I decide to prepare a meal and his "forgetting" to come home on time.

The sequence of events, when this occurs, is always the same. By the time he walks in, I have already tried calling several locations hoping to track him down. Dinner is ready and I mumble about the food getting cold. I suggest to my daughter that we begin without dad so that our food will still be hot. She senses my growing impatience. Later (what seems like years later) the door opens and I carefully plan my revenge—I will silently pout until he asks me, "What's wrong?" and then I will let him have it!

As he enters the room he greets us and seats himself, commenting about how good dinner smells. Then he cordially obliges by asking, "What's wrong?" and I jump at the opportunity to tell him. He defends himself and accuses me of being unreasonable. Things generally deteriorate from there. This particular plan of attack *never* works. I know this but my behavior belies this awareness.

However, something unusual happened one particular evening. The dinner scene was unfolding as usual when he walked through the door thirty minutes late. I was rehearsing to myself what I would say when he asked the million-dollar question. He predictably entered the room, said hello to us, sat down and began to eat. A couple of minutes passed and he did not inquire, "What's wrong?" "He's probably starving," I thought, reassuring myself that my attack was imminent. He then turned to my daughter and asked her how her day went in school. She launched into a ten-minute monologue consisting of the longest sentence I have ever heard. I thought she would never stop talking. After all, I was still waiting for my invitation to explode.

When she finally finished, instead of addressing me, my husband began to tell her some details of his day at work. She listened politely as I felt rage building inside: "What nerve, he didn't ask me why I am pouting!" I waited a while longer, though I couldn't help but become mildly interested in the conversation. Without realizing it I found myself joining the discussion. The remainder of the meal was very pleasant.

When I realized what had happened I asked my husband why he decided to talk to our daughter instead of asking about my silence. He replied, "You always tell your clients to do something different when they get stuck, but you never follow your own advice. I thought I would give it a shot." It's just awful to have your own weapons used against you! (Weiner-Davis, 1988, pp. 72–74.)

Since the writing of that article, I've smartened up and as a result Jim and I rarely fight about his not apprising me of his plans. I no longer interrogate him when he comes home later than I expect, and Jim (surprise, surprise) has gotten considerably more punctual and considerate when extenuating circumstances arise. So although doing something different isn't always easy, the alternative, not changing, is even harder.

2. *Where* Do Most of Your Arguments Occur?

Have you noticed that your battles usually occur in one particular location? Perhaps it's the bedroom, living room, during visits to friends or family or in the car. What is the pattern to the locations of your fights? After you've identified your usual battlefields, *try an entirely different location*. For example, if you usually argue in the bedroom, start your discussion in the living room. Or you might consider discussing matters while on a walk around the block. Some couples go out for dinner to discuss their differences knowing that they will not let things get out of hand in a public place.

A colleague of mine once told a couple that the moment they felt a fight coming on they were to go to the bathroom and continue in there. The couple reported that their trip to the bathroom made them start laughing and they were unable to continue sparring.

3. *When* Do Most of Your Arguments Occur?

When do you most often get into arguments with your spouse? Is it right after one or both of you return from work, right after a fight with the children, every Friday night, on the weekends?

Try Varying the Time of Day or Week You Deal with Bothersome Issues

If you usually fight the moment your spouse walks through the door at the end of the day, postpone it until after dinner. If you wait until weekends to work out your differences, try doing it during the week. If Friday nights are problematic, try talking things out Friday morning. Varying the time you confront a problem often changes the way it's handled.

Keep Peak Performance Times in Mind

"Timing is everything," people say, and while it may not really be *everything*, it is extremely important. People would be better off if they recognized the significance of timing. Clients tell me, "If she would just wait thirty minutes after I come home so that I can unwind, I'd be happy to discuss it with her," or "He wants to cuddle at eleven P.M. and by then I'm exhausted. If he came upstairs with me at nine-thirty, we would still have a sex life," or "I've noticed that if I talk to him on the phone when he is at work, he is not very warm." When people act at the appropriate moment, they frequently get more of their needs met.

Ask yourself: "When am I most likely to get the kind of response I want from my spouse?" Even if you think that there never seems to be a good time to discuss things, some times are clearly worse than others. Avoid those times at all costs.

Schedule Time-Limited Conflict Resolution Sessions

If fights happen intermittently and unpredictably throughout the week, you might try scheduling time-limited discussions once or twice a week and limiting all debates over the issues to those scheduled times. Many couples find the structure of scheduled discussion times to work out differences very helpful.

For example, Ann and Chuck sought therapy because Ann was having a very difficult time dealing with her feelings about an affair Chuck had had a year ago. Although he was no longer involved with the woman, Ann felt unable to move forward with their marriage. She felt anger and hurt each time she thought about the affair, which was quite often. In fact, Ann sometimes wondered if it wouldn't be easier to just call it quits.

Everything reminded Ann about Chuck's affair, clothing he wore, places they went, phrases he used. Each time she thought about it, she felt devastated. In an attempt to make herself feel better, she started asking Chuck questions about his relationship with the woman. She wanted to know everything from the dates and places they met, the content of their discussions and the nature of their sexual contacts. She hoped that once she had all of the uncensored information, she could put the affair in the past. Despite the fact that hearing the details never helped her feel better, she continued asking.

Ann complained that Chuck really wasn't being empathetic. She was convinced that he didn't understand her pain because, if he did, he would be more willing to answer her questions. Ann said that Chuck appeared fed up and impatient each time she tried to get information about the affair. His impatience was a signal to her that he "just wants me to snap out of this to make life easier on him." She felt that if Chuck were really compassionate he would understand the difficulty she was having "snapping out of it," and be more patient and loving toward her.

Chuck reported that he *was* frustrated because all of his attempts to answer her questions and help her feel better appeared fruitless. More information seemed to make Ann feel worse, not better. Furthermore, on the rare occasions when Ann felt reassured, it didn't last very long. He loved Ann very much, regretted the affair and wanted to move forward rather than continually focus on the past. His fear that the questions would never end made him impatient each time they began. He felt himself wanting to avoid her.

From Chuck's perspective, the questions (or the threat of being questioned) were ubiquitous. From Ann's point of view, Chuck was never available for questioning or calm discussion about the past. I asked Ann, "When you ask Chuck these questions, what do you want from him? What makes you feel better?" She said, "When he puts his arms around me and tells me how much he loves me, it reassures me." Then I offered them a suggestion.

Since their conflicts occurred frequently and unpredictably, ruining whatever positive feelings they might have been experiencing, I suggested that they structure their visits to the past. This would allow Ann to ask questions, thereby validating her needs, while at the same time limiting the question and answer period, thereby validating Chuck's need to move on.

I instructed them to choose at least two times in the next week (and the week that followed), for a half hour each time, when Ann could ask or say anything she wished about the affair. Chuck was to listen attentively during those times and answer all of her questions respectfully without debating the value of knowing the answers. Then, at the end of the half hour, Chuck was instructed to hold Ann and tell her how much he loved her. They were to repeat this procedure another time that week and twice in the following week. Ann was to limit all of her questions and comments to these four predetermined times.

Two weeks later, the couple returned appearing happy and acting loving toward each other. I asked about their visits to the past and they told me that they only needed to do it once. The first time they sat down, Ann asked her usual questions but felt, for the first time, that Chuck wasn't hurrying her to finish and she appreciated that. In fact, when she went well over the half hour limit, Chuck did not stop her, despite the fact that, according to the rules, he could have. She noticed his flexibility and appreciated that as well. At the end of their hour-long discussion, Chuck held her and verbalized his loving feelings about her. The discussion ended on a good note.

Ann and Chuck felt so good about their talk that Ann did not feel the need to bring it up again that week or in the week that followed. They reported that they were more affectionate, considerate and cooperative and that they had not gone a period of two weeks without a major blowup since the disclosure of the affair. They considered this a major accomplishment.

I asked them why they thought the homework assignment worked so well for them. Chuck said that he felt a great relief knowing that there was a limit to the questions. For the first time in a long time, he believed that there might be light at the end of the tunnel, that the questions would eventually stop and they could go on loving each other again.

Ann reported that Chuck was more compassionate, patient and eager to help her feel better. She now felt as if they were in it together rather than feeling like it was her problem to overcome. Interestingly, Ann stated that Chuck seemed more involved and attentive when she expressed other unrelated feelings during that two-week period. Pleased to hear the results, I suggested that they allow themselves the opportunity to meet twice a week in the weeks that followed should the need arise. However, upon last report, several months later, it hadn't.

Structuring time-limited conflict resolution sessions can solve other problems as well. Unlike the vast majority of tasks outlined in this chapter, which do not require both spouses to participate, the following task does. You may already have piqued your spouse's interest enough for him or her to be willing to try this one with you. If not, keep reading. There are many other ideas from which to choose.

For couples who feel they argue too much and that nothing ever seems to get resolved, the problem may be that both people are so intent on being heard that neither one is listening. Furthermore, when one or both partners are volatile, the smallest irritant can cause a major eruption. These battles can happen anytime and are likely to ruin many otherwise pleasant occasions. Couples fitting this category feel that there is always a fight just around the corner.

This pattern is easily interrupted by the structured-fight task. This exercise should not be confused with fair fighting, a program that establishes ground rules for couples to discuss heated topics. The structured-fight task simply interrupts a couple's habitual sparring style. Here are the steps:

1. Toss a coin to decide who goes first.
2. The winner gets to vent for ten uninterrupted minutes.
3. Then the other person gets a ten-minute turn.
4. Then there needs to be ten minutes of silence before another round is started with a coin toss. (de Shazer, 1985, p. 122.)

I usually suggest that the couple initially do the task twice a week, whether or not there's a perceived need. They are asked to confine all of their fights to the designated times. This requirement introduces a firm starting and stopping time for fighting, which in itself often reduces or eliminates the fights. Couples who do this task often tell me that after one session they had no need to repeat it and could not bring themselves to do it since they were getting along so well. In that case, I suggest that if they find themselves sliding back to old habits, they resume the task in the weeks that follow.

To reiterate, scheduled, time-limited conflict resolution sessions include three elements which interrupt unproductive patterns of interaction. Scheduling conflict resolution sessions insures that:

1. There *will* be a time to resolve problems.
2. These discussions are time-limited.

3. Spontaneous disagreements will be confined to predetermined times.

If you and your spouse seem to argue all the time and your arguments never seem to get resolved, it might be helpful to try this technique.

4. *Who* Is More Likely to Handle Certain Issues?

Many years ago when I was a rookie therapist I had an experience which taught me a great lesson about problem solving. A colleague was working with a mother who was unable to get her eleven-year-old daughter to school in the morning. The mother said her daughter had a school phobia. The school psychologist was also working with the daughter to help her overcome her so-called phobia. The father left their home early in the morning for work each day and was not aware of the problem because his wife didn't want to bother him with it.

But when the woman had to leave town suddenly because of a death in her family, the father reported to work later in the morning in order to take his daughter to school. Unaware of the girl's "phobia," he woke her, made her breakfast, prodded her along as she dressed, ignored her requests to stay home and drove her to school. When the mother returned, she couldn't believe that her husband had gotten their daughter to school without a major confrontation. The girl's school phobia had miraculously vanished! In light of this "miracle cure," the father agreed that he would take the girl to school until regular attendance was more of a habit.

Vary Who Handles the Problem

The lesson I learned from this family was that one way to introduce novelty into the habitual handling of problems is to change *who* handles the problem. We cannot conclude that the father was a better parent, we can only conclude that in regard to the school problem his actions, which differed greatly from his wife's, did not trigger his daughter's resistance about going to school.

Changing who is in charge of a particular decision or set of decisions can free couples from endless, unproductive debates about whose way of doing things is correct. Although there is rarely only one correct approach, this fact never stops people from trying to prove themselves champions in decision-making battles. As they debate, the problem persists and gains momentum.

For example, many couples I know have major disagreements about how to handle their children, creating a major source of conflict. Traditional wisdom suggests that parents must present a united front even when they disagree. In theory, that's fine and dandy, but in reality we all know that it doesn't always work that way. As the couple argues about the virtues of discipline versus the importance of TLC, the children continue to act out because the parents don't act, or if they do act, each action is undermined by the other parent in a battle for control. If this is a familiar pattern, rather than dispute the correctness of your approach or philosophy of life, you can break the destructive pattern in a number of different ways once you agree that it's okay to disagree with your spouse. But the question still remains: What do you do when you disagree?

Many couples have found it useful to flip a coin to determine which approach to use. Each time they find themselves about to embark on a "more of the same" battle, they stop and flip a coin. "Heads, TLC; tails, discipline." It is essential that the loser of the coin flip not interfere with his or her partner. The flipping of the coin bypasses the usual lengthy debates about who's right.

Child-rearing differences aren't the only problems resolved by coin flipping. This technique proved to be helpful for a couple who argued incessantly about many different issues. The most recent hotly debated issue was how to sell the remainder of the goods from a store they once owned. The husband accused the wife of being too impulsive about her actions, while she accused him of being too calculated. He thought that her failure to consider all the angles resulted in poor decisions. She thought his need to explore any and all alternatives prevented him from taking action.

Rather than argue about how the store remnants should be disposed of, I suggested the following: "If after a half hour discussion the two of you cannot reach a satisfactory agreement about the sale of the goods, you should flip a coin." They returned the following week reporting that they did not find it necessary to flip the coin and, in fact, were able to reach an agreement rather quickly. I asked how they accounted for their sudden cooperative teamwork. They said that since he hated the idea of flipping a coin because it left too much to chance, he was eager to find a solution within the time period allotted. She, in turn, was happy with their mutually agreed upon decision.

Avoid the Need for Joint Decisions by Delegating
Specific Responsibilities

Another way to eliminate the destructive "who's right" battle is to make the arbitrary decision that person A handles situations X, Y, Z and person B handles situations A, B, C. She decides which weekend night to go out and he decides where to go. She decides on the children's bedtimes and he sets the rules for table manners. Again, it is possible to alternate assigned responsibilities after a period of time.

One couple I worked with complained that at a specific time every year they would have enormous fights. They attributed their fighting to the fact that they were both organizers for a major fund-raising event. Occasionally, there were misunderstandings and confusion as to who was supposed to do what for the event. Other times, there were criticisms about how certain details were handled. They fought so much they considered relinquishing their positions as fund-raisers. When they started therapy, they realized that this would have been an unnecessarily drastic solution.

After discussing the fund-raising process, the couple agreed to delineate specifically each person's responsibilities. They also agreed not to comment on how a job was done if it was not within their domain. If either of them felt tempted to critique the work of the other, they were to write down the suggestion on a note pad, which was not to be reviewed until the end of the event.

Much to their surprise, they managed to go through the entire planning stage with only minor bumps, a vast improvement. This taught them that they need not abandon fund-raising if things get rough, they need only delegate responsibilities. By so doing, they earned money for their organization and saved their marriage.

Use the Odd Day, Even Day Method

An alternative method to interrupting the unproductive debates about whose method of handling things is more effective is called the odd day, even day approach. In advance of any crises, couples agree that on all even days that month, person A is in charge of all decisions and on all odd days, person B is in charge.

A couple I worked with was having a hard time deciding whether to make a long-term commitment or to part ways. William thought he and Cathy were compatible and believed the only way he could feel secure was for her to verbally commit to a lifelong relationship. Although Cathy cared about William, she felt less certain of their compatibility and wondered if they should simply cut their losses and separate. As the urgency to make a decision grew, so did the vacillating and the tension between them. Their need to make a decision about their future was interfering with their enjoying their present relationship. Prior to the time either of them required definition of their relationship they got along just fine. William's need for a verbal commitment strengthened Cathy's need for independence and vice versa.

As I observed the couple I noticed that despite Cathy's words of ambivalence their actions indicated that they were fairly committed to each other. They had been involved for many years and at no time had there been any separation. I felt that their current dilemma was more the result of a standoff of opposing positions than a real questioning of the viability of their relationship. In order to interrupt the usual way their conversations about the future occurred, I suggested the odd day, even day method.

On even days, they were to imagine themselves together forever and have future-oriented discussions about their lives. On odd days, they were to imagine themselves separating and have future-oriented discussions about their lives apart.

Two weeks later they returned, having learned something new about each other. Although Cathy had been the one leaning toward separating, she took the lead in making certain the homework assignment was completed. Every morning she reminded William whether it was an odd or even day, and initiated the corresponding conversations. Until that point, William felt that he was doing all the relationship work and found her initiative refreshing.

As the days passed, both partners realized that they had much more to talk about on even days, that is, on days when they visualized themselves together. They also realized that they felt better on the together days and even skipped doing the assignment on many odd days. The results of this exercise demonstrated that they were already committed to each other and, as the tension subsided, they started enjoying each other again.

UNCOMMON SENSE TECHNIQUE #2: INTRODUCE A STEP IN THE SEQUENCE

John and Marie had been married for ten years and had two children. John felt that when he had a bad day at work, he was more likely to be tense and take it out on Marie and the children. He said that on bad days he would yell at the kids and be more introverted at home. This meant that he paid less attention to Marie, which annoyed her.

Over a period of several weeks John worked hard changing how he responded to family members after trying days at work. Both he and Marie agreed that John had improved significantly. However, occasionally John would become impatient and get ir- ritated at the children or yell unnecessarily. John thought that an occasional bad day was to be expected and reacted badly when Marie confronted him, which she did immediately following each relapse. In John's eyes, Marie lost sight of the bigger picture, of how much he had changed, when she made such a big deal out of his minor setbacks. With each confrontation, John lost self- confidence, making it more difficult for him to get back on track.

John attended a session alone and we discussed this situation. After a few minutes, he thought of a great idea. He suggested that he and Marie each get a calendar. At the end of each day, they were to rate each other's behavior on a scale of 1 to 10. For example, if Marie noticed John really trying, she was to give him a 10 for that particular day. If John thought Marie was being critical, he might rate her a 5. However, they both agreed *not* to discuss their evaluations of each other until the end of the month, at which time they could go out alone and have a long discussion about their observations.

This plan worked like a charm for them. When John had a setback, he knew it, even without Marie's feedback. He got right back on track. Since Marie had to wait until the end of the month to give John feedback, she discovered that the vast majority of days during the month had been good ones. This allowed her to focus on the bigger picture and feel good about John's efforts to change.

What happened? By waiting until the end of the month, John and Marie interrupted the usual flow of things. A setback didn't lead to criticism, which, in turn, didn't lead to John's self-doubt. John became more self-confident and eventually setbacks were less frequent. By introducing an extra step in their marital ritual— privately rating each other on a daily basis rather than offering instant feedback—they were able to interrupt their usual pattern of interacting.

If certain debates have become rituals in your marriage, stop— and introduce an extra step in your usual pattern. If you are in the middle of a typical go-nowhere fight, stop momentarily and get a tape recorder to record it, or take a walk, eat lunch, read a magazine, make a telephone call, whatever. Inserting a new step in your predictable pattern will yield a less predictable, more desirable result.

Another therapist used this technique with a couple who complained of frequent arguments. After working with the couple for several sessions, she suggested that they go to the store and purchase two Groucho Marx plastic nose and glasses masks and the next time they felt an argument coming on they should both put on the masks before proceeding. They agreed to give it a whirl.

When they returned, they reported not being able to fight because of how ridiculous they both looked. They burst out laughing instead. Also, they commented that, "We really didn't realize how stupid our fighting was. This reduced what we were fighting about down to nothing."

In addition to preventing couples from fighting by introducing a step in the pattern, this technique often serves another purpose. It leads to unexpected insights about people's relationships, situations or the particular issue over which they had been so concerned. Many people are surprised at how much they have learned from doing a task that, on the surface, seems so silly or superficial. However, the reason for this enlightenment is simple: When people become more conscious of their typically automatic responses, learning about oneself and/or one's partner is often the by-product.

UNCOMMON SENSE TECHNIQUE #3:
TRY THE PREDICTION TASK
(de Shazer, 1988, p. 183)

A couple began therapy by complaining that they fought a lot. Each complained that the other was rude and insensitive. When asked when or why the fights began, they couldn't say. They felt that their fights were totally unpredictable. They rarely went a whole day without fighting and were never able to sustain a good period for very long. Each spouse felt as if he or she was a victim of the other's random mood swings.

After a couple of sessions, the therapist suggested a homework assignment. She asked the couple to sit down each night and predict whether the next day would be a good or bad day. Then they were to sit down at the end of the day and tell their partner whether, in fact, they thought the day had gone well or not. If both agreed that the day went well, they were to put a check mark on the calendar. If they disagreed, or if it had been a bad day, nothing more was to be said. Two weeks later they returned. They loved doing the assignment. Although things hadn't been perfect, they got along very well for the two weeks.

Why did the prediction task work? How did it stop them from bickering in their usual manner?

> Prediction tasks are based on the idea that what you expect to happen is more likely to happen once the process leading up to it is in motion. In pragmatic terms, this means that the prediction, made the night before, can sometimes be seen as setting in motion the processes involved in having a better day. No matter what guess the predictor puts down, the idea that he *might* have a good day is bound to cross his mind. Of course, having a good day is what he really wants and therefore a self-fulfilling prophecy might develop and this might prompt "better day behavior" the next day, right off the bat. (de Shazer, 1988, p. 184.)

Prior to doing this exercise, each believed that the next day would bring controversy and they behaved accordingly. By predicting each night whether the next day was to be a good or bad day, it allowed them to consider the possibility that tomorrow might be a good day. Furthermore, they realized the self-fulfilling nature of these kinds of predictions, which made each of them feel more in control of the outcome.

If you think your marital disagreements occur frequently and randomly, you might try the prediction task. If your spouse is not interested in doing it with you, you can do it alone. If you do, at the end of each day compare your previous night's prediction with your evaluation of the day. If there is a difference between your prediction and the actual outcome, account for the discrepancy. Notice what you learn about yourself and your marriage from doing this task.

UNCOMMON SENSE TECHNIQUE #4: DO A 180°
(Fisch et al., 1982, pp. 115–17)

Barbara sought therapy to solve a problem she was having with her husband, Jerry, in regard to his daughter, Linda, who lived with them. Barbara was very fond of Linda and they developed a very close relationship. Through Barbara's eyes, the longer they were married the more critical Jerry became of his daughter. Barbara thought that Jerry had unreasonable expectations of Linda and, when she failed to meet them, he severely criticized her. Furthermore, Barbara was very concerned that Linda's self-esteem would be damaged by Jerry's constant picking on her. Although Barbara admitted that Jerry's pickiness stemmed from his frustrations at work, she thought that Linda was too young to understand and she would internalize all of his negative comments. Furthermore, she began to resent Linda for driving a wedge between Jerry and her.

In my attempt to understand the situation further I asked Barbara, "What have you been doing to solve this problem?" to which she responded, "Every time Jerry criticizes Linda, I intervene on her behalf. I tell him to stop picking on her and then I tell her she's okay." When I asked Barbara if what she had been doing worked, she said that it hadn't. It only made him angrier at her and at Linda.

Clearly, the more Barbara defended Linda, the more Jerry felt the need to correct her. Since Barbara's strategy was backfiring, I suggested that she try a different approach. I asked her, "Although it's clear that you do not agree with Jerry's handling of Linda, can you appreciate that he really cares about her? After all, if he didn't love her he wouldn't bother. Is it possible that Jerry picks on Linda to help her make the most of her life, to be the best she can be?" Barbara responded, "I guess so."

I also suggested that perhaps Jerry felt left out of Barbara and Linda's close relationship and hypothesized that each time Barbara stood up for Linda in Jerry's presence, he felt more alienated. Barbara agreed. With this in mind I suggested that Barbara try the following experiment:

MICHELE: The first part of the experiment requires that you agree to stay out of any arguments between Jerry and Linda. Since you know that intervening doesn't work, this shouldn't be too hard. The second part will be more difficult and you might not like it at first. Instead of just staying out of the arguments, you must present a united front with Jerry in Linda's presence and observe the results.

BARBARA: That would be very hard for me to do.

MICHELE: I know, but I suspect all this fighting hasn't been very easy either. Am I right?

BARBARA: Yes, you're right.

MICHELE: Remember, this is just an experiment, you don't have to do it forever. Are you willing to give it a shot?

BARBARA: Sure, anything is better than what we've been doing lately.

Barbara left the session determined to give my suggestion a whirl and returned a week later with some interesting results. As she predicted, she found it difficult to do the assignment, but was pleased with the results. The first time she did not intervene, Linda trailed her around the house, attempting to pull her into the argument. She resisted the temptation by busying herself in the kitchen. Much to her surprise, Linda and Jerry somehow managed to end their battle without her!

Pleased with this unexpected ending, she felt encouraged to follow through with the second part of her assignment. According to Barbara, Jerry was lecturing Linda when Barbara decided to agree with him. Shocked, Jerry stopped dead in his tracks, and glanced at Barbara in amazement. Barbara's comment unbalanced Jerry enough for him to forget to lecture Linda. Barbara was as much in shock at Jerry's response as he was at hers.

As the week passed, Barbara noticed that the more supportive she was of her husband, the less he criticized Linda. In fact, Barbara reported that one night when the threesome were out to dinner, Jerry complimented Linda on her appearance and told her how proud he was of her accomplishments. Barbara added that compliments such as that were entirely unheard of prior to the changes in her actions. The icing on the cake, however, was that Barbara and Jerry were spending more time together, fighting less and enjoying each other more.

In Chapter 4, you learned how more of the same problem-solving efforts lead to more of the problem. Remember? In some cases, trying to cheer up depressed people makes them more depressed, pursuing more closeness leads to withdrawal, trying to get others to be more responsible by setting an example allows them to be irresponsible, stressing the importance of nurturing and understanding in child rearing yields an even more firmly held conviction about the importance of firm discipline, and so on.

Similarly, Barbara learned that protecting Linda from Jerry's criticism resulted in his being more critical. When it became clear that what she was doing wasn't working, that in fact it was making things worse, I suggested that Barbara do a 180°. Doing a 180°

required that she identify her "more of the same" behavior and do exactly the opposite of what she had been doing in order to reverse its effect.

If, like Barbara, you have noticed that your efforts to fix things have only made things worse, you might try to do a 180°. Keep in mind that this technique is a variation of technique number one—do *anything* different. It differs in that instead of trying anything new it directs you to specifically do the opposite of what you've been doing. Which technique you experiment with first is simply a matter of personal preference. If you decide to do a 180°, here are the four steps you need to follow:

Step # 1: Describe what you see as the problem.
Recall what your spouse does that provokes you. In Barbara's case, she detested it when Jerry criticized Linda.

Step # 2: Assess how you have been handling the problem thus far.
What single approach do you most commonly use to change your spouse's behavior? (Although you may have tried varied approaches, which is most typical?) Barbara's approach was to defend Linda.

Step # 3: Do a 180°.
This step requires a leap of faith and is therefore the most diffi-cult. You must begin doing the opposite of whatever you have been doing and do it in a credible and sincere manner. For instance, Barbara had to join Jerry in his criticism of Linda. If your new behavior seems ungenuine, it won't work.

Step # 4: When your spouse starts changing, stick with this plan. The worst mistake you can make is to go back to your old habits as soon as you see your spouse starting to act differently. It may be quite tempting to relax, but you must keep up your new behavior until you are convinced that your partner's changes have become habits.

Comment

Some people tell me that they are afraid to do a 180° because they anticipate dire consequences. They think the worst will happen. A man worries that he cannot stop pursuing his estranged wife for fear that he will really lose her if he stops showing interest. Iron-ically, these very same people fail to realize that the real risk is the continuation of "more of the same" behavior. I tell people, "I can't guarantee that this will work, but I *can* guarantee that if you keep doing what you've been doing, it *will* make things worse." Here is another example.

I worked with a woman who wanted her husband to spend less time with his colleagues and more time with the family in the evening. Over the years he usually socialized with associates once a week. However, when this woman came to my office, he was going out two or three times a week. She didn't mind his spending time with friends, she minded the frequency.

She told me that because he was going out so often, they were fighting constantly. On the nights he was home, there was so much tension they didn't enjoy being together. She felt they were stuck in a vicious circle and wanted a suggestion to break out of it.

I asked what she had been doing to try to get her husband to curtail his outings and she said, "Mostly, I've been asking him to come home, telling him that the kids miss him and that I hardly see him anymore. But since that hasn't been working, lately I've gotten angry at him and we do a lot of yelling on the phone." I wondered whether his nights out had increased, remained the same or decreased since she stepped up her efforts to have him come home; as I expected, he was going out more often.

Therefore, I suggested that she try something different. "Tomorrow when he goes to work, call him and tell him that you have realized that he has a great deal of pressure at work and spending time with colleagues helps him unwind. Confess that you hadn't realized this before. Suggest that he make some plans for the evening rather than rushing home that night."

Fearful that he might take her up on it, she hesitated until she realized that he was likely to go out anyway. I suggested that she repeat her invitation for him to stay out one other time that week, adding that she had her own plans. I recommended that she get a sitter and go somewhere—to a friend's house, a movie or out shopping.

The next day she called her husband at work and, in a loving manner, encouraged him to stay out. Taken aback by her suggestion, he agreed to make plans, but returned at 8 P.M. instead of 10 P.M., the usual time. She noticed his early arrival but said nothing about it. Instead, she asked whether he had a good time and when he said that he had, she said she was glad. They put the children to bed and enjoyed what remained of the evening together.

Later that week, she called him at work and told him not to bother coming home early because she had plans. He was curious and asked about her plans. She said she wasn't sure yet whether she was going to a movie with a friend or to meet for a glass of wine.

When she returned from her evening out, her husband was there, the babysitter had been taken home and the children were sound asleep. He asked about her evening and, again, they spent enjoyable time together. And although she was curious, she never asked why he came home early.

Over the weeks this woman realized that encouraging her husband to stay out drastically reduced his evenings away from home. He returned to the original level of going out once a week and, in some weeks, skipped going out entirely. Interestingly, the woman continued going out approximately once a month because she discovered that she loved it! She realized that her life had become too routine and she did not want to go back to living that way. Furthermore, she reported that she and her husband started going out more as a couple, which, in her eyes, was a real bonus.

Since it is important that you understand the mechanics of doing a 180°, and since this technique defies common sense, here is one more example. When Joe started therapy he said he was depressed. He had been out of work for three years due to a back injury. At the time that I saw him, he was drawing unemployment. He told me that no one wanted to hire him because they knew that he hurt his back several years before. Because of this, he felt like less than a man. He said that he was trying very hard to find employment and was willing to settle for anything he could get. However, after several sessions, there was still no job and no relief from his depression.

I asked if Joe minded if his wife attended a session and he said no. In contrast to his morose demeanor, Ellen was perky and energetic. When I asked her about Joe's predicament, she offered a very different picture of their situation. She said that Joe moaned and groaned a lot about not having work, but in reality did very little to find employment. Most of the time he lay on the couch complaining about his aches and pains and feeling sorry for himself.

As she spoke, it became clear that Joe's condition was more a problem for her than for him. In fact, the real reason for Joe's coming for therapy became evident; by showing that he was experiencing emotional problems due to the back injury, his lawyer was helping him build a legal case. Granted, he was feeling down, but his level of motivation to change was questionable. Based on this, I asked Ellen to come alone for a session.

Ellen cried as she described what a burden Joe had become. Not only hadn't he earned any income for their family for years, he was an emotional drain on her. Ellen was his only social outlet. He was not interested in being with friends and relatives, and when he made a concession to be with extended family, he was pretty grouchy and unpleasant to be around. Joe was no longer the man Ellen married, but because they had two children, Ellen didn't want to leave. Although she was pained to see him so down, she was angry that he wasn't taking a more aggressive approach to "getting off his butt."

I asked Ellen what she had been doing to try to help Joe. I was not surprised to hear her say that she had been giving him pep talks, reassuring him that he could find a job, circling jobs in the classified section of the newspaper, reminding him to pick up job applications and coaching him prior to the few interviews he managed to get. When they weren't talking about job hunting, she was urging him to get out of the house and do something, anything. She was clearly worried about his mental health and couldn't understand his defeatist attitude, since she was so positive about her own life.

I asked her whether her pep talks were working and she said, "Absolutely not. He has only gotten worse over the last few years." I expressed my opinion that Joe had taken to a childish form of rebelling against her good advice. She concurred. I asked if she were willing to try a new approach that might have a better chance at good results and she was eager to hear my suggestion.

Since he was in a rebellious mode, I said, it was essential that she stop encouraging him to find work, get out of the house or be happy. Her encouragement was not only working, it appeared to be backfiring. She nodded as I spoke:

> So my suggestion is the following: As strange as it may seem, you should tell Joe that you now realize that you have been overestimating him. Apologize for pushing him too much. Tell him that your expectations have been too high. Apparently, your expectations must have been based on how you remembered him several years ago, but now you realize that your memory has been playing tricks on you.
>
> Go on to tell him that another reason you have been pushing him so hard is that you have been in denial about his condition. Now you realize that you must admit to yourself that he will always be unhappy and he will never be employed again. Coming to grips with this reality has been hard, but at least you are finally facing the truth.
>
> In addition to giving him this message, you must stop encouraging him completely. Go out and get brochures from nursing homes and leave them around the house without commenting on them. If he asks about them, just tell him that you are simply thinking about the future.

Ellen immediately liked the suggestion and was eager to try it even though it sounded unusual.

Two weeks later she returned and told me that she had followed through with the suggestion with some good results. Joe's spirits had lifted and he had been putting forth a genuine effort to find employment. Additionally, he had been more active around the house and even socialized with neighbors. What surprised Ellen the most was that Joe did not complain even once about his back or his health. "What happened when you told him you were expecting too much from him?" I asked. She said, "He told me I was crazy."

I congratulated her for helping Joe change and impressed upon her the importance of remaining skeptical of his changes. "If you get excited about the improvement, he'll rebel by getting worse again. So keep bringing home nursing home brochures!" She laughed and said, "I get the message."

Comment

Sometimes, after reading about doing a 180° people wonder, "Isn't this technique like game playing? Isn't it manipulative?" Continuing to do the same old thing even though it doesn't work is no less game-like than doing something different. In fact, since relationships are like seesaws, if one person expresses all the optimism and confidence, the other person is free to feel all the pessimism and insecurity. Spouses often balance each other in this way. When one person's views are extreme, it forces his or her partner to adopt an equally extreme view in the opposite direction.

When Ellen was absolutely confident about Joe, he felt insecure. Surely, Ellen had her doubts about Joe deep down inside, but she never expressed them. By keeping her doubts private, Ellen's response was not particularly authentic either. Once she finally expressed her reservations about Joe, it allowed him the opportunity to get in touch with his own strength, which enabled them both to feel better about their lives.

Some say that the 180° technique is really a form of reverse psychology and in a sense it is. Parents know the wisdom of telling their young children, "Don't you dare eat all that broccoli" or "I bet you can't clean this room in ten minutes." Why, when we recognize the effectiveness of appealing to a young person's desire to do it his own way, do we forget that adults are often motivated by the same need for independence? Many people just don't like being told what to do. No matter how good your suggestion, the mere fact that it feels like control sends them reeling in the opposite direction. Sound familiar? If so, do a 180°.

UNCOMMON SENSE TECHNIQUE #5: ACT AS IF . . .

Amanda and her husband, Keith, had one major problem in their marriage, a second marriage for both of them. Amanda said that they get along very well until Keith's college-age daughter, Chrissy, comes home from school for a visit. The couple agreed that Chrissy's visits sparked fights between them, but disagreed as to why they happened. Amanda told her side of the story first:

> Keith and I have disagreements about our children. I think he favors Chrissy and lets her have anything she wants, but he's much more strict with my boys. If I say anything less than positive about his princess, he punishes me by withdrawing. He stops talking to me completely. And he stops being affectionate to me when she's here. It happens every time she visits. I can predict exactly when he will pull away from me.

As Amanda spoke, Keith's facial expression suggested that he did not agree. I asked him about his perspective and he said:

> I do not get angry. I don't know what she's talking about. All I know is that when Chrissy comes into town, Amanda gets strange. There's a lot of tension because I feel that she is standing over me watching, waiting to criticize my handling of the children.

I asked Keith, "When you think that Amanda is watching you like a hawk and it makes you tense, what do you do then?" He responded, "I withdraw."

So they both agreed that Keith withdraws when Chrissy visits, but for different reasons. Amanda sees the situation like this:

Chrissy visits
▼
I say something about Chrissy.
▼
Keith punishes me by being silent.
▼
I get mad at Keith.
▼
Keith withdraws further.

However, Keith sees their situation like this:

Chrissy visits.

▼

Amanda scrutinizes me.

▼

I withdraw out of discomfort.

▼

Amanda gets mad at me.

▼

I need some time out.

Since Keith did not agree that he got angry at Amanda, I asked Amanda, "How can you tell the difference between the times when Keith is quiet, signaling that he is in fact angry at you, or when his quietness indicates that he is just thinking about something else, or he has had a bad day at work, or he is just a quiet kind of guy?" Without hesitation, she insisted, "I can just tell."

Keith wasn't so sure however. He felt that she often accused him of being angry when he wasn't feeling angry. He saw Amanda as someone who liked to talk about things in order to sort them out. He, on the other hand, preferred to think things through before talking about them. He felt that his silence during the time he processed information was misread by Amanda to mean that he was irritated, which angered her.

After listening to both of their points of view, I noticed a common denominator: Problems arose between them because of anticipated rejection. Keith anticipated criticisms and Amanda anticipated withdrawal. Chrissy's visits triggered expectations of trouble in the couple, which changed the usual way they acted with each other. Keith became unusually quiet anticipating Amanda's criticisms, and Amanda became unusually guarded anticipating Keith's withdrawal. In a sense, their mutual expectation of trouble forced each of them to behave in ways that brought about the self-fulfilling prophecy.

I postulated that if either of them were able to act in their usual manner when Chrissy arrived, it would interrupt the problematic pattern of interaction. In other words, if Keith continued being affectionate and attentive to Amanda in Chrissy's presence, Amanda would feel more relaxed and be less inclined to watch over Keith, or if Amanda were to be complimentary and relaxed around Keith in Chrissy's presence, he wouldn't fear her criticisms and would respond by being affectionate.

I offered the couple a suggestion pertaining to Chrissy's next visit home. To Amanda: "The next time Chrissy comes home, if you sense that Keith is starting to withdraw, act as if he is just thinking about something else and that nothing is wrong. Behave as you do when everything is okay between you and notice what happens." To Keith: "On Chrissy's next trip home, if you observe Amanda starting to glare at you, assume she's wanting to be close to you and act as you normally do when you want to be close to each other and notice what happens." They agreed and we scheduled another appointment for two weeks.

Keith and Amanda returned appearing much happier than the previous session. I asked how the assignment went and they reported that it had worked really well for them. Tension built twice in two weeks but it did not turn into a fight because they handled it differently than before. The first time, Amanda felt Keith pulling away, instead of feeling rejected and getting angry, she said, "Now remember, I'm assuming you're just thinking about something. How long do you need to be by yourself? Can I kiss you while you're thinking?"

They both laughed and the tension passed immediately. The second time, Keith felt Amanda tensing up and he hugged her, saying in a joking manner, "Remember, act as if . . ." They both chuckled as they described how they averted two major confrontations and felt they had taken a critical step in their marriage. Granted, the difficulty between them wasn't completely resolved yet, but they could both see that it was possible to get along even in Chrissy's presence.

If you anticipate a negative response from your mate such as, "I know he will be angry at me when I walk through the door," or "I know he won't accept the idea I have," or "I'm convinced we'll have a fight at this party tonight," you probably change *your* behavior in subtle and not so subtle ways. As a result, you may inadvertently trigger the very response you are hoping to avoid. Your tension—the way you walk, look and speak—may provide cues that signal hostility without your even knowing it.

To avoid setting yourself up for failure, ask yourself: *"How would I act differently if I expected _____ (him to be pleased to see me, her to agree with me, or the evening to go well)?* Be as specific as possible. Perhaps another example will help.

A woman admitted that she was anticipating a fight with her husband when he returned home from work that evening. I asked her to predict the sequence of events after his arrival. She said that when he entered the house she would be making dinner. He would walk into the kitchen and she would avoid his eyes, waiting for him to greet her first. She anticipated feeling tense and, in an effort to calm herself and avoid conflict, she would continue making dinner, paying little attention to him.

Then I asked how she behaves when she's had a great day and is eager to see her husband. Without hesitation she responded, "I greet him at the door with a hug and a kiss. I ask about his day and tell him about mine. Then we relax for ten minutes or so; he reads the paper and I read the mail. He tells me that I hum when I'm happy, so I probably hum when I'm done reading the mail."

You can see how different the backdrop for the getting-along scene is as compared to the backdrop for the showdown. The scenes are the contexts which influence moods, feelings, perceptions and, last but not least, actions. I suggested that this woman set the scene for cooperative interactions by acting as if she expected cooperation. She did and, much to her surprise, they had a very pleasant evening together.

Although the woman in the above case wasn't totally convinced that the evening would go smoothly when she agreed to do the task, she committed herself to acting as if it would, and thereby accomplished her goal. Many people say that they appreciate the "act as if . . ." task, saying they feel more in control of their lives because they recognize that feelings needn't dictate actions or outcomes.

UNCOMMON SENSE TECHNIQUE #6: ACTIONS SPEAK LOUDER THAN WORDS

I recently heard a story over the radio which illustrates this technique extremely well. A woman wrote to an advice columnist to describe the creative way in which she solved a chronic marital problem. She said that her husband insisted on eating his meals with his shirt off, a habit which she found irritating for all of their married life. In light of the fact that they were currently seventy years old, the woman's irritation had reached enormous proportions.

Her letter related to the columnist that for many years she had begged, pleaded and reasoned with her husband to have the decency to dress before meals, but her requests were not honored. After so many years of being ignored, one would have thought this elderly lady would have just given up, but she didn't. Her persistence and a flash of ingenuity finally paid off.

One morning she made an especially lovely breakfast and called her husband to the table. As usual, he sat down topless. After a moment, she quietly rose from the table, went into the bathroom, disrobed and, without a word, sat down naked next to her husband and began eating her breakfast. Her husband looked up, left the table, returned fully clothed and never sat down without a shirt again.

Have you ever said to your spouse, "I talk until I'm blue in the face" or "If I've told you once, I've told you a million times"? If you have, you've been relying too heavily on words to communicate your needs. You are not alone. Most people believe that relationship failures can be traced to a breakdown in the way people talk to each other. "Improving communication skills" is one of America's most popular endeavors. Corporate executives, salespeople, doctors, spouses and parents are taking workshops and training themselves to talk better.

For many, the emphasis on improved talking skills is worthwhile. After all, words are an extremely powerful vehicle for transmitting ideas. However, others find that no matter *how* something is said, paraphrased, emphasized or reworded, the effect is still the same—no response.

For example, many self-help books and marriage enrichment courses instruct couples to use "I messages," nonblaming statements which describe feelings rather than accusations. "When you talk to me like that, I feel hurt" (an I message) is preferred over "You are so insensitive" (a you message). Although I messages are often the most effective way of communicating to others, they don't always work.

There are a variety of reasons that even properly constructed statements of feelings and requests are ignored. One such reason is that words lose their power if one's partner has stopped listening. Words go in one ear and out the other because, no matter how you phrase it, your efforts to change things via talking sound like nagging to your partner. Regardless of what you say, all of your comments get lumped together: "There he goes again with his trying to pressure me to do it his way" or "Why can't she stop bitching about this all the time?" Even I messages fall on deaf ears when someone has grown impervious to words.

Before jumping to the conclusion that your marriage is over because your spouse isn't responding to your patient verbal requests, take a lesson from the naked seventy-year-old woman: For some, actions speak louder than words. Her naked body at the breakfast table got her husband's attention in a way that fifty years of talking never did. For him, seeing was believing.

You might be wondering exactly which action to take to make your point. Experience has taught me that most people already know what they need to do, they just haven't done it yet. Although the particular action you take depends on your situation, it might be useful to ask yourself: *"What wild ideas have you had about what could be done to solve this problem?"* (Heath and Atkinson, 1989, pp. 56–57).

I once asked that question to a woman who struggled for years with her husband to get him to be more prompt. Her biggest complaint was that when they were invited to a social event he was always slow to get ready and, as a result, they would be late. Although he thought nothing of it, it embarrassed her greatly. For years she pleaded with him to try harder to be on time. Occasionally, he would agree to try but they never managed to get out the door punctually.

When I asked her, "What wild ideas have you had about what could be done to solve this problem?" she said, "For years I've been thinking that while he is getting ready, I should just leave quietly and surprise him by not being there when he walks out of the bedroom. I just haven't done it." Two weeks later she left without him, and the next time they went out together, he was prompt. Although leaving unannounced is a far more sedate solution than getting naked for breakfast, it nevertheless seemed farfetched to her because she had still been hoping that reasoning with her husband would work.

Here's another example that shows the effectiveness of action after years of fruitless talk. When Sally finally gave up talking and reasoning with her husband, Tom, and started acting instead, the marriage improved dramatically. Sally came alone to discuss her concern about her husband's anger. Although there was no physical violence, his anger had increased over the last year.

In order to get a clearer picture, I asked Sally, "When he starts ranting and raving, what does he usually do?" She replied that he yelled, pounded on the table and often worked himself up to the point where he would leave the house. "What do you do when he is screaming?" I asked. "I just look at him in awe and say, 'How old are you?' I know this irritates him because he starts parodying my voice and then attacking the way I say something rather than dealing with the issues." Our conversation went as follows:

MICHELE: If he were here now, how would he say you have been handling the situation recently?

SALLY: He'd say I talk too much, that I would make a good lawyer. He always tells me that I am "making a case" when I talk to him. I guess I refer to research and theories when I tell him my point of view. To me, this is only rational, but he doesn't like it. I think it intimidates him.

MICHELE: So he doesn't like the rational approach?

SALLY: No, it never works with him. It just makes him madder.

Sally's comment that her husband thought she talked too much was the first sign that she might be a good candidate for the "actions speak louder than words" technique. At least we had a clear picture of what wasn't working. Later in the session:

SALLY: One thing we fight about is how late he sleeps on weekends. He usually sleeps until noon. It ruins our day together because we get such a late start.

MICHELE: What do you usually do when he wakes up?

SALLY: I talk to him about how nice it would be if he would wake up earlier and then we usually get into a fight.

MICHELE: What would happen if, instead of your talking to him about rising earlier, you were gone when he awoke? What would happen if you made plans with some friends and by the time he opened his eyes you were already out and about?

SALLY (Smiling):   That would really blow his mind! I've never done that before.

Since Sally told me that Tom thought she talked too much, I suggested that instead of talking, she take action. She immediately liked the idea. At the end of the session I complimented her on her openness and suggested that she get a large piece of paper, perhaps a poster board, and, with markers, write in large letters: JUST DO IT! Without telling her anything more specific, I hoped the sign would serve as a reminder for her to stop talking and start acting. She laughed, and said that it sounded like a good idea.

Sally returned two weeks later having taken action on several occasions. She said that the first weekend when Tom was sleeping in, instead of arguing with him about it, he awoke to find her gone. She had taken the dog for a walk and gone to visit a friend.

When she returned, he was up, dressed, looking refreshed and curious about her absence. In fact, he was attentive and they spent a very pleasant day together. The following day he even got up earlier than usual. Sally was so pleased by these results that she felt the "Just do it" slogan held a lot of promise.

She also reported handling something else differently. In the previous session, Sally complained that Tom never wanted to go anywhere or do anything. They fought about this a great deal. Rather than discussing her feelings about his apparent lack of motivation to go out as she usually did in the past, she simply got theater tickets and announced that they had plans in two weeks. When she did, his eyes lit up. Tom seemed delighted. This shocked Sally, since she had convinced herself that he was a total couch potato. She told me that she now thought about Tom in a new light. As long as she started the ball moving by taking some action rather than discussing her feelings, he rarely resisted. In fact, he apparently enjoyed it. Furthermore, when she stopped talking and trying to get him to commit to seeing things her way and, instead, just took action, Tom was more pleasant and less angry. Indeed, life had been peaceful for the past two weeks. Sally's lesson? Sometimes talking things out is not the best solution—particularly if it doesn't work!

If talking about things has gotten you nowhere fast, stop talking and start acting! Imagine you are not *able* to talk. How would you get your message across then? That's what you need to do.

UNCOMMON SENSE TECHNIQUE #7: THE MEDIUM IS THE MESSAGE

It has been my experience that the manner in which a message is delivered often influences whether it is received. Speaking clearly and succinctly into a dead telephone results in no message being transmitted. You have already read how it might be necessary to communicate through actions rather than words. The message doesn't change, but the communication method or the medium changes.

There are other ways you can change the medium to get your message heard. Many people tell me that writing their spouses in-depth letters explaining their feelings has had a positive impact on the marriage. Despite the fact they've expressed these same feelings orally "a million times," for some reason the letters were better received.

Similarly, some couples say that, while they have a great deal of difficulty dealing with controversy when they are face-to-face, they can talk about heated issues over the phone.

Since there is no single correct way to deliver a message, if your usual medium doesn't get the job done, try another.

UNCOMMON SENSE TECHNIQUE #8: WAIT OR DO NOTHING

The worst advice a newlywed couple could be given is: "It is important to be open and honest with your feelings at all times." Although the open expression of feelings is a prerequisite for any successful marriage, there definitely is a time and place for it. Intense feelings often cloud perceptions, making clear assessments of problematic situations difficult.

Most people assume that if they are angry they must act on it immediately. It is crucial to remember that no matter what you are feeling, you have a choice as to how you respond. Anger doesn't *force* you to say you're angry, yell, pout or walk out. You choose how you react. Feelings are just feelings; they come and go. You are not an innocent victim of your raging emotions and they need not dictate what you do.

When your alarm goes off at 5:30 A.M. you don't *feel* like getting up, but because you want to keep your job, you get yourself up. You dread April 15 because you don't *feel* like doing your taxes, but for obvious reasons, you do it anyway. You see someone eating a scrumptious chocolate sundae and would love to have one, but because you are on a diet, you forego the pleasure. Clearly, we can feel one way but choose to act in another.

Knowing that feelings don't cause actions is essential to marital problem solving because you can decide whether telling your partner how you feel is in your best interest. When you feel anger you need to stop, take a deep breath and ask yourself: "If I say (do) this to him (her), how will he (she) respond? Is that really what I want?" If your partner's likely response is not what you want or need, don't express your feelings (or take action) unless a catharsis is your goal. There are other options.

One option is for you to wait and see how you feel later when you are more clearheaded. This will give you the opportunity to be more strategic in your approach. More time will allow you to determine the best possible plan to achieve your goal. It will also permit you to decide whether the confrontation will be worth your effort. You may decide that you overreacted and feel relieved you didn't stir up bad feelings unnecessarily.

Another option is to do nothing. If you and your mate *never* let anything slide, your tit-for-tat interactions do nothing but increase hostility. While being able to say what's on your mind is an extremely valuable skill, true assertiveness entails picking and choosing the important battles, not having a knee-jerk reaction to every provocative situation.

Of course, if your "more of the same" behavior is to keep silent when something bothers you, this technique is not for you since you need to be more expressive.

UNCOMMON SENSE TECHNIQUE #9: AS A LAST RESORT, TRY THE LAST-RESORT TECHNIQUE

Whether your spouse has already filed for divorce or you are already separated, it may still not be too late to save your marriage. Although this technique doesn't always work, it is worth trying when all else has failed. Even if your marriage is dangling by a thread, you still may be able to turn things around.

The last-resort technique is really no different from the 180° technique. The reason that it is listed separately is because of its importance. When there are marital difficulties and a person fails to do a 180°, the problems get worse. However, when a marriage teeters on divorce and a person fails to use the last-resort technique, divorce is almost inevitable. I'll explain why.

When one person wants the marriage to work, but the other doesn't, fairly typical patterns emerge. The spouse who wants to preserve the marriage desperately pursues his mate, trying to reverse the momentum of the alienation. Usually there's pleading, begging, crying, threatening—anything—to try to win back the departing spouse. "I know deep down inside you still love me," she says, in an effort to convince him to keep trying. Or "What about all these years together? We have a history that shouldn't be thrown away," he tells her hoping she will see the light. "I promise I'll change, I know it can work," he tells her, praying she will give him one more chance.

Although these acts of desperation are understandable, they unfortunately have the paradoxical effect of increasing the chances of divorce. The more desperate the spouse wanting to keep the marriage alive appears, the less appealing he or she becomes. The result? The reluctant spouse becomes more certain that the decision to divorce is the right one and withdraws even further.

Pursuers have other things in common. As the marriage deteriorates, they often become obsessed with wanting to know their mate's whereabouts and daily activities. If separated, they call many times a day, sometimes to check on their mate, other times to be reassured. These calls are usually met with anger or apathy, hardly the reassurance the caller needed. In fact, the distancing mate feels that the pursuer is trying to control him or her, which inevitably leads to resistance.

In addition to becoming undesirable and controlling, there is another downside to trying to convince a distancing spouse that the marriage is workable. Over the period of weeks or months this pursuit continues, the pursuer's behavior allows the other spouse to avoid thinking about or feeling the real consequences of divorce. As long as the struggle between the polarized spouses is intense, the distancing spouse can focus on the struggle while defocusing on feelings of loss.

Furthermore, the more person A worries about the marriage, confesses love and commitment, fears for the future of their children, aches for the closeness of times past, the less person B does. As I've illustrated, relationships are like seesaws: The more one spouse worries about the breakdown of the marriage, the less the other spouse has to worry. The result? If you have been working overtime to convince your spouse that your marriage is worth saving, you love each other or you're worried about the children, you are making it easy for him or her *not* to think or feel these things because you are doing all the work. The solution? Stop the chase. In fact, it's not enough just to stop the chase, you must do a 180°! Here's an example.

Randy, a twenty-nine-year-old laborer, was referred to me by an attorney who thought he seemed depressed about his imminent divorce. When Randy entered my office I could tell he had been crying. His wife, Angie, had taken their three-year-old son and had gone to live with her mother. She told Randy that she did not want to be married anymore because he couldn't give her what she needed to be happy in a marriage.

Randy had been married once before and definitely did not want this marriage to end. He loved Angie and felt certain that their problems could be overcome with a little bit of perseverance. The whole time he talked about his wife and little boy, he fought back tears. I asked what he had been doing recently to try to save their marriage. As I expected, he said, "Calling her daily, promising changes, asking to get together and letting her know how the separation is destroying me."

I wondered when and under what circumstances they still got together. He told me that Angie would pick up the mail and drop off their son for short periods on the weekends. Additionally, since their separation occurred over the holiday season, they agreed to spend Christmas together for the sake of the family.

I asked Randy whether he thought his current strategy to save the marriage was working. He replied, "If it were, I wouldn't be here. I don't know what else to do." Wanting more information, I asked, "When Angie comes over to pick up the mail or drop off your son, what do you usually do?" He responded, "Lately I've been depressed a lot and so when she walks in, she can tell I've been crying. I try to engage her in a conversation to prolong her visit. Sometimes the conversations are pleasant, but there's always a gnawing feeling inside that it's not going to last. Then she leaves."

I asked him how he thought he appeared to his wife when he was depressed. He said, "I bet she wonders why she is with me." I agreed and told him that he had better present the more desirable side of himself if he wanted to win her back. Ready to construct a plan, I asked, "What could you do that would take Angie completely by surprise?" He wasn't quite sure how to answer the question at first, but after a while he listed several things he could do which would be totally uncharacteristic of his handling of the situation thus far. They included the following:

1. Stop calling her.
2. Be unavailable when she stops over.
3. Seem happy (like his old self) when she visits.
4. Be more involved with their son.
5. Make social plans for himself after work.

I told him that it was essential that the proposed changes be ones she could notice. In other words, if he were to change his behavior at work, no matter how dramatic the change, she would not be present and consequently his efforts would go unnoticed. However, the majority of the changes he suggested would be observable by her. Change number five, making social plans after work, while not something she could see, would help him feel better, which would make the rest of the changes easier to accomplish.

I told him that although there were no guarantees it would work, I could assure him that pursuing Angie would push her in the opposite direction. He agreed to implement the new plan and seemed relieved as he walked out the door.

The second session he returned looking more hopeful. He went the whole week without calling Angie, and much to his surprise she called him twice that week, which was unprecedented. She even stopped by at work once to say hello. Randy said that in addition to her usual weekend visits Angie used the excuse of needing to get some clothes to make an unannounced visit. While she was getting her clothes, Randy played with their son. When she walked out, they were in the midst of playing a game and Angie seemed very pleased. Finally, Randy went out after work with a few buddies and returned home to discover a message on his answering machine. Angie had been looking for him.

Although there was no talk of reconciliation yet, Randy could tell that he was on the right track. He felt considerably more optimistic and upbeat, which made it easier for him to stick to the plan. He found it tempting to beg her to come home, since he felt she was more affectionate. However, he resisted the urge and stayed interested but not eager.

Over time, they started dating again and gradually spending more time together as a family. Within two months of their separation, Angie told Randy she was considering coming home. Together they worked out the conditions for her return, and she and their son moved back home, marking the end of therapy.

If, after reading this, you realize that you've been in the midst of a cat-and-mouse chase that's going nowhere, it's time to stop, take a deep breath and try the last-resort technique. To determine what you need to do differently, ask yourself: *"What could I do to shock my spouse? What could I do that would give my spouse the impression that my life is going on without him (her)?"* and start doing it! The changes may not be as immediate as in Randy's case, but stick with it for a while before you decide whether it's working.

If it does work, as in Randy's case, resist the impulse to ask for more of a commitment or of seeming too eager. If you don't allow enough time for the positive interactions to take hold, you may go back to square one. You *must* continue your new behavior until you are absolutely convinced your spouse's changes will last. Don't get complacent too soon or your spouse will become distant again. When this method fails to save the marriage, people tell me that it has, nevertheless, saved their self-esteem. Feeling desperate and meeting with rejection makes people feel negative about themselves, whereas acting more independently helps them feel more in control and self-determining, a prerequisite to an improved sense of self-esteem.

Perhaps another example might help. George started therapy because he feared that his wife, Alicia, was ready to file for divorce. Both George and Alicia were married when they met. They had an intense affair before they decided to leave their spouses and marry. For a while, their marriage was also intense, but as is usually the case, the fire eventually subsided.

As things cooled off between them, their sexual relationship slowed down. George complained that they made love less frequently and that the level of excitement had also subsided. Although this decrease in sexuality is a predictable by-product as a marriage moves out of the honeymoon stage, George started wondering whether something was wrong. This in itself was not necessarily a problem, but eventually he became excessively suspicious. Alicia was repulsed. She threatened to leave him unless he started acting normal again. By the time George came for therapy, Alicia had gone to stay with a friend for a few days to sort things out.

George informed me that he suspected she was having an affair with a fellow employee. They frequently worked on projects together, sometimes until late at night. George found himself looking through her personal belongings and continually driving past the fellow's house to see if Alicia's car was there. Occasionally it was, but she swore it was because they were working.

The more insecure George became, the more he called her at work to check up on her and seek reassurance. When she was not available to come to the phone, he questioned her for long periods of time. At night she was so angry about his constant accusations she did not feel like making love. Each time she rejected him, he took it as a sign she didn't love him anymore and that there was someone else in the picture.

All George could think of was Alicia. He imagined her in intimate scenes with her colleague and this enraged him. He was no longer able to concentrate at work and, for that matter, neither was she. Alicia told him that she could no longer live with someone who did not trust her and that she was strongly considering getting out of the marriage. Devastated, George sought an answer to his problem.

After asking George what he would need to do to surprise Alicia, he listed the following:

1. Stop calling her at work.
2. Stop initiating sex.
3. Make plans for himself.
4. Keep busy around the house when Alicia was present.
5. Act normally (not desperate and more focused on work).
6. Stop questioning her about her whereabouts.

In the sessions that followed, George managed to get his marriage back on track by doing the unexpected. Alicia did not file for divorce. In fact, she noticed the change in his behavior immediately. During the period between two sessions, George wrote me a letter updating me about their progress:

> I seem to have found peace and no longer check in during the day to get an update on Alicia. I'm sure she notices this. I find her calling me, just to see if I'm okay. I continue to do things she doesn't expect. As a result, I see her thinking and wondering what's up. This is a pleasant turn of events for me. Life is not quite so predictable for her anymore.
>
> The bedroom is even more interesting, as we seem to be shifting roles. I'm not quite at the point where I'm fighting her off but *she* has been the initiator. I even had fun telling her I was too tired a few nights ago—that got her thinking! Please call or write if you have any more great ideas to keep this momentum rolling. I'm a willing guinea pig based on results so far.

WHEN TECHNIQUES DON'T YIELD THE BEST RESULTS

If you have tried a particular technique but it didn't seem to make a difference, there are several possible explanations. It is important to try to determine which one fits your situation in order to know what to do next. The following may account for unsatisfying results:

1. The Different Approach Isn't Different Enough

Make sure that what you are doing is unusual. While screaming and quiet bargaining are certainly different behaviors, they may both be experienced as intrusive. Be certain that your new behavior bears little resemblance to your "more of the same" behavior.

2. It's Too Soon to Tell

It's essential that you wait a while to see if a particular intervention is working. Not all results are immediate. Since your problem did not develop overnight, you must be patient while your new behavior effects change in the problem pattern. However, after a couple weeks of no change, it may be time to try another method.

3. You're Overlooking Small Changes

Eager to see your marriage improve and have things back to normal, you may fail to notice the small changes. If you do, you may incorrectly decide that your new approach isn't working and switch strategies. Remember general problem-solving rule number one: "If it works, don't fix it." Therefore, although you still may have a ways to go, be sure to look for *any* signs of improvement. It's essential that you do.

4. Your Heart Isn't in It

If you make a halfhearted attempt to implement a new approach, you might as well not bother. You won't be believable and it won't work. If you don't feel completely comfortable with a particular technique, you won't seem sincere. Don't do anything that doesn't feel right for you. There are enough choices from which to choose. If your heart isn't in it, do something different.

5. You Find Yourself Reverting to Old Ways

Sometimes people say that a technique has failed, but when we examine what actually happened that week, we discover that in fact the beginning of the week showed some improvement. However, as soon as things improved, the person returned to the habitual ways of responding, which explains the lack of positive results later in the week. In this case, return to the more effective approach and stick with it.

P.S.

Don't forget to have fun. Have you ever wondered why you can laugh with your kids, laugh with your friends but are dead serious with your mate? Humor can be the best antidote for marital problems:

> People in chronic problem situations tend to find those situations anything but humorous. Chronic problems are often described with negative imagery that ranges in intensity from annoying . . . to quite frightening. . . . It is often the very seriousness with which a problem is viewed that inhibits the flexibility of thought and the creativity that are so helpful in changing things. The ability to find the humor in a situation that had previously produced only clenched teeth and knotted stomach is a big change and is often enough, in itself, to influence events positively. (Molnar and Lindquist, 1989, p. 39.)

Do whatever you need to do to get yourself in the proper state of mind. Doctor's orders: Watch a Woody Allen movie, go to a comedy club, recall a humorous memory, crack a joke. Do whatever tickles your fancy, just don't be so serious!

Now you know what to do to change your relationship. If it works, don't fix it. If it doesn't work, do something different. But what if your relationship still hasn't changed? Make yourself happy. The next chapter will tell you how.

CHAPTER 7

Make Yourself Happy for a Change

Have you ever noticed that when you point a finger at your spouse, three other fingers point back at you? Maybe your spouse has been inattentive, inconsiderate or uncaring, but there are steps you can take besides complaining, trying to change him or her or being miserable. *Make yourself happy.* When you focus less on your spouse and more on yourself, you can start making your life enjoyable again.

This chapter is the counterbalance to Chapter 4, "It Takes One to Tango," which focused on things *you* can do to create change in your marriage. The aim of the techniques in that chapter is to bring about changes in your relationship with your spouse. The purpose of this chapter is different. It is to remind you that regardless of what happens with your marriage it is you who are responsible for your own happiness and to help you identify ways to achieve it independently of your relationship.

You may be thinking, "I don't think I should have to meet my needs outside my marriage," or "The only reason I'm unhappy is because of him," or "I don't think I'm the one who needs to change." If this sounds familiar, you and your spouse have probably gotten into escalating struggles. Your "more of the same" behavior can be characterized by the following persistent message to your mate: "*You* need to change because you're the problem." This provokes your mate's "more of the same" response: "No, *I'm* not the problem, you are. You change."

These tugs-of-war not only make you miserable, they enervate you. You have no energy left to help yourself. Furthermore, the challenge of getting your spouse to change is so enticing, you forget a most important fact: You are the only one who can make yourself happy. If you have lost sight of this fact, this chapter will help you identify ways to refocus your attention and energy onto yourself.

Unhappy marriages consist of unhappy people. Although marital unrest can lead to individual unhappiness, it also works the other way around. If you are dissatisfied with your life, everything is colored by that fact. Little irritants become major crises. You've got a shorter fuse with the kids and you're more likely to respond rashly to your mate.

When your own life is in order, you feel better about yourself, which helps you be more clearheaded about your marriage. Options open up that were once invisible. In fact, many people tell me that once they focused on themselves and suspended their efforts to change their mates, their marriages improved. Particularly when two people have been involved in a "You change first" standoff, shifting the focus to yourself can have a noticeable effect on the relationship.

Wendy is a good example of someone whose life improved dramatically when she stopped trying to change her husband and made herself happy instead. Wendy looked tired when she walked into my office the first day we met. After hearing about her unsuccessful five-year struggle to change Matt, her husband, I understood the reason for her fatigued appearance.

Matt had a problem with alcohol. When they married, he drank socially, at parties, on the weekends or when they went out for dinner. However, over the past five years, his drinking had increased tremendously. He frequently stopped at bars on his way home from work and came home drunk. On nights when he came straight home, he would drink martinis until he fell asleep. Socializing with friends became a nightmare for Wendy because, although Matt was never violent or abusive, his loud behavior embarrassed her. Mutual friends confided in Wendy about their concern for Matt.

I asked Wendy about her goals. She was adamant that she did not want to leave the marriage because of their four children, but she couldn't stand being miserable. We discussed what she had been doing over the past five years to improve the situation. She told me that she had tried everything she could think of to get Matt to stop drinking, including reasoning, pleading and threatening to leave. She begged him to get help and even got information about treatment centers for him to read. He wasn't interested because he didn't think he had a problem. Wendy went on to say that she even had friends talk to him, hoping that he would be more open to hearing the suggestion from someone outside the family. He wasn't.

What triggered Wendy to make the call for therapy was when she realized that Matt's drinking was ruining her life. She waited up for him at night and lectured him when he came home. She hid bottles of vodka, hoping he wouldn't drink. She'd empty his glass, hoping he'd think he finished his drink and go to bed. One morning Wendy woke up and looked at herself in the mirror and realized that she had become obsessed with Matt's drinking problem and that it was making her miserable.

Short of leaving the marriage, Wendy was eager for some suggestions to improve her situation. I asked her, "If Matt were here now, how would he say you have been trying to handle things lately?" She replied, "That's easy. He'd say all I do is nag, nag, nag." "Wendy, has your reasoning with him about his drinking helped?" I asked. "Nothing I've done has helped stop his drinking. He just gets worse all the time."

I could tell that Wendy was so fed up with Matt and her obsession with his behavior that she was a good candidate to focus on herself for a change. When I then asked, "If, all of a sudden, Matt no longer had a drinking problem, what would you do with all the time you have been spending worrying about him?" she replied, "I haven't the foggiest idea. I have been paying so much attention to Matt, I've forgotten all about myself." She went on to tell me that she didn't see friends anymore, never went to cultural events, which she used to love to do, had been less active in the children's school activities and so on. The picture was clear; Wendy had put her life on hold.

As Wendy's list of forfeited activities grew longer, so did her awareness that she needed to make some changes. She agreed to completely stop trying to get Matt to change and focus on herself instead. She would no longer reason with him, beg him or even remind him that he had been drinking too much. Rather, she agreed to keep herself busy with her children, recontact friends and make plans for herself. At night, she was to go to bed before Matt returned home. If she couldn't go to sleep, she was to be reading or watching TV when he entered the room and treat him as she would if he hadn't been drinking. No lectures, no questions, just "Hi, dear."

Wendy thought it would be difficult to remain quiet when Matt came home drunk or when he drank himself into oblivion. I agreed that it would be hard. I asked her to keep track of the times she feels tempted to scold him and be aware of what she did instead. Although the change wasn't immediate, a couple of months later, Wendy felt as if she had a new lease on life. She invested her energy in her children, her friends and herself. She was more active and even took up a new hobby, restoring antiques. The less she worried about Matt, the happier she became. She reminded me that, although she felt much better, it still wasn't always easy to remain quiet when Matt overindulged. "Whoever said this was going to be easy?" I asked her.

In our last session, Wendy commented that something intriguing had happened: Matt told her that he thought he had been drinking too much. She even noticed that he had been coming straight home from work on most days and drinking less at home. Although she did not assume that his problem drinking days were over, she was nevertheless amazed that Matt even admitted to having a problem. She considered this admission icing on the cake because her real goal in changing herself was changing herself.

Comment

Wendy learned several important lessons. She recognized that she was responsible for her own happiness. Her happiness could not hinge upon Matt's sobriety. She also learned that the more she nagged Matt, the less he had to face his own weakness. Instead, he could react to her and focus on the struggle for control. Once Wendy quit trying to change him and he had to face himself, he didn't particularly like what he saw. He finally admitted that his drinking was out of control. In an ironic way, Wendy's attempt to change and protect Matt prolonged his denial.

Not everyone in Wendy's shoes can do what she did. Nor does every spouse respond as Matt did. However, when married to a person who is chemically dependent, the spouse has three choices. One is to continue being miserable. The second is to get out of the marriage. The third is to become detached so that the chemical dependency doesn't ruin your life. Wendy chose option three and wished she had done it five years earlier.

Whether you shift your focus to making yourself happier as a way to implement change in your marriage or because you realize that no one else can do it for you, the message is to DO IT. If you were to decide to leave your marriage because of feeling unhappy, when you become single *you* will be solely responsible for your happiness. *You* will need to pull yourself up by the bootstraps. You won't be able to point a finger at your spouse because he or she won't be there anymore. Whether the marriage works or fails, you will need to find satisfaction in your life, so why not start now?

Gina, age thirty-nine, was convinced she was wasting her life as long as she remained in her marriage to Robert. Gina and Robert had been married for fifteen years and had two daughters, ages five and nine. During the first session, Gina cried as she told me of the emptiness she felt.

For much of their fifteen years together, Gina felt lonely and sad. Her dissatisfaction with their marriage confused her because years ago she wanted nothing more than to be married to Robert and have children. Theirs was a "white picket fence" dream story come true. Robert was a successful engineer, and Gina a committed stay-at-home mom. They had all the things money could buy, a lovely home, two healthy, beautiful and bright little girls, occasional vacations to exotic places, respect in the community. But something wasn't right. Gina felt a gnawing inside, she just wasn't happy.

She was tired of being the primary caregiver of their children, fed up with the never-ending upkeep of their house and frustrated with Robert's lack of help around their home. Gina also spoke of her resentment toward Robert for his preoccupation with work and lack of energy for doing anything with the family. According to her, when he came home at the end of the day, he "zoned out," read his newspaper and was oblivious to everything going on around him.

Gina's upcoming fortieth birthday impacted tremendously on her feelings about her life. For the first time ever she realized that she was not immortal and a feeling of urgency overcame her. "I never expected to have a career when I was forty but I did expect to be happy. I'm not happy now and my time is running out," she told me. She believed that leaving Robert was her only hope. At least she would have a chance of meeting someone with whom she could share the rest of her life and, maybe, could finally be happy.

I asked Gina what steps she had taken over the years to get Robert to be more involved with her, their children and the upkeep of their home. "Every once in a while I asked him for help, but he never did what I asked," she explained. "When he was unresponsive, what did you do then?" I inquired. "What could I do?" she said. "What good would it have done anyway? He wouldn't have changed."

The longer we spoke, the more clear it became that, despite how miserable Gina had been all these years about Robert's lack of involvement and responsibility at home, she had actually done very little to change it. She suffered inwardly but never took a strong stand for fear of alienating or angering him. Now, fifteen years later, exhausted from perpetual resentment, she wanted out. For the first time in her life, she felt she was taking care of herself. This announcement shocked Robert, who until then had absolutely no idea that she was unhappy.

Later in the session, after exploring some of their relationship issues, I said to Gina, "You have been unhappy for a long time now." She shook her head in agreement. "What have *you* done to make *yourself* happy?" Puzzled by my question, she thought for a moment and asked, "What do you mean?" To clarify, I offered some examples. "Sometimes when people feel dissatisfied in their lives, they begin a new hobby, take a course, go out with friends more often, work part-time or treat themselves to buying something new. What have you done recently to spice up your life?" Other than going out to lunch with a friend a month ago, she admitted having done nothing for herself. Robert told her many times that he would be happy to watch the children if she wanted to take a class or get out in the evening, but she never took him up on it.

In a sense, Gina was right in thinking that she hadn't been looking out for herself, but Robert wasn't her only obstacle. She was standing in her own way by failing to recognize the role she played in her unhappiness. By not standing her ground with Robert and taking some initiative for making her own life more fulfilling, she was placing the entire responsibility for her well-being in Robert's hands. When he failed to make her happy, Gina believed *Robert* was the problem, thereby crediting him with more power than he actually had.

In order for their marriage to work, Robert had to make changes, but Gina needed to take more responsibility for the quality of her own life. Had Gina focused more on herself and the options she had available to her, things might not have deteriorated so badly in their marriage.

As a result of our sessions, Gina was willing to see if making her life more fulfilling would affect her feelings about their marriage.

She decided to work part-time in a busy office. She realized that even if she were to divorce Robert, she would have to start working and this would give her the opportunity to get her feet wet. She discovered she enjoyed the contact with other people and that she enjoyed her children more when she came home from work. She also learned that she felt less urgency to have Robert's attention the moment he walked in the door because of the contact she had with others throughout the day.

Robert felt relieved that he wasn't her only contact with the outside world, and he found himself interested in her daily activities. With some hesitation, Robert admitted that he now respected Gina more for taking some action to help herself. This respect translated into his being more helpful at home. Robert's changes surprised Gina since she really didn't expect him to change as a result of her working. Because she was feeling better about her own life and more optimistic about the possibility of permanent changes at home, she decided to make her marriage work.

Gina is just one of many people who have changed their minds about the viability of their marriages once they took steps to change their own lives. Another woman told me that she was convinced she wanted to leave her husband. "In fact," she said, "I'm not sure why I even came today. I thought about canceling and going to an attorney instead."

She was planning on leaving the session to tell her husband of her decision. I asked about her future plans and she said she had none. The woman had never worked a day in her life, her husband had full control of their finances and she rarely went anywhere by herself. Furthermore, she told me that she predicted her husband would be vindictive about money if she said anything about divorce.

I wondered how she was going to care for herself financially after the divorce and where she was going to live. She hadn't considered these issues or any other future problems. By the end of the session I suggested that she hold off announcing her decision until she had a plan sketched out. She thanked me for the suggestion and wondered why she hadn't thought of it herself.

Two days later she called to tell me that a friend had offered her a job. She was delighted about the timing of the offer. She also had suggested to her husband that he share the responsibility for the family finances with her so that she could learn more about handling money and feel more independent. He agreed. By the end of our phone conversation she said, "Who knows, maybe I won't have to leave. Maybe I should have done this years ago." "Who knows?" I said and congratulated her on the strides she had made. "Good luck" were my parting words.

The difficulties in your marriage may or may not be due to dissatisfaction in your life. However, if you think there is the slightest possibility that there is something *you* can do to improve the quality of *your* life, by all means do it. If you are unhappy with your lot in life, it's up to you to do something about it. Although many people recognize this to some degree, they still hold on to the deadly illusion that another person can supply them with happiness. Here are three common forms this illusion takes:

DEADLY ILLUSION #1: "I AM NOT HAPPY BECAUSE HE OR SHE DOESN'T SATISFY MY EMOTIONAL NEEDS"

There's an old joke about a man who goes to his doctor with several broken fingers asking, "Doctor, when my fingers mend, will I be able to play the piano?" When the physician replies yes, the man says, "Great! I never knew how to play before I broke my fingers!"

Contrary to any fantasy you may have that knight(ess) in shining armor will make you happy, unless you know how to make *yourself* happy, you will be sorely disappointed. There is nothing magical about being married. You won't find marriage fulfilling if you aren't satisfied with the rest of your life. David Viscott, a psychiatrist, has this to say about the efficacy of getting one's needs met through a relationship:

> The way to live with another person is to start with the right person. But you can't start with the right person until you know exactly who you are.
>
> Before you have that clear perception of yourself, you aren't secure about your identity or your life choices. And then you tend to use the relationship to make up for a lack of self-esteem. You become dependent on the relationship to make you feel good—and less dependent upon it once you find yourself. Most people who have found themselves are not going to allow other people's neediness to dictate their lives. (Viscott, 1991, p. 13.)

Although loving someone can be one of life's most gratifying experiences, it must be the icing on the cake. In the same way that eyeglasses sharpen images as opposed to giving vision to the blind,. you must be whole in order to feel whole with your mate. Sometimes couples in love appear to be like one. Their individualities seem to mesh frictionlessly. However, sound marriages are in reality more like three. There's you, me and us—three separate identities. Unless your life has definition and meaning without your mate, your relationship is doomed from the start. Marriage is one area that defies mathematical logic—one-half plus one-half *do not* equal a whole. They equal divorce.

You need to remember that in even the best of marriages one person cannot satisfy all the emotional needs of the other. Too many people lose sight of this. To the man who admits he wants to have sex at least once a day but his wife prefers having it no more than three times a week, I ask, "In what other ways do you satisfy your need for intimacy besides sexual intercourse with your wife?" or "In light of the fact that you two have different sexual needs, how do you take care of *yourself* so that you don't run off and have an affair?"

To the wife who adores nothing more than verbal communication as a way of connecting but whose husband is a man of few words, I ask, "In what other ways do you get your communication needs met other than by talking with your husband?" or "In what other ways do you connect with people besides talking?"

These questions are often met with blank stares because people fail to recognize that there are ways to get one's needs met without relying solely on one's partner. People worry, "If I have to rely on my friends to have intimate conversations, doesn't that mean that something is wrong with my marriage?" or "If I have to masturbate or fantasize about someone else, doesn't that mean there's something wrong with our sexual relationship?" Heavens no!

Human needs are far too complex to have any single outlet. No matter how much you love your mate, you will have unmet needs. Regardless of how successful your marriage, you will need other people and other interests to make your life meaningful. Give up on the fantasy that your knight(ess) in shining armor will shield you from the pressures and frustrations of the world and you will live happily ever after, because you won't. *You* have to make yourself happy.

Leo Buscaglia writes:

> We are totally responsible for ourselves. We cannot look for reasons outside of us. Still, we are forever blaming outside forces for our feelings

and actions, seldom asking, "Why am I choosing to act or react that way?" Happiness and true freedom come only when we assume full responsibility for who and what we are. As long as we feel comfortable putting blame on others, we will never be required to evaluate and change our own behaviors. (Buscaglia, 1984, pp. 96–97.)

Several months ago I was eating lunch with colleagues in a diner and we were waited on by a particularly perky waitress with a sparkle in her eyes. When we finished the meal and stood up to put on our coats, she handed us our bill, smiled and said, "Make a nice day," and left. I thought about her comment for a moment and then understood the reason for the sparkle in her eyes.

DEADLY ILLUSION #2: "MY SPOUSE WON'T GO PLACES I LIKE TO GO OR DO THINGS I LIKE TO DO AND THAT'S WHY I'M UNHAPPY"

Many of my clients complain that they are unhappy because their spouses don't like to go to parties, visit relatives, get together with friends or go to museums. These people say that their lives have become stagnant because their spouses are unwilling to do anything fun. So I ask, "What's different about the times you do the things you enjoy without your spouse?" After a period of silence, I usually hear, "I don't."

Where did people ever get the idea that spouses have to do everything together? It's absurd. Yes, it would be nice if your wife enjoyed going to your parents' house as much as you. And it would be wonderful if your wife had the same artistic interests as you, but she doesn't. Staying home consistently because your mate doesn't feel like doing what you suggest is one surefire way to destroy your marriage. The resentment will build gradually until one morning you will wake up feeling life is passing you by. Don't let this happen to you. Martyrdom isn't very becoming and it doesn't work very well either. Take charge of your own life.

If you want to be more sociable and your spouse is a grouch, let him be a grouch and go out anyway. Besides, you know that the few times you've convinced him to go along, you spent the whole time worrying about him and he spent the whole car ride there and back complaining. His company is not worth the aggravation. Allow for the two of you to be different and nurture *your* needs. It's the only way marriage can work.

DEADLY ILLUSION #3: "I CAN'T DO WHAT I WANT BECAUSE MY SPOUSE WOULDN'T APPROVE"

Sometimes people hesitate taking care of their own needs for fear that their spouse may not approve. I'm not referring to major decisions which involve both parties such as where to live or whether to have children; these are joint decisions. However, some people act as if even minor decisions require unanimous approval; unless person A gets the unequivocal green light from person B, no action is taken. Then I hear, "He (she) doesn't want me to," which leads to resentment, distrust and eventual withdrawal.

If you are consistently seeking approval for every step you take, it's unlikely that you will get it. No two people think alike all the time. If you allow differences of opinion to stop you from doing the things necessary to make yourself happy, you are heading for disaster. Remember, it's important to agree to disagree at times. It is impractical to think marriage can thrive in any other way. I guarantee that if you spend half a lifetime backing down because your mate disagrees, you will spend the next half backing out of your marriage. Should you remarry, you might be surprised to discover that your new spouse won't always agree with you either. Then what?

In addition to believing that our spouses are responsible for our happiness, there are other self-limiting beliefs that serve as roadblocks to attaining personal satisfaction. Here are two of the most common ones:

SELF-LIMITING BELIEF #1: "I CAN'T PUT MY OWN HAPPINESS BEFORE MY CHILDREN'S"

"I work forty hours a week, how can I do something just for myself on the weekend after not spending time with my son during the week?" Or "I'm not working, I don't feel right getting a babysitter just to go and work out in an aerobics class." Does this sound familiar? If it does, it is time for you to reconsider your position. If you are not happy, if you don't take time for yourself, you can't be the best possible parent.

If you think about it objectively for a moment, when you are burned out you cannot really be available to your children. You have nothing left to give. Furthermore, since you know that children learn by example, if you take charge of your life and feel good about yourself, you are setting an example for your children to follow in their own lives. If instead you continually make sacrifices to spend time with your children, you are bound to feel resentment, which will be reflected in your interactions with them. Taking even a small breather can go a long way toward restoring a positive outlook or peace of mind.

SELF-LIMITING BELIEF #2: "HOW CAN A MINOR THING LIKE DEVELOPING A HOBBY HELP ME WHEN MY PROBLEMS ARE MAJOR?"

A friend of mine told me that his wife was ready to call it quits on everything in her life. She hated her career, she was frustrated with the kids, furious at her husband, felt badly about herself and just had a fight with her best friend. She wasn't sure exactly what, but something needed drastic changing. Her husband was a strong contender on the list of things needing replacement.

As she thought about it, she realized that she had so much responsibility that she felt overwhelmed. She longed for the days when she used to treat herself to a new dress, even if it was too expensive, or go out in the evening with a friend and be totally unaccountable to her husband. In the middle of her reminiscing about past carefree days, her husband suggested that she do something—anything—"delightfully irresponsible."

The following Friday night she went out with undefined plans. With the whole evening to herself, she decided to buy a new dress and meet a friend for a movie. She returned home feeling refreshed and as if a small piece of her old self had resurfaced.

In the weeks that followed, her negative outlook all but vanished. She expressed her amazement at how some seemingly trivial acts, such as shopping and seeing a movie with a friend, could have such a profound impact on her psyche. She acknowledged that, despite how complex and intractable her difficulties initially appeared, the solution was far less dramatic than she had anticipated. The woman decided to institutionalize "irresponsible" evenings out on a regular basis to prevent marital and familial burnout.

When despair hits, it is easy to believe that no solution exists, let alone a simple solution. But I have seen this type of situation alleviated time and time again. If you are feeling overwhelmed by the grip problems between you and your mate seem to have on you, having coffee with a friend, taking a course, going for a hike, being "irresponsible"—any small step you take to make yourself happy may have a surprisingly large impact.

It has been my experience that the more convinced people are that small changes won't make a difference, the less likely it is they have tried it. Those reluctant to focus on themselves and make manageable changes in their own lives are more likely to blame their mates for their unhappiness. As you know, blaming gets you nowhere fast. So stop pointing a finger and make some small improvement in your life. You've got nothing to lose and everything to gain.

"WHAT DO I NEED TO DO TO MAKE MYSELF HAPPY?"

Perhaps you are ready to make personal changes but aren't sure how to proceed. If so, there are two steps you will need to take. First, because the same principles apply here, it will be helpful to review Chapter 4, which outlines goal-setting guidelines and various effective techniques. As you review the techniques, apply them to yourself instead of your relationship. For example, instead of answering the question "What's different about the times the two of us get along?" ask: "What's different about the times in my life when I'm feeling happy?"

Second, it is important that you answer the following questions to help you clarify what you need to change in your life to make it more fulfilling. As you go through the questions, you might notice that some of them seem similar in that they ask about related information. You are absolutely correct. Several extra questions are included in this section in case you are having trouble answering any one in particular. If after answering the first few you have a clear vision of your personal goals, move ahead to the next chapter.

1. If the Problems Between You and Your Spouse Got Resolved All of a Sudden, What Would You Do with All the Time and Energy You Have Been Spending on Fixing or Worrying About the Marriage? Describe What You Would Do Instead.

Arguing and arguing about arguing takes a tremendous effort and uses up precious time. Even when you aren't having an overt battle, your mind is often filled with negative thoughts about your spouse. When problems are eliminated, people find themselves with time on their hands, time that was once used to plan battle strategies. What will you do with the excess time and energy when your problems disappear? Again, limit your response to activities you can do independently. Then start doing them.

2. If You Went to Sleep Tonight and a Miracle Happened So That All Your Marital Difficulties Disappeared, What Would You Be Doing Differently Tomorrow? In What Ways Would Your Life Change? (de Shazer, 1988, p. 5)

Keep in mind, you must limit your response to changes that don't depend on your spouse changing. You should envision your life without marital struggles and catch a glimpse of yourself and what you will be doing.

For example, in response to this question, one woman told me that after the miracle happened, she would have more time for her children and her friends and she would feel more relaxed. As a result of feeling more relaxed about her marriage, she would put her energy into redecorating her house. She had wanted to redecorate for some time but felt too absorbed with her marital problems.

Later in the session, we explored specifically what she would do with her children and her friends. In regard to her children, she said she would take them places, such as the zoo, more often and be more attentive and play with them more. In regard to her friends, she said she would spend time with them, something she hadn't done in a long time. Also, since she was so self-absorbed recently, she felt that she hadn't shown much interest in her friends' lives. This too was something she wanted to change. After our discussion, it became clear to this woman what she could do to improve the quality of her own life, regardless of the state of her marriage.

3. When You Feel Happier, What Will You Be Able (or Want) to Do That You Haven't Been Doing Lately?

Perhaps you have said to yourself, "My marriage makes me feel so lousy I don't feel like doing anything for myself. If things were better between us, I would feel happier and more motivated to do something for myself." Although this might be valid to some extent, it is more productive to remember that a change in your feelings will *follow* a change in your behavior or actions. Once you identify what you will be doing when you feel happier, you can start doing these things immediately, which *will* help you feel better.

4. If Your Mate Were to Die Suddenly or Leave Abruptly, How Would You Rearrange Your Life? As You Imagine What You Might Do Differently, Can You Identify Which of These Changes You Could Make Immediately?

It's too easy to believe that our mates prevent us from being happy. This question asks that you try to imagine your life without spousal constraints to see how you would structure it. You probably cannot make *all* of these changes, but identify what you can change and do it now! Furthermore, answering this question will help you sort out how much of your unhappiness is due to your spouse and how much would still be there even if he or she were gone.

5. If You Just Learned That You Have a Life-Threatening Illness and Only Have a Short Time to Live, What Experiences Would You Need to Have in Order to Consider Your Life Complete?

Many of us live our lives as if we were going to live forever. We waste time worrying excessively and holding ourselves back from achieving our dreams. We tell ourselves "There's always tomorrow" and retreat to our safe but unstimulating existence. Perhaps your spouse hasn't helped much these days in terms of giving your life dimension, but what *else* is missing? How can you inject excitement and meaning in your daily existence? What would be different if you were to live your life as if each day were the last, and why not start doing some of those things right now?

6. What Might Be One or Two Small Things You Can Do This Week That Will Take You One Step Closer to Your Goal?

Remember, think in behavioral terms. Perhaps you can call a friend, get a health club membership, go for a run, read a novel. Commit to doing one or two new small things this week. Note how you feel during and after you do them.

7. What, If Anything, Might Present a Challenge to Your Taking These Steps This Week, and How Will You Meet the Challenge?

Is there anything that may happen that would offer you a reason *not* to follow through with your new plan? It may be a busy schedule, a discouraging glance from your mate, demands from your children. What will you do differently so that these hurdles are not obstacles but challenges to your taking the necessary steps? Planning how you will handle any challenges makes overcoming them simpler.

For instance, after a man told me about his plans to confront his boss, an action he felt was way overdue, he said his wife might thwart his plans by making a critical comment. In the past when he discussed his intentions to confront his co-workers, his wife disagreed with his strategy, which usually stopped him in his tracks. When I asked him how he would overcome that particular challenge, he replied, "I guess I can just tell her, 'Thanks for the feedback,' and go ahead with my plans." That's exactly what he did.

In addition to answering these questions and reviewing Chapter 4, there are many books on personal growth and programs available that will help you realize your goals. Check the recommended reading list at the end of this book.

It is also important to remember that you may take a two-prong approach to achieving more happiness in your life. While you work on your personal goals and feel better about yourself, you can also try to implement change in your marriage. Conversely, while you are working on your marriage by utilizing the techniques in Chapter 4, you can also begin to work on your personal goals. Improvement in one area will undoubtedly lead to improvement in the other.

Once you start feeling better about yourself and your marriage, you may experience a mixed reaction. You're likely to feel tremendous joy and relief, but you might also feel anxious about whether the changes will be permanent. You probably want some reassurances that the pleasant feelings you are having aren't going to disappear. Chapter 8 describes the techniques you'll need to make these positive changes last.

PART III

Keeping the Changes Going

Frequently, WHEN PEOPLE BEGIN TO SEE IMPROVEMENT, THEY start to wonder how long the changes will last. "My spouse is on her best behavior and I don't see how it can last much longer," they say. Or "It's easy for me to remain calm now, but if he starts pushing my buttons, I'm afraid I'll go back to my old ways." Years ago, before I practiced SBT, I used to think that these people were being resistant. In other words, I thought they were subconsciously trying to undermine their therapeutic progress. Now I perceive their tentativeness in a very different light.

When a marriage is on the rocks, people build walls to protect themselves from being hurt. As the marriage improves, defenses drop and the walls begin to crumble. Vulnerability and uncertainty replace tough facades. With that come the questions "Can I trust him/her?" and "Is this going to last?" I now recognize tentativeness as a sign that for the first time in a long time people are opening themselves up to the possibility that life can really be different.

It's natural to worry about old habits sneaking up on you, and, believe it or not, there are some definite benefits to being concerned about it. As long as you are concerned, you will be less likely to unconsciously return to your old negative habits. Your cautiousness will help you be more aware of your actions and reactions. You will be in control of your responses rather than your responses controlling you. So remain cautious until the new way of relating becomes an old habit.

However, it is important to point out that staying cautious is different from expecting failure. Too many people, therapists included, fear that relapse is inevitable. It isn't! Remember the Butterfly Effect? If you accept the premise that a small change leads to bigger changes, it seems logical that, with time, you and your mate will build on your initial changes. There are studies substantiating this assertion.

My colleagues have done some interesting follow-up research six to twelve months after therapy ended where they asked clients, "Have any old problems that were not directly dealt with in therapy improved since you finished therapy?" (de Shazer, 1985, p. 156). Approximately two-thirds of the people who made changes during therapy said that additional changes were made during the six-to-twelve-month period following it. In other words, their lives were even more satisfying than when therapy ended.

For example, one person responded to a three-month follow-up question by saying, "When my husband and I came for therapy, we were most concerned about a lack of communication and this is what we worked on during our sessions [the ultimate goal]. Although we did not directly focus on our sex life during our sessions, we have noticed that, because of improved communication, our sex life has also improved."

With this in mind, instead of worrying about relapsing, why not envision a future that is even brighter than that which you are currently experiencing? At the same time, though, don't take progress for granted. It's essential to find a balance between these two perspectives; this chapter will help you do just that.

LOOKING A GIFT HORSE IN THE MOUTH

People superstitiously avoid dissecting or analyzing successes for fear that they will disappear. However, this fear is unwarranted. In fact, the best way to maintain positive changes is to carefully identify how they happened so you can do more of what has been working.

Here are seven steps you must take to keep the ball rolling once you've made some progress:

1. IDENTIFY THE CHANGES

Ask Yourself: "What's Happening That I Want to Continue to Happen?"

It's great that you are feeling better, but it is important to determine specifically what contributes to your positive state of mind. As before, make sure that your responses are as concrete as possible. Instead of saying, "She's been more responsive," say, "She's asking me about my day, touching me more and accepting my invitations to do things together."

Be certain to include all of the changes you have observed. Think carefully about the last few weeks and try not to leave anything out. As you think about your answer, you might reflect on changes in your mate, your own changes or changes the two of you have made as a couple. Additionally, perhaps something extraneous has changed—a new work schedule, a move, a baby out of diapers—any of which might have made life easier for you. Note these changes too.

How Have Changes in Your Relationship Affected the Rest of Your Life?

Feeling better about your spouse and your marriage has undoubtedly changed your perspective and the way you interact with others. This question asks that you pay attention to the ripple effect of your relationship changes. Have you been more relaxed at work or with the children? What changes have others noticed? Have your friends or colleagues mentioned that you seem happier? Have the children been bickering less? Have you felt more inclined to engage in your hobby or avocation? What other signs of movement in your life have you observed?

In What Ways Have These Changes Helped You to Feel Better About Yourself, Your Mate and Your Marriage?

In addition to your outlook and behavior having changed, you probably have noticed that you feel differently. How so? How have these new positive feelings enabled you to get along better and persist in doing what is necessary to keep the changes going? For instance, if you feel more secure, you are less likely to misinterpret your partner's actions or comments. If you are feeling more loving, you are more likely to be sensitive and responsive to your partner's needs.

2. TO WHAT DO YOU ATTRIBUTE THESE CHANGES?

Now that you recognize the changes, you need to ask yourself:

"How Did I (We) Get That to Happen?"

You must identify exactly what each of you is doing differently now that the problem has disappeared. It's important to remember that difficulties don't just come and go on their own; you were part of the problem and now are part of the solution. Some people say, "I'm not doing anything different, he/she's been kinder to me." Even if your partner is being kinder, *you* are now behaving in ways that bring about kindness rather than self-centeredness. What are you doing differently?

Another way to ascertain what you are doing right is to ask yourself:

"What Would My Partner Say Are the Changes That He (She) Would Want to Continue to Happen?"

As usual, be as specific as possible. Answering this question will give you some insight as to which of your actions has increased your partner's desire to meet your needs. Remember: "If you scratch my back, I'll scratch yours."

There is another advantage to identifying your role in bringing about positive responses from your mate rather than giving him or her all the credit for the changes. The flip side of giving credit is blaming. If things aren't going so well, you might be inclined to blame the whole situation on him or her too. Believing that relationship difficulties have unilateral beginnings or endings will not help you determine what you currently need to do to maintain your changes nor will this attitude help you steer clear of problems in the future.

3. DESCRIBE WHAT YOU NEED TO DO TO KEEP THESE CHANGES GOING

The key to maintaining positive changes in relationships is to keep doing what works. When a car runs out of gas, no one would ever assume that one stop at the gas station would keep the car running forever. Similarly, health-conscious individuals would be foolish to think that one fierce workout at their health club would allow them to stop exercising, or that a day or two of dieting would take off unwanted weight forever. There is no magic to making lasting changes. With this in mind, it will be helpful to clearly outline exactly what you need to keep doing in the weeks that follow in order to continue moving forward. As you list these things, you will notice that they are similar, if not identical, to your list of what's working. And that's because you're applying the "If it works, don't fix it" philosophy. Just keep doing what works.

In addition to maintaining the changes you've already made, you might be interested in building on the changes. The following questions will help you figure out what you need to do to build on your successes:

On a Scale of 1–10, with 10 Being "Great" and 1 Being "Awful," How Would You Rate Your Marriage Prior to Your Making the Changes. (Lipchik and de Shazer, 1988, pp. 113–14)

Think back to how things were before your marriage improved. Recall your feelings and some of the incidents contributing to these feelings. Rate your relationship as it was at that time.

Since the Changes, Where on This Scale Would You Rate Your Marriage Now?

Appraise honestly how much of an improvement you have observed.

Are You Satisfied?

There are three ways you might respond to this question. The first is to say that you are satisfied and have accomplished your goals. If so, that's great! Congratulations!

The second response is that your current level is satisfactory, but more time is needed at the current level in order for your goals to be met. In other words, as long as the changes last, there is no need for additional drastic changes. If you feel this way, you should ask yourself: *"How long will these changes have to last in order for me to feel more confident that they will become a habit?"* Is it two more days, three weeks, two months or longer?

This question is not simply asking you to wager how long your spouse will be on his or her best behavior. You need to know how much longer it will take for you to feel more confident that, no matter what your partner does or doesn't do, you will be able to respond effectively the majority of the time.

A third possible response is "Not yet." If you would like to see additional improvements, ask yourself: *"Where on the scale would I need to be in order to feel satisfied?"* Keep in mind that no marriage is ever perfect. (Sorry, no 10s.)

For example, some people say, "We've gone from a 2 to a 6 and we need to be at an 8. To build on these improvements, I ask: *"What are one or two things you can do next week to bring you up from a 6 to a 6½ or a 7?"* Think very specifically about what changes, if they were to occur, would make you evaluate the quality of your relationship one-half a notch higher than the week before. Visualize steps *you* can take next week to make things better. If your spouse is open to it, you can suggest specific steps he or she can take as well. If not, just focus on actions that are within your power to change. During this week, keep your eyes open for any and all 6½ or 7 occurrences and keep track of them. Continue identifying half steps up the scale until you arrive at your goal.

For example, one woman said that she had gone from a 2 to a 6 between the first and second sessions. She based this evaluation on the fact that she and her husband spent more time together, he had been more considerate of her feelings and he helped more around the house. Since her goal was an 8, I asked: *"What are one or two small things you could do this week to bring your 6 to a 6½ or a 7?"* She said, "We still need to talk more. So I guess if I initiated a few conversations, that would help. Also, we need to continue spending time together. With that in mind, if he doesn't ask me to do something with him, I need to ask him." I felt confident that she had a clear idea of what she needed to do to build on the changes she had made.

4. ASCERTAIN POTENTIAL CHALLENGES

The smart planner considers all the contingencies. Although it varies with everyone, it is important to remind yourself that there will be challenges ahead. Once you identify potential challenges and develop a strategy to avoid or handle them effectively, you will feel confident that you're able to maintain your changes.

The following questions are designed to help you forecast these rough spots in order to circumvent them. Ask yourself: *"Is there anything that might occur in the upcoming weeks that would present a challenge to my doing what's necessary to keep the changes going?"* As you think about this question, reflect on three areas: extraneous occurrences, your partner's actions and yourself. Take extraneous occurrences first.

Perhaps you have noticed that every time your mother-in-law visits (and you happen to be due for a visit next week) tempers flare. Or it has come to your attention that you and your spouse get tense around April 15, tax time, which your calendar tells you is just around the corner. Maybe especially busy weeks make it harder than slower-paced ones to maintain a Zen-like detachment when things go wrong. Look at your schedule in the upcoming weeks and determine if any such event is heading your way. If so, what is it?

Now think about your spouse. Is there anything in particular you should be aware of about the weeks that follow regarding him or her? Does he or she have to give a nerve-racking presentation, will an upcoming birthday give cause for pouting? Try to pinpoint what he or she might do that would be a challenge for you.

Finally, turn your sights inward. Carefully consider whether you are expecting anything to happen soon that might lower your resistance to negativity. Are you planning a confrontation with a colleague at work, stopping smoking, entertaining an unappreciative relative? See if you can isolate anything that might rub you the wrong way, making it more challenging for you to remain level-headed or cooperative.

As you think about ways that you might interfere with your own progress, don't forget the possibility of having unpredictable feelings that threaten your staying on track. Sometimes old feelings might creep up on you, and tempt you to resort to "more of the same" behavior. If you do, here is a suggestion: *If you find yourself tempted to do the same old thing (even though you know it won't work), notice what you do to overcome the temptation. Keep track of what you do instead* (de Shazer, 1985, p. 132).

For example, do you walk out of the room, go for a walk, count to ten or call a friend? What do you do to resist the urge to do more of the same? You might want to keep a running list of things you do to overcome the temptation to give in to old habits.

5. DEVELOP A PLAN TO OVERCOME CHALLENGES

Once you identify any potential hurdles, ask yourself, *"How will I handle this situation differently this time? What do I need to do to get the results I want?"*

One couple told me that although things had greatly improved they feared that a visit from his relatives would hurt their chances of continued change. She said, "Each time his relatives come into town, he ignores me entirely and I get resentful. When I feel that way, I am critical of him and we get into fights." I asked how they would handle the visit differently this time. At first they weren't sure, but after considering the question for a while, she said, "I guess if he would take even five or ten minutes each day to be alone with me so that we can touch base with each other, I would feel better about his relatives being here." He readily agreed to her proposal.

In the example above, both partners were present to consider how they might handle the potentially sticky situation in a new way. However, if you are working on this question alone, you can ask yourself the question: "How will I handle this situation differently this time? What do I need to do to get the results I want?"

Carefully detail how your spouse will recognize from your new handling of things that things are different. And be as specific as possible. If the woman in the example above had answered the question without her husband present, she might have said, "If I notice that I'm starting to feel resentment, I will suggest to my husband that just the two of us go out for a cup of coffee."

6. DEFINE BACKSLIDING

Realistically speaking, you probably won't divert or overcome every single challenge in your path, even if you carefully plan for it. Everyone has his or her off days. Reverting to old, unproductive habits is considered backsliding. However, you can minimize the impact of off days and keep them from becoming off weeks or off months. There are two things you must do to prevent old habits from settling in.

The first is for you to remember that real change, the kind that sticks, is often three steps forward and two steps back. If you backslide a bit and fail to remember this, you might incorrectly think that you are regressing to where you started and get unnecessarily frustrated. Experiencing setbacks once in a while teaches you how to handle them better in the future. Don't be self-recriminating, don't feel sorry for yourself, just do whatever it takes to get back on track and do it promptly.

The second thing you must do to prevent a mini setback from becoming a major setback is to define backsliding *before* it happens. When things are going well, ask yourself: *"If we were to backslide, what would we be doing?"* Make sure your description is concrete, since this will clue you in as to when some intervention is needed. For example, "If we stop spending time together or spend less time talking to each other, we will be backsliding" is a typical response to this question. Knowing what to look for will allow you to diagnose your setbacks quickly and, therefore, you will be able to intervene effectively.

7. DEVELOP A PLAN TO REVERSE BACKSLIDING

Ask yourself: *"If I notice that we're backsliding, what will I do?"* Some people choose a sign that will serve as a reminder to get back on track. For example, an argumentative couple knew that the husband would tug on his ear and the wife would point to her eye when either one felt picked on. Another woman who had been overly dependent on her husband's approval of her actions wrote a note to herself which read "Just do it!" and posted it on her refrigerator door. Any time she felt herself slipping, she reminded herself to read her note.

Perhaps a similar reminder might help get you back on track. The reminder can be something you do by yourself or it can be a sign you and your spouse agree upon jointly. As long as you build in a plan to prevent cataclysmic avalanches, you will keep moving forward.

In addition to predicting rough spots, it is also useful to foresee *who* might be the first one to notice when you're headed off course. Will it be you or your spouse? Will your children be the first to recognize backsliding? When one little girl told her parents, "You guys are acting like kids," they reminded themselves to get back on track. Once you predict who will be the first to notice, see if you can identify what he or she will do to call for a time-out.

THE STUMBLING BLOCKS TO AVOID

In addition to knowing the seven steps you must take to keep the ball rolling, you must also know what to avoid. Over the years, I have learned a great deal from couples who inadvertently sabotaged their efforts to change. On the basis of my observations of these couples, I have been able to extract a formula which will help you learn from their mistakes. The following outlines the major stumbling blocks to success. Avoid them at all costs.

1. DON'T EXPECT TOO MUCH TOO SOON

Once you have gotten a taste of improvement, you might become impatient to experience further improvements. If you only focus on the ultimate goal, you are bound to overlook smaller achievements. Each accomplishment is a building block to the next step forward. When you acknowledge and appreciate even minute steps forward, goal achievement becomes more of a reality. If you expect too much too soon, you will be disappointed, and this will make it harder for you to stay on track. Be patient—lasting change takes time.

2. DON'T EXPECT PERFECTION

I once had a client whose marriage was falling apart. After several months, things vastly improved and she felt she had a new lease on life. At that point, she felt therapy was no longer needed. Three months later, I bumped into her at a store and asked her how things were going. She said okay. Since there was some hesitation in her voice, I asked, "Just okay?" She answered, "Things are basically fine with my husband, but I still get upset with him once in a while."

As things improve between you and your partner, you may begin to fantasize about a life without problems. Nip that fantasy in the bud because you will only be disappointed. There is no panacea to marital ups and downs. If you expect perfection, the next disagreement will send you reeling in a downward spiral. Don't let this happen to you.

3. DON'T EXPECT FAILURE

Expecting failure is about as dangerous to your marital health as expecting perfection. By now, you know about the power of self-fulfilling prophecies. If you expect failure, you often get it. If you believe you and your spouse will get sidetracked, you will behave in ways that will bring about these results.

If, on the other hand, you are just being cautious about getting too excited too quickly, that represents sound reasoning. After noticeable improvements some cautious people comment, "We've had good times before, and then things backslide. This is nothing new." If this sounds familiar, ask yourself the following questions:

1. In the past, how long have good periods usually lasted?
2. What was the longest peaceful period?
3. How long have things been better now?
4. How much longer will things have to remain this way for me to be able to say to myself: "Something different is going on here. This isn't just another false start. It looks like things are really beginning to change."

The last question asks that you choose a specific date that will connote a turning point in your confidence about the changes. Be reasonable. Factor marital ups and downs into the equation and mark on your calendar the date you've chosen. As you quietly observe the results in the days that pass, act encouragingly and refrain from being a doubting Thomas(ina).

I worked with a couple who fought constantly about family finances. The woman complained that she worked her butt off for their family as a secretary while her husband went from job to job with limited financial security. He claimed his erratic employment history was due to his lack of interest in the particular jobs he held. She claimed it was due to his immaturity and lack of stick-to-it-iveness. He was unemployed at the time of our initial session.

Several weeks later he found a new sales job which interested him a great deal. However, because the position offered a commission as opposed to a salary, his wife continued to worry about family finances and resented his decision to accept the job. Even though he invested energy into getting his new job off the ground, she said, "This is another one of his pie-in-the-sky ideas."

Although there was good reason for her to be cautious, I was concerned that her pessimism would eventually be contagious, hardly an appropriate mental state for a salesman. So I asked her, "What would he need to do, or what would need to happen to make you think that this career is going to work out financially for everybody?" She thought about it for a moment and said, "If he goes out on calls every day and makes at least one sale a week."

He agreed that this was a reasonable expectation. He realized the importance of keeping her informed of his progress so that she knew of his efforts. He was determined to prove to her that he could handle this responsibility, and, as it turned out, he had no problem making at least one sale a week. When she saw this, she was more supportive, which led to his feeling better about his decision, which in turn led to increased sales. She eventually cut back on her work until she was working part-time, an arrangement they both preferred.

The turning point for this couple was when they identified what it would take to move from skepticism to optimism. If you are feeling skeptical, you need to ask yourself this question: *"What will it take for you to become just a bit more optimistic about the possibility of lasting change?"* If you don't ask yourself this question, your pessimism might keep you from achieving your marital goals.

4. DON'T TAKE CHANGE FOR GRANTED

One mistake people make is to assume that they can sit back and relax once changes have occurred. The *reason* changes have occurred is because you are responding in new ways. If you take the improvements for granted and start slipping back to the old you, you might as well say goodbye to the changes.

It is easy to take progress for granted if you incorrectly believe that your spouse is now a changed person. In other words, perhaps you are thinking that because things are better, your spouse has undergone a major *personality* overhaul. It is essential to remember that changes in your spouse's behavior are reflections of the changes in you and vice versa. If you stop behaving productively, your spouse's personality will appear to change once again. Remember, your *patterns of interaction* have changed, not just your spouse. If you revert to your old ways, so will your spouse.

As you have read through the how-to portion of this book, you probably have noticed that the underlying message is "Try it, it works!" But some people, despite their best efforts, fail to make progress on the home front. If, after implementing some of the strategies for change in this book, you haven't seen positive results, you may be wondering what to do next. The next chapter, "Is Working on My Marriage Working?" outlines what to do if you and your spouse are still locking horns.

CHAPTER 9

Is Working on
My Marriage Working?

It is my hope that anyone reading this book wishing to preserve his or her marriage will be able to do so. However, I know this is not always possible. You may need additional resources to help you solve your marital difficulties. And, unfortunately, some marital problems are not resolvable.

Perhaps you are someone who has read this book with great interest, understood the principles, applied the techniques, yet for some reason your marriage has not improved. It is important to identify when your efforts to improve your marriage aren't working so you can do something different that might bring change or decide that you have tried hard enough. This chapter would not be complete without mentioning the important fact that some marriages should be terminated. But which ones?

The reasons a person should leave a marriage are rarely black-and-white and can't be neatly categorized. A particular kind of problem doesn't necessarily lead to divorce; it is the unwillingness to change that destroys marriages. The type and even the severity of a particular problem tells less about the chances for eventual happiness than does an honest commitment (or lack of it) to change.

Having said that, it is essential to point out that physical abuse should never be tolerated. If you are married to someone who is physically abusive, who does not recognize the problem and isn't willing to get help, it is crucial that you remove yourself from the threat of violence and get professional help. No one, under any circumstances, should endure physical abuse. Thankfully, most marital problems are not so severe. Nevertheless, even less severe problems that remain unresolved can be excruciatingly painful.

If you wake up each morning feeling pain because no matter what you have done your marriage seems impervious to change, you need to know what to do next. This chapter will answer the question "Now what?" if you haven't made any progress. By the end of this chapter, you will be able to determine when working on your marriage isn't working, when to seek additional help, why some people avoid seeking professional help, what to expect from therapy, how to locate a qualified marital therapist and why therapy doesn't always work.

If you have made no progress after implementing the techniques in previous chapters, don't panic. Go through the following four-point checklist:

1. HAVE YOU GIVEN A PARTICULAR APPROACH ENOUGH TIME?

If you've been experimenting with one of the techniques and your spouse hasn't immediately responded positively, it is important not to jump to the conclusion that nothing is working. It may just take some more time. The question is how much more time? Unfortunately, since every situation is different, there is no definitive answer. However, if after two to three weeks of using a particular method no visible results can be observed, it is time to try something else.

2. HAVE YOU TRIED ANOTHER APPROACH?

If you've stuck to one or two methods, then read through the technique chapters and select a different strategy. Experiment again for two to three weeks and observe the results. If nothing changes, it may be time to consider option three.

3. HAVE YOU TALKED TO FRIENDS, RELATIVES OR CLERGY?

If nothing you try on your own is effective, you might consider getting another perspective from friends, family or clergy. If you share your concerns with a compassionate person who has had a similar experience, you may get some excellent advice. If nothing else, you will feel supported.

However, if you decide to talk to others about your marital problems, make sure that the discussions don't end up as "bitch sessions." These blaming sessions only make you angrier and offer absolutely nothing in the way of solutions. You may temporarily feel validated if your confidante agrees with you when you complain, but that feeling of victory doesn't last and it certainly won't help in the long run.

Instead, confide in someone who can suggest new perspectives or new actions you can take to improve the quality of your life. If after talking to friends, relatives or clergy you still haven't made any progress, signal the seriousness of the situation by asking your spouse to consider going for therapy.

4. HAVE YOU ASKED YOUR SPOUSE TO GO FOR THERAPY?

Perhaps you have been trying to get your partner to change, but he or she doesn't recognize the fragility of your marital bond or the depth of your dissatisfaction. Your spouse may have tuned out your complaints and figures you'll get over it. If the majority of your attempts at describing what needs to change or how unhappy you are have occurred in the midst of fights or anger, anything you say can be easily interpreted as, "She/he didn't really mean that, she/he is just angry." If you think that your spouse hasn't been taking you seriously, short of serving him or her with divorce papers, it behooves you to think of a way to wave the proverbial red flag. When you are *not* fighting, mention calmly that unless things improve, you will need to make some changes. Tell him or her that you would prefer going to a therapist together, but you *will* go alone if necessary.

Frequently, the need to go to a therapist signals to both partners that the marriage has hit rock bottom. Since many people don't make changes unless there's a risk of losing something or unless they have become desperate, requesting to seek professional help sometimes jolts an overly complacent spouse into action.

"I Know Therapy Would Be Helpful, But . . ."

It has come to my attention that the majority of people deciding to dissolve their marriages do not seek professional counseling, a fact which I find to be both amazing and disturbing. Since we now know how devastating divorce can be for everyone involved, it is hard to imagine that anyone would opt to get out of a marriage without seeking professional advice. I would think most people would want to feel they left no stone unturned before making such a critical decision. Apparently, not everyone agrees.

"I Don't Have a Lot of Faith in Therapy"

People's reasons for not going to therapy vary. Some say, "I don't have a lot of faith in therapy. I think it's a bunch of baloney." Frankly, I can understand many people's skepticism about psychotherapy as a profession. Too many therapy experiences have yielded questionable results, and only after considerable financial and emotional hardship.

SBT has had wide appeal for this very reason. If either you or your spouse has rejected the idea of therapy in the past, now, after understanding that not all therapy is created equal, you might reconsider. SBT has won over many therapy skeptics and proven successful with those who have had disappointing therapy experiences. In the worst-case scenario, SBT won't help you accomplish your marital goals, but, unlike other approaches, you and your therapist will know this quickly, which will spare you expense, time and false hopes.

"My Spouse Won't Consider Therapy, So What's the Use?"

Another reason people hesitate going for therapy is that their spouse won't go. By now, it should be clear that if you want your marriage to work, going to a therapist might help you figure out what *you* need to do to get the ball rolling. Remember, if one person changes, the marriage must change. Besides, sometimes a reluctant spouse may decide to join you once you've already started the therapy process. But it's not necessary in most cases to have both partners present. If, when you begin therapy, the therapist you choose tells you your spouse *must* come in or therapy won't be successful, you may want to get another therapist.

"Therapy Is for Women"

Men often dislike the idea of going for therapy. The reasons for this vary, but some say that the male ego makes it difficult for men to ask for help. That's possible, but there is another possible explanation.

Traditional therapy is primarily a stereotypical female process. First, the focus is on talking, a familiar and comfortable focus for women. Secondly, many therapists emphasize the discussion of *feelings,* home turf for women once again. Clients analyze and express feelings, get reminded to make eye contact and reprimanded when talk about feelings shifts to a discussion of rational thoughts. A man's tendency to speak in other than terms of feelings wins him the psychotherapy booby prize, a distinction which makes therapy a less appealing option for men.

SBT, on the other hand, is attractive to men in that it does not favor a feminine problem-solving style. Although it is a form of talk therapy, it is goal- and action-oriented and it is highly structured. It asks the question, "What do you need to do to achieve your goals?" This solution orientation suits most men, which makes their active participation in the solution process considerably more likely. Women appreciate this.

"It's Not My Problem, My Spouse Needs Help"

Another reason people reject the idea of therapy is that they think that their spouses are the ones with the problem and, therefore, the ones who need help. Remember, too many marriages go down the tubes as spouses debate who has the problem. Even though this book has taught you that patterns of interaction rather than people create problems, you may still be convinced your spouse is to blame. If so, a competent therapist can help you figure out what you can do to effect changes in your spouse.

"It's Too Late"

Finally, people occasionally reject the idea of seeking therapy because they think it is too late. Maybe it is. Maybe there's nothing you, your spouse, a therapist or God can do to prevent the breakup of your marriage. But what do you have to lose? Having helped a fair number of couples resurrect "too late marriages," I'm now convinced that it can be done.

Have I left anything out? Have you thought of additional reasons to procrastinate picking up the phone and making an appointment? Whatever it might be, forget it. Just go and find the best therapist in your area and get started. In "How Do I Find a Therapist" on page 226, you will be offered some suggestions to help you find the right person for you. But first you need to know what to expect from the therapy process so you can make informed choices about your therapist.

WHAT CAN YOU EXPECT FROM THERAPY?

Obviously, if you are embarking on long-term insight therapy, your expectations will differ dramatically from what you would expect from an SBT therapist. Since my expertise lies in the area of SBT, I will describe what you can expect from a short-term, solution-oriented approach.

1. You Should Feel Comfortable with Your Therapist

Although your relationship with your therapist will be time-limited, he or she will play an extremely important role in your life. You will depend on your therapist to help guide you beyond the rough times. Because your therapist plays such a pivotal role, you must feel comfortable with him or her. You should feel as if your therapist respects you and that your thoughts and feelings are being acknowledged.

This is not to say that you will always agree with or love everything your therapist says or does. It is your therapist's job to suggest new ways of looking at your situation. Some new perspectives may challenge your usual way of perceiving your marriage—and that's good. However, you should never feel that your way of seeing things is incorrect or invalid. Although it's difficult to quantify, you should sense that your therapist likes you and values the information you impart during the session.

2. Goals Should Be Set Within the First Two Sessions

This book has stressed the importance of goal setting if problem solving is to be successful. The same holds true in the therapy context. If you don't identify where you're going, you won't know when you get there and neither will your therapist. Therapy will ramble and be unfocused. Each session will be an opportunity for you to react to the most recent crisis instead of making headway toward a specific goal. Conversations during the therapy session will begin to sound more and more like the conversations you and your spouse have in your living room and you don't need a therapist to do that.

It is essential that you and/or your spouse spell out your goals specifically so that you and your therapist have a contract. This need not be in writing, but goals should be clearly stated, early in therapy, so that therapy gets off to a good start and no time, energy or money is wasted. If your therapist doesn't *ask* you about your goals within the first two sessions, make sure you tell him or her. Then make sure the therapy is structured around the accomplishment of your goals. In other words, it is important that your therapist help you continually monitor progress toward your goals and make suggestions when progress has halted.

3. You Are the Experts, You Set the Goals

It is essential that you and/or your spouse be the ones in charge of establishing goals. You know yourselves the best. Although your therapist may have extensive training and education in human behavior and marital relationships, each marriage is different. Every person is different. Your therapist just met you. *You* must determine what you hope will happen as a result of seeking therapy, not your therapist.

The reason I am emphasizing that *you* must identify what you want to change is that some therapists will make that determination for you if you don't. Sometimes therapists suggest that you should change something that you don't find problematic. Other times, therapists suggest that what they consider the real root of your problem requires focusing on something you find extraneous, irrelevant or uncomfortable. Remember that you have hired your therapist to do a job for you. Although you should respect his or her professional skills, ultimately you are the boss. If something doesn't feel right to you, it isn't. Discuss your feelings immediately with your therapist and, if you don't feel understood, get yourself another therapist.

4. Therapy Needn't Be Very Painful

I have often heard it said that the expression "no pain, no gain" applies to the therapy process. In other words, growing is painful. If during therapy you are expected to explore painful memories of your childhood, this philosophy makes sense. However, you now know that you can solve marital problems without painful journeys into the past. I am certain that the vast majority of SBT clients would not say that therapy is painful.

Another reason traditional therapy can be uncomfortable is that a trademark of many of these approaches is confrontation. The therapist boldly confronts clients about behavior considered self-destructive or unproductive. Sometimes these attacks occur before a person is willing to deal with an issue or are totally inconsistent with a person's self-concept. Naturally, this harsh and dissonant feedback is disturbing and, in my experience, rarely effective in helping a person change. Typically, one digs one's heels in deeper when feeling attacked.

Confrontation is not necessary during therapy. Most people take the initiative to address issues and concerns they are willing to change. If they don't raise certain issues, it's because they are not willing or ready to deal with them. Therapists should respect people's intuitive sense of direction and self-protection and follow their client's lead.

Obviously, problem solving isn't always pleasurable or fun, that goes without saying. However, guard against therapy increasing rather than decreasing the stress you are feeling. Rather than feeling pained by going to therapy, you should look forward to sessions for the relief they offer.

5. The Therapist Must Be an Ally to Both Partners

Therapists who are trained to work with couples have an in-depth understanding of how relationships work. They are trained to observe patterns between people rather than merely focusing on intrapsychic phenomena or personal problems. They see marital problems stemming from a series of interactions rather than from ill-meaning individuals. They understand, for example, why "irresponsible" spouses are matched up with "overresponsible" mates.

This nonjudgmental perspective enables therapists to generate varied solutions to relationship difficulties. It also prevents therapists from feeling the need to take sides. Although it may momentarily feel good for a therapist to take your side in the presence of your spouse, this maneuver usually backfires. It is human nature to harden one's stance when challenged. If a therapist takes sides, it is likely that the attacked spouse will intensify his or her perspective or actions and/or drop out of therapy. What good will that do anyone? A good therapist will make it possible for both spouses, regardless of their divergent views, to leave the session feeling supported and validated.

6. There Should Be Improvement Within Three or Four Sessions

Although the rate at which you can expect improvement varies from therapist to therapist, you should expect some change within weeks rather than months or years. This is not to say that all of your difficulties will be resolved instantly. But within several weeks you should see definite signs that your marriage is headed in the right direction. If it isn't, discuss your concern with your therapist. If the explanation offered makes sense, be patient and hang in there. If not, trust your instinct and shop around for a new therapist.

Clearly, if you were to go to a psychodynamic therapist, it is unlikely that you would see results so quickly. For reasons described in detail in Chapter 3, traditional therapy takes considerably longer to work. Unfortunately, when change occurs slowly, pessimism about the future often consumes couples.

7. Therapy Sessions Should Not Be Complaining Sessions

Make sure you are not just complaining to or about each other. If you start arguing in the therapist's office in a familiar way and your therapist doesn't redirect the session, ask for suggestions. Don't waste your time arguing.

Now that you have a clearer idea of what to expect from a therapist, you may be wondering how to find one.

HOW DO I FIND A THERAPIST?

Word of mouth is the best way to find a qualified therapist. Network with friends, relatives and neighbors who have had positive therapy experiences. A satisfied customer is living proof of positive results. Keep in mind, though, that although a word-of-mouth referral is the best way to find a therapist, it is not foolproof. Your friend or neighbor might click with someone who might turn you off. As always, you must be the final judge. If you trust and respect the person making the referral, more likely than not you will also have a good experience. In any case, it's a good place to start.

Additionally, it is possible to get a listing of qualified marital therapists by contacting the American Association for Marriage and Family Therapy (AAMFT). They will send you a list of clinical members of AAMFT in your area. AAMFT clinical members have a minimum of a master's degree, including specific training in marriage and family therapy, and have completed at least two years of supervised clinical practice with couples. Write to the following address for referrals in your area:

AAMFT—Referrals
1100 17th Street N.W., 10th floor
Washington, D.C. 20036

The AAMFT has published a helpful brochure entitled *A Consumer Guide to Marriage and Family Therapy,* obtainable at the same address. You can also call 800-374-AMFT, AAMFT's referral line.

QUESTIONS TO ASK

Before scheduling an appointment you should interview the therapist over the phone. There is no point in paying for a session unless you both agree on expectations for therapy. You may be uncertain as to the kinds of questions you should be asking. This section will suggest some important areas to cover but the list is not, by any means, comprehensive. All of the following questions, with the exception of number ten, were taken from the AAMFT brochure.

1. What Is the Therapist's Educational and Training Background?

In most cases, the professional will answer this question in terms of his or her graduate education. The therapist may have a doctorate or a master's degree in marriage and family therapy or in an allied discipline such as psychiatry, clinical social work, psychiatric nursing or the ministry. If the professional's degree is not in marriage and family therapy, you could ask about additional postgraduate training he or she has completed in marriage and family therapy.

2. Is the Therapist a Clinical Member of the American Association for Marriage and Family Therapy (AAMFT)?

Therapists who attain Clinical Membership in the AAMFT meet the educational supervision and training standards of the association. These standards meet or surpass the training and experience requirements for licensing in the states that license marriage and family therapists.

3. Does the Therapist Have Experience Treating Your Kind of Problem?

Make sure the therapist understands and has had experience with the type of difficulty you are having.

4. How Much Does the Therapist Charge? Are Fees Negotiable?

If you cannot afford the therapist's fee, some therapists are willing to negotiate a lower fee.

5. Are the Therapist's Services Covered by Health Insurance?

Many insurance policies cover 50 to 80 percent of the therapist's fee. It pays to ask.

6. Where Is the Office and What Are the Office Hours?

If you require evening or weekend appointments, make sure the therapist is available.

7. How Long Do Sessions Last?

Forty-five to sixty minutes is common.

8. How Often Are Sessions Held?

Although many therapists schedule sessions once a week, brief therapists often see clients less frequently, particularly once there is improvement.

9. What Is the Average Length of Treatment?

The average length of treatment varies depending on a number of factors: the approach used, the skill of the therapist, your motivation and the seriousness of the problem. However, many brief therapists see clients for ten sessions or less. Since sessions are not necessarily scheduled on a weekly basis, ask that the average length of treatment be stated in the number of sessions usually required to accomplish goals rather than the number of weeks or months. For example, it may take three months to have five sessions.

10. What Percentage of the Couples Coming to This Therapist Are Able to Resolve Their Difficulties Without Divorcing?

Your therapist might not have specific data about these percentages; however, as he or she discusses this question, a great deal of information can be gleaned about the therapist's views of marriage and divorce.

THERAPY DOESN'T ALWAYS WORK

Therapy doesn't work all the time. Once you start going to a therapist, you may find that despite your best effort, nothing is changing. Perhaps you are asking yourself, "Why isn't my marriage improving? Why doesn't my spouse seem to notice or care about the changes I'm making?" Again, there are no universal answers to these questions. Every person and every marriage is different. However, here is one reason that your marriage might not be improving.

Your Spouse Has Already Made Up His or Her Mind to Leave

Although one's partner may not have formally announced that he or she is leaving, sometimes the decision has already been made and efforts to solve marital problems come too late. In these cases, no matter what person A does, person B is disinterested and unimpressed. There may even be another person waiting in the wings for the marriage to dissolve.

If your spouse is absolutely convinced that he or she must leave the marriage, there probably isn't much you can do to turn things around. You can't make a person *want* the marriage to work if he or she is determined to get out. Sometimes there is absolutely nothing that will change a person's mind about leaving. You may be doing everything right and it still doesn't work.

You may be wondering how you will know if things are hopeless. Trust your instincts. Continue working on your marriage until *you* are absolutely convinced it's over. Don't let anyone else tell you it's time to abandon ship. You are the expert on your life, you decide whether it's time to rethink your goals. There are no experts and no books that can tell you whether or when to end a marriage. You must be the one to make this decision.

If you do decide to divorce, you will need to determine what you will need to do to get on with your life, and, if you have children, the best way to handle telling them and dealing with their feelings. Some people opt to seek a therapist's help to sort out their thoughts and feelings. Friends and relatives can often provide similar support during the transitional period. There are many excellent books available to assist you through your divorce.

Additionally, a therapist or a divorce mediator can help you and/or your spouse make decisions about post-divorce issues concerning the children and other family matters. Increasing numbers of people are opting to use the services of a divorce mediator rather than a lawyer to iron out issues concerning future family matters.

After reading this section you may be wondering how it is possible to maintain a positive attitude when working through difficult issues. While it is true that many marriages will end in divorce, you must also remember that the vast majority of the people who seek help for their marital problems *are* able to improve their relationships. It is my hope that you are merely skimming through this chapter because you have already noticed changes indicating that working on your marriage *is* working. However, if little has improved, do what you must to get the support you need to help you feel good about yourself and to keep moving forward in your life.

CHAPTER 10

Parting Words

Congratulations! You have read this entire book. This shows that you obviously care a great deal about your commitment to your spouse and your family. Caring and commitment are two necessary components for making your marriage work, but there is a third, equally important component—and that is the ability to take *action*.

It is my assumption that you have already started to implement the ideas in this book. If you haven't, don't wait a minute longer. The longer you wait, the more difficult it will be to do something different because inertia sets in. This book will not have served its purpose if you have simply been intrigued by the techniques but have not taken action. The ideas proposed here should have inspired you enough to stop reading and start doing.

Inaction isn't the only obstacle to your getting the results you want. Lack of forgiveness is a close second. Too many people go through the motions of putting the pieces of their marriage back together when, in reality, they bear grudges about past injustices which prevent them from moving forward. Even the best problem-solving techniques in the world won't penetrate the resentment one feels from the lack of forgiveness.

Leo Buscaglia, an author who has written extensively on the topic of love, has this to say about forgiveness:

> When wronged by those we love, we seem to devalue years of a relationship—a relationship that may have brought us many joys and which required much intellectual and emotional energy to have lasted so long. Still, with a single harsh statement, a thoughtless act, an unfeeling criticism, we are capable of destroying even the closest of our relationships. We quickly forget the good and set out to rationalize scenarios of hate. We do this rather than take up the challenge of honest evaluation and confrontation. We ignore the possibility that in the act of forgiving and showing compassion we are very likely to discover new depths in ourselves and new possibilities for relating in the future. We are too proud. We engage rather in self-defeating activities which keep us from forgiving; beliefs that if we withdraw and run from the situation we will hurt the other and absence will heal us; the fantasy that in avoidance there can be closure; the naive hope that in hurting, shaming, blaming and condemning we will be made to feel better. We fail to realize that when we refuse to engage in forgiving behaviors, it is we who assume the useless weight of hate, pain and vengeance which is never ending, and, instead, weighs upon us rather than the wrongdoer. (Buscaglia, 1984, pp. 96–97.)

You might be asking yourself, "But how do I forgive when I still feel hurt?" My guess is that some of your hurt relates to the past, but your hurt lingers because your relationship hasn't been repaired in the present. You will notice that as your communication improves and as time spent together becomes more pleasant, your hurt and resentment will fade. I've seen it happen that way time and time again.

If you are feeling resentful, as a symbolic gesture you might consider taking the time to sit down and write a long letter to your spouse outlining everything he or she did in the past that hurt, angered or disappointed you. It's essential that you take painstaking care not to omit any critical incident. As you recall the past, allow yourself to relive the feelings, writing the details as the pictures flash through your mind. Once you feel certain you've left nothing out of your letter—burn it.

Whether you do this exercise or not, do yourself a favor. Don't pretend that you are putting effort into your marriage when you have a mental ledger book detailing your spouse's every wrongdoing. As long as you are holding on to resentments of the past, you can't be forgiving. As long as you are not forgiving, you can't be loving. As long as you aren't loving, you can't do what it takes to make your marriage work. So decide. Are you going to carry a grudge and stand by while you and your spouse become a divorce statistic or are you going to rid yourself of the shackles of the past which have held *you* prisoner? Forgive your spouse and start anew.

In the popular movie *Back to the Future* characters traveled through time. They recognized that changing the course of past events would irreversibly change the future. Although we can't time-travel nor can we change the past, we *can* change what we are doing in the present that alters our future paths.

Start by imagining that you have a family photo album filled with photographs taken ten or twenty years from now. Picture exactly what you, your spouse and your family will be doing then. Take time to envision the details of Thanksgiving gatherings, vacations, Christmas dinners, birthdays, graduations, bar mitzvahs, anniversaries and births of new family members. Notice how gratifying it feels to be together with your spouse and your family on those occasions. In an ever-changing world, experience how comforting it is to know that some things don't change.

Once these images are indelibly imprinted in your mind's eye, return to the present. Know that what you're doing at this very moment is shaping your future. If you want intimacy, caring and companionship five, ten or thirty years from now, start making it happen *now*. Start creating the good old days right this moment.

> By starting to make changes, by growing in bits and pieces, you can slowly but steadily change your life. Like the rock thrown into the still pond, you create ripples that grow larger in the future. It's often the littlest thing, viewed over time, that makes the biggest difference.
>
> Think of two arrows pointing in the same general direction. If you make a tiny change in the direction of one of them, if you push it three of four degrees in a different direction, the change will probably be imperceptible at first. But if you follow that path for yards and then for miles, the difference will become greater and greater—until there's no relation at all between the first path and the second. (Robbins, 1986, pp. 349–50.)

People often ask me how I can do marital therapy so much of the time without getting depressed and taking other people's problems home with me. Before practicing SBT, I definitely used to pick up other people's frustration and depression and then give it to members of my family like in a game of tag, but this is no longer true. For me, SBT has been an antidote to intractable problems. There are fewer therapeutic impasses, more optimism and increased numbers of satisfied clients who decide that staying married is worth the effort. I can't imagine anything in the world more gratifying than knowing that I've helped people harness their inner resources to resolve difficulties and rediscover the unequaled joy of a lifelong partnership.

Until now my enthusiasm about dissolving problems in marriage could only be passed on to my clients and to marital therapists who have trained with me. This book has given me an opportunity to reach thousands of people and remind them that the vast majority of relationship problems *are* solvable and the vast majority of marriages *are* worth the effort required to make them work.

People in the throes of marital problems who are considering divorce need to get the message that working it out instead of getting out *is* a viable solution. It is my hope that this book is a harbinger of the nineties being the decade of alternatives to divorce. Close friends and colleagues tell me that I'm a hopeless optimist. But I tell them, "That's okay, it's a communicable disease."

Selected Bibliography

Bateson, G., et al. 1956. Towards a theory of schizophrenia. *Behavioral Science*, Vol. 1.

Beck, Aaron T. 1988. *Love is never enough.* New York: Harper & Row.

Bergman, J. 1985. *Fishing for barracuda.* New York: Norton.

Berman, C. 1991. *Adult children of divorce speak out.* New York: Simon & Schuster.

Bogdan, J. 1986. Do families really need problems: why I am not a functionalist. *Family Therapy Networker*, July/Aug: 35.

Buscaglia, L. F. 1984. *Loving each other: the challenge of human relationships.* New York: Fawcett.

Coyne, J. 1985. Book review of *The process of change* by Peggy Papp. *Family Therapy Networker*, Mar/Apr: 60–61.

de Shazer, S. 1982. *Patterns of brief family therapy.* New York: Guilford.

de Shazer, S. 1985. *Keys to solution in brief therapy.* New York: Norton.

de Shazer, S. 1988. *Clues: investigating solutions in brief therapy.* New York: Norton.

Fisch, R., J. Weakland, and L. Segal. 1982. *The tactics of change: doing therapy briefly.* San Francisco: Jossey-Bass.

Gottman, J. M., and R. W. Levenson. 1986. Assessing the role of emotion in marriage. *Behavioral Assessment* 8: 31–48.

Heath, T., and B. Atkinson. 1989. Solutions attempted and considered: broadening assessment in brief therapy. *Journal of Strategic and Systemic Therapies*, Vol. 8, Nos. 2 and 3.

Heidbreder, E. 1933. *Seven psychologies.* New York: Appleton-Century-Crofts.

Hendrix, H. 1988. *Getting the love you want: a guide for couples.* New York: Holt.

Hetherington, E. M., M. Cox, and R. Cox. 1981. Effects of divorce on parents and children. In M. Lamb, ed., *Nontraditional families*, pp. 233–88. Hillsdale, N. J.: Erlbaum.

Hetherington, E. M., A. S. Tryon. 1989. His and her divorces. *Family Therapy Networker*, Nov/Dec: 58.

Kahn, M. 1966. The physiology of catharsis. *Journal of Personality and Social Psychology* 3: 278–98.

Kiser, D. 1990. As quoted in Brief therapy on the couch. *Family Therapy Networker*, March-April.

Lederer, W. J., and D. Jackson. 1968. *The mirages of marriage.* New York: Norton.

Lipchik, E., and S. de Shazer. 1988. Purposeful sequences for beginning the solution-focused interview. In E. Lipchik, *Interviewing*. Rockville, Md.: Aspen.

Medved, D. 1989. *The case against divorce*. New York: Donald I. Fine, Inc.

Molnar, A., and B. Lindquist. 1989. *Changing problem behavior in schools*. San Francisco: Jossey-Bass.

Napier, A. 1990. Fixing the between. *Newsweek*: July 2, p. 43.

Nord, K. 1989. Charting rough waters. *Family Therapy Networker*, Nov/Dec: 26.

O'Hanlon, W. 1987. *Taproots: underlying principles of Milton Erickson's therapy and hypnosis*. New York: Norton.

O'Hanlon, W., and M. Weiner-Davis. 1989. *In search of solutions: a new direction in psychotherapy*. New York: Norton.

Rachman, S. 1963. Spontaneous remission and latent learning. *Behaviour research and therapy* 1: 133–37.

Robbins, A. 1986. *Unlimited power*. New York: Simon & Schuster.

Rosenthal, R., and K. L. Fode. 1963a. The effect of experimenter bias on the performance of the albino rat. *Behavioral Sciences* 8: 183–89.

Rosenthal, R., and K. L. Fode. 1963b. Psychology of the scientist. V: Three experiments in experimenter bias. *Psychological Reports* 12: 491–511.

Rosenthal, R., and L. Jacobson. 1966. Teachers' expectencies: determinants of pupils' I.Q. gains. *Psychological Reports* 19: 115–18.

Rosenthal, R., and L. Jacobson. 1968. *Pygmalion in the classroom*. New York: Holt.

Rosenthal, R., and R. Lawson. 1964. A longitudinal study of the effects of experimenter bias on the operant learning of laboratory rats. *Journal of Psychiatric Research* 2: 61–72.

Sheehy, G. 1974. *Passages*. New York: Dutton.

Siegel, B. 1986. *Love, medicine and miracles*. New York: Harper & Row.

Stuart, R. 1980. *Helping couples change*. New York: Guilford.

Synder, D. K., and R. M. Wills. 1989. Behavioral versus insight-oriented marital therapy: effects on individual and interpersonal functioning. *Journal of Consulting and Clinical Psychology* 57(1): 39–46.

Synder, M., and P. White. 1982. Moods and memories: elation, depression, and the remembering of the events of one's life. *Journal of Personality* 50(2): 149–67.

Tanenbaum, J. 1989. *Male and female realities: understanding the opposite sex*. Sugar Land, Tex.: Candle Publishing Co.

Tannen, D. 1990. *You just don't understand: women and men in conversation*. New York: Morrow.

Ullmann, L. P., and L. Krasner. 1969. *A psychological approach to abnormal behavior*. Englewood Cliffs, N. J.: Prentice-Hall.

Viscott, D. 1991. Interview in *Special Report*, May–July.

Wallerstein, J. S., and S. Blakeslee. 1989. *Second chances*. New York: Ticknor & Fields.

Watts, A. 1966. *The book: on the taboo against knowing who you are*. New York: Pantheon.

Watzlawick, P., J. Weakland, and R. Fisch. 1974. *Change: principles of problem formation and problem resolution.* New York: Norton.

Weiner-Davis, M. 1988. Doing it my way. *Journal of Strategic and Systemic Therapies* 7 (2).

Weiner-Davis, M., S. de Shazer, and W. Gingerich. 1987. Constructing the therapeutic solution by building on pretreatment change: an exploratory study. *Journal of Marital and Family Therapy* 13(4): 359–63.

Weiner-Davis, M. 1990. In praise of solutions, *Family Therapy Networker*, Mar/Apr: 43–48.

Weitzman, L. J. 1985. *The divorce revolution.* New York: The Free Press.

Recommended Reading

SELF-HELP

Beck, Aaron T. 1988. *Love is never enough*. New York: Harper & Row.

Lerner, H. G. 1985. *The dance of anger*. New York: Harper & Row.

Robbins, A. 1986. *Unlimited power*. New York: Simon & Schuster.

DIVORCE

Berman, C. 1990. *Adult children of divorce speak out*. New York: Simon & Schuster.

Medved, D. 1989. *The case against divorce*. New York: Donald I. Fine.

Wallerstein, J. S., and S. Blakeslee. 1989. *Second chances*. New York: Ticknor & Fields.

Weitzman, L. J. 1985. *The divorce revolution*. New York: The Free Press.

SOLUTION-ORIENTED BRIEF THERAPY

de Shazer, S. 1985. *Keys to solution in brief therapy*. New York: Norton.

O'Hanlon, W., and M. Weiner-Davis. 1989. *In search of solutions: a new direction in psychotherapy*. New York: Norton.

MARRIAGE

Lederer, W. J. , and D. Jackson. 1968. *The mirages of marriage*. New York: Norton.

Nichols, M. P. 1988. *The power of the family*. New York: Simon & Schuster.

COMMUNICATION

Tannen, D. 1990. *You just don't understand: women and men in conversation*. New York: Morrow.

INDEX

INDEX

About the Author

Michele Weiner-Davis, M.S.W., is a therapist in private practice specializing in Solution-Oriented Brief Therapy. Her highly acclaimed workshops on Brief Therapy have earned her national recognition among professional audiences. She publishes extensively in professional journals and her work has been written about in popular magazines and newspapers across the country. Michele is happily married and lives with her husband and two children in Woodstock, Illinois.